AAT

INTERACTIVE TEXT

Technician Unit 16

Evaluating Activities

In this May 2001 edition

- Layout designed to be easy on the eye - and easy to use

- Icons to guide you through a 'fast track' approach if you wish

- Numerous activities throughout the text to reinforce learning

- Thorough reliable updating of material to 1 May 2001

FOR 2001 AND 2002 DEVOLVED ASSESSMENTS

BPP Publishing
May 2001

First edition 1998
Fourth edition May 2001

ISBN 0 7517 6517 1 (previous edition 0 7517 6222 9)

British Library Cataloguing-in-Publication Data
A catalogue record for this book
is available from the British Library

Published by

BPP Publishing Limited
Aldine House, Aldine Place
London W12 8AW

www.bpp.com

Printed in Great Britain by Ashford Colour Press

We are grateful to the Lead Body for Accounting for permission to reproduce extracts from the Standards of Competence for Accounting, and to the AAT for permission to reproduce extracts from the Mapping and Guidance Notes.

BPP
PUBLISHING

HOW TO USE THIS INTERACTIVE TEXT

Aims of this Interactive Text

> To provide the knowledge and practice to help you succeed in the devolved assessment for Technician Unit 16 *Evaluating Activities*.

To pass the devolved assessment you need a thorough understanding in all areas covered by the standards of competence.

> To tie in with the other components of the BPP Effective Study Package to ensure you have the best possible chance of success.

Interactive Text

This covers all you need to know for the devolved assessment for Unit 16 *Evaluating Activities*. Icons clearly mark key areas of the text. Numerous activities throughout the text help you practise what you have just learnt.

Devolved Assessment Kit

When you have understood and practised the material in the Interactive Text, you will have the knowledge and experience to tackle the Devolved Assessment Kit for Unit 16. This aims to get you through the devolved assessment, whether in the form of the AAT simulation or in the workplace. It contains the AAT's sample simulation for Unit 16 plus other simulations.

Recommended approach to this Interactive Text

- To achieve competence in Unit 16 (and all the other units), you need to be able to do **everything** specified by the standards. Study the text very carefully and do not skip any of it.

- Learning is an **active** process. Do **all** the activities as you work through the text so you can be sure you really understand what you have read.

- After you have covered the material in the Interactive Text, work through the **Devolved Assessment Kit**.

- Before you take the devolved assessment, check that you still remember the material using the following quick revision plan for each chapter.

  ○ Read through the **chapter learning objectives**. Are there any gaps in your knowledge? If so, study the section again.

  ○ Read and learn the **key terms**.

  ○ Look at the **assessment alerts.** These show the sort of things that are likely to come up.

  ○ Read and learn the **key learning points,** which are a summary of the chapter.

  ○ Do the **quick quiz** again. If you know what you're doing, it shouldn't take long.

  This approach is only a suggestion. You college may well adapt it to suit your needs.

Remember this is a **practical** course.

- Try to relate the material to your experience in the workplace or any other work experience you may have had.

- Try to make as many links as you can to your study of the other Units at Technician level.

- Keep this Text - (hopefully) you will find it invaluable in your everyday work too!

TECHNICIAN QUALIFICATION STRUCTURE

The competence-based Education and Training Scheme of the Association of Accounting Technicians is based on an analysis of the work of accounting staff in a wide range of industries and types of organisation. The Standards of Competence for Accounting which students are expected to meet are based on this analysis.

The Standards identify the **key purpose** of the accounting occupation, which is to **operate, maintain and improve systems to record, plan, monitor and report on the financial activities of an organisation**, and a number of key roles of the occupation. Each key role is subdivided into units of competence, which are further divided into **elements of competences**. By successfully completing assessments in specified units of competence, students can gain qualifications at NVQ/SVQ levels 2, 3 and 4, which correspond to the AAT Foundation, Intermediate and Technician stages of competence respectively.

Whether you are competent in a Unit is demonstrated by means of:

- *Either* a Central Assessment (set and marked by AAT assessors)

- *Or* a Devolved Assessment (where competence is judged by an Approved Assessment Centre to whom responsibility for this is devolved)

- Or *both* Central *and* Devolved Assessment

Below we set out the overall structure of the Technician (NVQ/SVQ Level 4) stage, indicating how competence in each Unit is assessed. In the next two sections, there is more detail about the Standards of Competence and the Devolved Assessment for Unit 16.

BPP PUBLISHING

NVQ/SVQ Level 4 - Technician qualification structure

Units 8, 9, and 10 are compulsory. You can choose one out of Units 11 - 14, and then three out of Units 15-19.

Unit of competence   **Elements of competence**

| Unit 8 Contributing to the management of costs and the enhancement of value

Central Assessment *only* | 8.1 Collect, analyse and disseminate information about costs |
| | 8.2 Make recommendations to reduce costs and enhance value |

Unit 9 Contributing to the planning and allocation of resources **Central Assessment** *only*	9.1 Prepare forecasts of income and expenditure
	9.2 Produce draft budget proposals
	9.3 Monitor the performance of responsiblity centres against budgets

Unit 10 Managing accounting systems **Devolved Assessment** *only*	10.1 Co-ordinate work activities within the accounting environment
	10.2 Identify opportunities to improve the effectiveness of an accounting system
	10.3 Prevent fraud in an accounting system

| Unit 22 Monitor and maintain a healthy, safe and secure workplace (ASC)

Devolved Assessment *only* | 22.1 Monitor and maintain health and safety within the workplace |
| | 22.2 Monitor and maintain the security of the workplace |

| Unit 11 Drafting financial statements (Accounting Practice, Industry and Commerce)

Central Assessment *only* | 11.1 Interpret financial statements |
| | 11.2 Draft limited company, sole trader and partnership year end financial statements |

| Unit 12 Drafting financial statements (Central Government)

Central Assessment *only* | 12.1 Interpret financial statements |
| | 12.2 Draft central government financial statements |

| Unit 13 Drafting financial statements (Local Government)

Central Assessment *only* | 13.1 Interpret financial statements |
| | 13.2 Draft local authority financial statements |

Unit of competence

Elements of competence

Unit 14 Drafting financial statements (National Health Service) **Central Assessment *only***	14.1 Interpret financial statements
	14.2 Draft NHS accounting statements and returns

Unit 15 Operating a cash management and credit control system **Devolved Assessment *only***	15.1 Monitor and control cash receipts and payments
	15.2 Manage cash balances
	15.3 Grant credit
	15.4 Monitor and control the collection of debts

Unit 16 Evaluating current and proposed activities **Devolved Assessment *only***	16.1 Prepare cost estimates
	16.2 Recommend ways to improve cost ratios and revenue generation

Unit 17 Implementing auditing procedures **Devolved Assessment *only***	17.1 Contribute to the planning of an audit assignment
	17.2 Prepare capital allowances computations
	17.3 Prepare related draft reports

Unit 18 Preparing business taxation computations **Devolved Assessment *only***	18.1 Adjust accounting profit and losses for trades and professions
	18.2 Prepare capital allowances computations
	18.3 Prepare Capital gains tax
	18.4 Account for Advance Corporation tax and Income tax payable or recoverable by a company
	18.5 Prepare Corporation tax computations and returns

Unit 19 Preparing personal taxation computations **Devolved Assessment *only***	19.1 Calculate income from employment
	19.2 Prepare computations of property and investment income
	19.3 Prepare Capital Gains Tax computations
	19.4 Prepare personal tax returns

BPP PUBLISHING

UNIT 16 STANDARDS OF COMPETENCE

The structure of the Standards for Unit 16

The Unit commences with a statement of the **knowledge and understanding** which underpin competence in the Unit's elements.

The Unit is then divided into **elements of competence** describing activities which the individual should be able to perform.

Each element includes the following.

- A set of **performance criteria.** This defines what constitutes competent performance.

- A **range statement.** This defines the situations, contexts, methods etc in which competence should be displayed.

- **Evidence requirements.** These state that competence must be demonstrated consistently, over an appropriate time scale with evidence of performance being provided from the appropriate sources.

- **Sources of evidence.** These are suggestions of ways in which you can find evidence to demonstrate that competence. These fall under the headings: 'observed performance; work produced by the candidate; authenticated testimonies from relevant witnesses; personal account of competence; other sources of evidence.' They are reproduced in full in our Devolved Assessment Kit for Unit 16.

The elements of competence for Unit 16: *Evaluating Current and Proposed Activities* are set out below. Knowledge and understanding required for the unit as a whole are listed first, followed by the performance criteria and range statements for each element. Performance criteria and range statements are cross-referenced below to chapters in this Unit 16 *Evaluating Activities* Interactive Text.

Unit 16: Evaluating activities and proposed activities

What is the unit about?

Unit 16 is concerned with current and proposed activities. Its central theme is decision making in all its facets. Element 16.1 is primarily about the collection of costs to assist in making decisions. Element 16.2 emphasises the application of techniques of assistance in long-term and short-term decision making.

Compared with many other units, the performance criteria are expressed in abstract terms. This is inevitable if the emphasis is to be placed on outcomes. Guidance as to content and depth therefore has to be found in the range statement and the underpinning knowledge and understanding.

Knowledge and understanding

Accounting techniques

- Basic statistical methods: index numbers, time series (Element 16.1)

- Marginal costing, absorption costing, opportunity costs (Elements 16.1 & 16.2)

- Interpretation of cost data, the use of overhead rates (Element 16.1)

- The identification of fixed, variable and semi-fixed costs and their correct use in cost analysis (Element 16.2)

- The identification of relevant costs (Element 16.2)

- The identification of limiting factors (Element 16.2)

- Methods of project appraisal: payback, discounted cash flow methods (NPV and IRR) (Element 16.2)

- Basic principles of risk analysis: Expected Monetary Return (Element 16.2)

- A basic understanding of the tax implications of capital expenditure (capital allowances and their effect on future cash flows) (Element 16.2)

Accounting principles and theory

- Cost behaviour (Elements 16.1 & 16.2)

- The economic basis of pricing policies (Element 16.1)

- The principles of DCF, comparison of different methods (Element 16.2)

- Risk and uncertainty (Element 16.2)

The organisation

- Understanding that the accounting systems of an organisation are affected by its organisational structure, its administrative systems and procedures and the nature of its business transactions (Elements 16.1 & 16.2)

- A knowledge of the sources of information about labour, material and overhead costs (Element 16.1)

BPP PUBLISHING

Element 16.1 Prepare cost estimates

Performance criteria		Chapters in this Text
1	The extent of the information to be contained within estimates is agreed with those who commission them	8
2	Appropriate staff are consulted about technical aspects and any special features of work activity and projects which impact upon costs	Throughout
3	Current material, labour and other variable costs are identified and future trends assessed	2
4	Estimates account for the effect of possible variations in capacity on fixed overhead rates	2
5	Estimates are prepared in an approved form and presented to the appropriate people within an agreed timescale	1, 8

Range statement

1	Estimates prepared for: price fixing; submitting tenders or quotations; costing proposed activities and projects	8

Element 16.2   Recommend ways to improve cost ratios and revenue generation

Performance criteria	Chapters in this Text
1 Information relevant to estimating current and future costs and revenue is identified and used as the basis of analysis	6, 11
2 Critical factors which may affect costs and revenue are analysed using appropriate accounting techniques and clear conclusions are drawn from the analysis	12
3 The views of appropriate specialists are gathered and used to inform analysis and any conclusions drawn	8
4 The assumptions made and the degree of accuracy which exists in conclusions are clearly stated	8
5 Potential options and solutions are identified and evaluated for their contribution to improving cost ratios and revenue generation	6
6 Recommendations to inform decisions are based on clearly stated conclusions drawn from an accurate analysis of all relevant information	8
7 Recommendations are presented to the appropriate people in a clear and concise way and are supported with a clear rationale	8, 11

Range statement	
1 Type of decisions: decisions relating to operational activities of the 'make or buy' type; decisions relating to strategic planning and future project activity	5
2 Types of information:	7
- internal information: accounting information, technical data, cost estimates	
- external information: competitor prices, supplier prices, market information	
3 Techniques related to: the identification of fixed, variable and semi-fixed costs and their correct use in cost analysis; marginal costing; opportunity costs; the identification of limiting factors	1-4, 6, 9, 11
- methods of project appraisal: payback; discounted cash flow methods NPV and IRR	
- risk analysis: identifying Expected Monetary Return	
4 Methods of presentation: verbal presentation; written reports	1

ASSESSMENT STRATEGY

This unit is assessed by *devolved* assessment.

Devolved Assessment

Devolved assessment is a means of collecting evidence of your ability to carry out **practical activities** and to **operate effectively in the conditions of the workplace** to the standards required. Evidence may be collected at your place of work or at an Approved Assessment Centre by means of simulations of workplace activity, or by a combination of these methods.

If the Approved Assessment Centre is a **workplace**, you may be observed carrying out accounting activities as part of your normal work routine. You should collect documentary evidence of the work you have done, or contributed to, in an **accounting portfolio**. Evidence collected in a portfolio can be assessed in addition to observed performance or where it is not possible to assess by observation.

Where the Approved Assessment Centre is a **college or training organisation**, devolved assessment will be by means of a combination of the following.

(a) Documentary evidence of activities carried out at the workplace, collected by you in an **accounting portfolio**.

(b) Realistic **simulations** of workplace activities. These simulations may take the form of case studies and in-tray exercises and involve the use of primary documents and reference sources.

(c) **Projects and assignments** designed to assess the Standards of Competence.

If you are unable to provide workplace evidence you will be able to complete the assessment requirements by the alternative methods listed above.

Part A

Cost behaviour and cost information

1 Cost information

Chapter topic list

Learning objectives

On completion of this chapter you will be able to:

	Performance criteria	Range statement
• Understand techniques related to cost analysis		16.2.3
• Identify information relevant to estimating current and future costs and revenue, for use as the basis of analysis	16.2	
• Prepare written reports in formats appropriate to their purpose	16.1, 16.2	16.2.4

1   COSTS

1.1   Consider what a ballpoint pens is made up of. There is probably a red plastic cap and a little red thing that fits into the end, and perhaps a yellow plastic sheath. There is an opaque plastic ink holder with red ink inside it. At the tip there is a gold plastic part holding a metal nib with a roller ball.

1.2   Let us suppose that the manufacturer sells biros to wholesalers for 20p each. How much does the little ball cost? What share of the 20p is taken up by the little red thing in the end of the biro? How much did somebody earn for putting it there?

1.3   To elaborate still further, the manufacturer probably has machines to mould the plastic and do some of the assembly. How much does it cost, per biro, to run the machines: to set them up so that they produce the right shape of moulded plastic? How much are the production line workers' wages per biro?

Production costs

1.4   Any of these separate production costs could be calculated and recorded on a unit cost card which records how the total cost of a unit (in this instance, a biro) is arrived at. These costs are known as **direct costs** because they can be traced directly to specific units of production.

BIRO - UNIT COST CARD	£	£
Direct materials		
Yellow plastic	X	
Red plastic	X	
Opaque plastic	X	
Gold plastic	X	
Ink	X	
Metal	X	
		X
Direct labour		
Machine operators' wages	X	
Manual assembly staff wages	X	
		X
		X
Direct expenses		
Moulding machinery - operating costs	X	
Assembly machinery - operating costs	X	
		X
Total direct cost (or prime cost)		X
Overheads (production)		X
Manufacturing cost (or factory cost)		X
Overheads (administration, distribution and selling)		X
Total cost		X

Don't worry if you are a little unsure of the meaning of some of the terms in the unit cost card above as we will be looking at them in detail as we work through the Text.

Cost units

> **KEY TERM**
>
> A **cost unit** is a unit of product which has costs attached to it. The cost unit is the basic control for costing purposes.

1.5 The only difficult thing about this is that a cost unit is not always a single item. It might be a batch of 1,000 if that is how the individual items are made. In fact, a cost per 1,000 (or whatever) is often more meaningful information, especially if calculating a cost for a single item gives an amount that you cannot hold in your hand, like 0.003p. Examples of cost units are a construction contract, a batch of 1,000 pair of shoes, a passenger mile (in other words, the transportation of a passenger for a mile) and a patient night (the stay of a patient in hospital for a night).

Cost centres

> **KEY TERM**
>
> **Cost centres** are the essential 'building blocks' of a costing system. They act as a collecting place for certain costs before they are analysed further.

1.6 A cost centre might be a place, and this is probably what you think of first because the word 'centre' is often used to mean a place. On the other hand it might be a person. For example, the company solicitor would incur costs on books and stationery that were unique to his or her function. It might be a group of people, all contributing to the same function, the accounting staff, say, or the laboratory staff. Or it might be an item of equipment such as a machine which incurs costs because it needs to be oiled and maintained.

1.7 Cost centres may vary in nature, but what they have in common is that they **incur costs**. It is therefore logical to **collect costs** initially under the headings of the various different cost centres that there may be in an organisation. Then, when we want to know how much our products cost, we simply find out how many cost units have been produced and share out the costs incurred by that cost centre amongst the cost units.

Profit centres

1.8 We have seen that a cost centre is where costs are collected. Some organisations, however, work on a **profit centre basis**. Cost centres only have costs attributed to them. Profit centres, on the other hand, also receive revenues associated with those costs. For example, an organisation with two departments each making a different product will allocate the revenues from each product to the department where each product is made. This ensures that the organisation has some idea as to the relative profitability of each product.

> **KEY TERM**
>
> A **profit centre** is similar to a cost centre but is accountable for both costs *and* revenues.

1.9 Profit centre managers should normally have control over how revenue is raised and how costs are incurred. Not infrequently, several cost centres will comprise one profit centre.

Investment centres

1.10 You might also come across the term **investment centre**. The term may be applied by a company to its divisions where the divisional manager is allowed some direction about the amount of investment undertaken by the division.

Overheads

1.11 Overheads (or indirect costs) include costs that go into the making of the biro that you do not see when you dismantle it. You can touch the materials and you can appreciate that a combination of man and machine put them together.

1.12 It is not so obvious that the manufacturer has had to lubricate machines and employ foremen to supervise the assembly staff. He also has to pay rent for his factory and for somewhere to house his stock of materials, and he has to pay someone to buy materials, recruit labour and run the payroll. Others are paid to deliver the finished biros to the wholesalers; still others are out and about persuading wholesalers to buy biros, and they are supported at head office by staff taking orders and collecting payments.

1.13 Also, certain costs that could be identified with a specific product are classified as overheads and not direct costs. Nails used in the production of a cupboard can be identified specifically with the cupboard. However, because the cost is likely to be relatively insignificant, the expense of tracing such costs does not justify the possible benefits from calculating more accurate direct costs.

1.14 Instead of keeping complex and time consuming records which might enable us to trace such costs directly to specific units of production, we try to apportion them and other overheads (indirect costs) to each cost unit in as fair a way as possible.

1.15 Overheads are the biggest problem for cost accountants because it is not easy to tell by either looking at or measuring the product, what overheads went into getting it into the hands of the buyer. Overheads, or indirect costs, unlike direct costs, will not be identified with any one product because they are incurred for the benefit of all products rather than for any one specific product.

Make sure that you understand the **distinction between direct and indirect costs,** as it is a very important part of your studies. Note that an expense can only be classified as direct or indirect when it is related to an activity, and not by any analysis of the expense in isolation.

Direct and indirect costs

1.16 To summarise so far, the cost of an item can be divided into the elements of **materials, labour** and **expenses**.

Each element can be split into two, as follows.

Materials	=	Direct materials	+	Indirect materials
+		+		+
Labour	=	Direct labour	+	Indirect labour
+		+		+
Expenses	=	Direct expenses	+	Indirect expenses
Total cost	=	Direct cost		Overhead

Activity 1.1

List all of the different types of cost that a large supermarket might incur. Arrange them under headings of labour, materials used and other expenses.

Fixed costs and variable costs

1.17 One other important distinction is that between **fixed costs and variable costs.**

(a) If you produce two identical biros you will use twice as many direct materials as you would if you only produced one biro. Direct materials are in this case a **variable cost**. They vary according to the volume of production.

(b) If you oil your machines after every 1,000 biros have been produced, the cost of oil is also a variable cost. It is an indirect material cost that varies according to the volume of production.

(c) If you rent the factory that houses your biro-making machines you will pay the same amount of rent per annum whether you produce one biro or 10,000 biros. Factory rental is an indirect expense and it is **fixed** no matter what the volume of activity is.

1.18 The examples in (b) and (c) are both indirect costs, or overheads, but (b) is a variable overhead and (c) is a fixed overhead. The example in (a) is a variable direct cost. Direct costs usually are variable although they do not have to be. We are elaborating this point because it can be a source of great confusion. Variable cost is *not* just another name for a direct cost.

1.19 The following distinctions can be made.

(a) **Costs are either variable or fixed, depending upon whether they change when the volume of production changes.**

(b) **Costs are either direct or indirect, depending upon how easily they can be traced to a specific unit of production.**

Activity 1.2

Are the following likely to be fixed or variable costs?

(a) Charges for telephone calls made
(b) Charges for rental of telephone
(c) Annual salary of the chief accountant

(d)　Managing director's subscription to the Institute of Directors

(e)　Cost of materials used to pack 20 units of product X into a box

---

2　WHY RECORD COST INFORMATION?

2.1　In case you are beginning to think that recording cost information is far more trouble than it is worth we shall now consider why we bother. There are a number of very good reasons.

Determining the selling price

2.2　In the first place, if an item costs 50p and it is sold for 35p then the seller makes a loss on every sale. Before long he will go out of business. It is therefore important to know how much things cost so that a suitable selling price can be set.

Decision making

2.3　Before deciding on the selling price, the seller had to decide whether to make the item at all. Suppose he could make one or other of two items, either of which could be sold for £1 each. If one cost 80p to make and the other cost 90p then it would be better to make the one that cost 80p. Costing is therefore essential to **decision making**.

Planning and budgeting

2.4　Having decided to make the item it is then necessary to work out the best way of going about it. Sellers are limited as to the number of items they can sell and as to the amount of money they have available to invest in a project. You might conduct market research that told you you could sell 10,000 items. You would then need cost information so that you could plan what quantity of materials you could afford to buy, how many staff to employ, and how long to keep the machines running each day. Costing is thus an integral part of **planning** for the future. Another term for planning of this sort is **budgeting**.

> **KEY TERM**
>
> We can think of a **budget** as a plan that shows how much money you expect to make and how much it will cost to produce the items (or services) that bring this money in.

Control

2.5　There is, of course, no guarantee that everything will go according to plan. You might make and sell your 10,000 items for 50p each, only to discover that the actual cost of each item had gone up to 70p, perhaps because the suppliers of materials had put their prices up, or because workers had demanded higher wages.

2.6　Costing is not a one-off exercise. Costs can be predicted in advance but they must also be monitored as they are actually incurred. If this is done then an increase in materials costs, say, can be spotted as soon as it arises and the implications for the

future assessed. It may be possible to buy cheaper materials and keep costs down to the level planned or it may be necessary to draw up an entirely new plan. The recording of cost information in such a way that it can be monitored is thus vital to maintain **control of the business**.

Reporting

2.7 Finally, **costs have to be recorded so that a business can report its results**. Companies have to prepare accounts to comply with the Companies Acts and all businesses need to have some records so that the Inland Revenue knows how much tax is due and Customs and Excise know whether VAT is being properly accounted for. Senior managers judge the performance of their subordinates according to whether they have managed to meet targets which include targets for cost control. Cost information is essential for **reporting**.

Activity 1.3

(a) Give five reasons for recording cost information.
(b) How can costs be used to control a business?
(c) Who is interested in cost information?

---

3 PRODUCT COSTING

Job costing

3.1 There are several different ways of arriving at a value for the different cost elements (material, labour and expenses) which make up a unit cost of production. The most straightforward case is where the thing to be costed is a **one-off item**. For example, a furniture maker may make a table, say, to a customer's specific requirements. From start to finish the costs incurred to make that table are identifiable. It will cost so much for the table top, so much for the legs, and so on. This form of costing is known as **job costing**.

Batch costing

3.2 An item like a biro, however, will be produced as one of a **batch** of identical items, because it would clearly be uneconomical to set up the machinery, employ labour and incur overheads to produce each biro individually. There might be a production run of, say, 5,000 biros. The cost of producing 5,000 biros would be calculated and if we wanted to know the cost of one biro we would divide this total by 5,000. The answer would however be a fraction of a penny and this is not very meaningful information.

3.3 This method of costing is called **batch costing** and it applies to many everyday items. So far as costing techniques are concerned, job and batch costing are much the same.

Process costing

3.4 Another approach can be used when the product results from a series of continuous or repetitive operations or processes, and is not distinguishable as a

separate unit of product until the final stage. A can of baked beans, for example will start off as a much larger quantity of beans which go through the processes of adding ingredients, baking, cooling, canning, and labelling. Some of the original beans are subjected to different processes and become 'barbecued baked beans'; others end up in cans with sausages. Thus it is only at the canning stage that we can identify separate units of production.

3.5 The costing method used in these circumstances is called **process costing**. It causes problems because **the same process may give rise to different final products**. A bean may end up as an ordinary bean, a barbecued bean or a bean with a sausage. Further problems arise because production is of a continuous nature. To put a cost to production at a particular point in time we have to decide how complete the beans in a particular process are at that time. If they are only half-baked, perhaps they should be costed at only 50% of the total baking cost!

Accounting for overheads

3.6 Whether job costing, batch costing or process costing is used, there is still a problem in attributing to units of product overhead costs like factory rental, canteen costs and head office lighting. The pros and cons of trying to work out an amount per unit for such costs are open to debate. Most businesses actually do try to do this in practice, and one very good reason for doing so is to make sure that all costs are covered when prices are set.

3.7 This practice of working out an amount per unit for overheads is known as **absorption costing**. Absorption costing is a technique that is used in conjunction with the product costing methods described above. We will look at absorption costing in Chapter 3.

Activity 1.4

For each of the items listed below decide which type of costing would be used. Mark an X in the appropriate column.

	Job	*Batch*	*Process*
Suit (off the peg)			
Suit (tailored)			
Soap			
Yoghurt			
House decoration			
Car alarm			
Paper			
Poster			
Audit			

4   FUNCTIONAL COSTS

4.1 When we talk about functional costs we are not talking about a different **type** of cost to those we have met already, but about a way of grouping costs together

according to what aspects of an organisation's operations (what **function**) causes them to be incurred.

Functional cost	Description
Production costs	Materials and labour used and expenses incurred to make things and get them ready for sale.
Distribution and selling costs	Costs incurred both to get the finished items to the point where people can buy them and to persuade people to buy them.
Administration costs	A vague term - you might like to think of these costs as the materials and labour used and the expenses incurred in co-ordinating the activities of the production function and the distribution and selling function.
Financing costs	The expenses incurred when a business has to borrow to purchase fixed assets, say, or simply to operate on a day to day basis.

4.2 These divisions are not the only ones that could be made, nor are there rigid definitions of what is a production cost, what is an administration cost and so on.

5 STANDARD COSTS AND VARIANCES

5.1 When we were talking about the purposes of costing we hinted that it might involve not only recording what costs were, but also predicting what they ought to be.

5.2 Recognising the usefulness of cost information as a tool for controlling what goes on, many businesses adopt what are known as **standard costs**. They decide what the cost of each element that makes up a product *should* be in advance of the actual cost being incurred. Once the cost has been incurred it is compared with the estimated standard cost and if there is a difference (a **variance**) somebody is asked to explain why.

5.3 To set a standard cost it is necessary not only to know what the level of cost was in the past but also to have an idea of what it is likely to be in the future. In Chapter 9 we shall look at the various problems involved in setting standard costs.

5.4 **Standard costing** is not an alternative to job, batch or process costing, nor to absorption costing. It is an approach that can be used in addition to those methods.

Activity 1.5

Explain the following terms in your own words.

(a)	Cost unit	(f)	Overhead
(b)	Functional cost	(g)	Cost centre
(c)	Fixed cost	(h)	Variable cost
(d)	Standard cost	(i)	Budget
(e)	Indirect cost	(j)	Direct cost

Activity 1.6

The managing director of your organisation, a manufacturer of garden furniture, disagrees with you over the need for a costing system within your organisation. He says that the only requirement for the classification of costs is by the financial accountant into cost of sales, distribution cost and administration expense for the published accounts and anything beyond that is unnecessary.

Task

Write a report to the managing director stating your case as to why you believe he is wrong and specifying the following.

(a) The manner in which he has classified cost in his statement

(b) Four alternative classifications of cost and the ways in which they can assist management decision making, planning and control

6 WRITTEN REPORTS

6.1 Accounting Technicians and accountants are much involved in the presentation, dissemination and interpretation of information. We now look at how information can be disseminated in reports.

ASSESSMENT ALERT

Your Unit 16 assessment could involve quite a lot in the form of written reports. Presenting the necessary information effectively is important.

What is a report?

6.2 There are a variety of formats and styles of reports.

(a) You may think of reports as **extensive, complex documents**, but a **single page may be sufficient** in many contexts.

(b) **Routine reports are produced at regular intervals.** An example of a routine report is a budgetary control report, the preparation of which we will be looking at later in this Interactive Text. **Special reports may be commissioned for 'one-off' planning and decision-making purposes** such as a report on a proposed project or particular issue.

(c) Reports may be **for professional purposes,** or they may be **for a wider audience of laymen** or people from other backgrounds, who will not necessarily understand or require the same information or language.

6.3 Reports are meant to be **useful**. The information contained in a business report might be used in several ways.

(a) **To assist management,** as they rarely have time to carry out their own detailed investigations into the matters on which they make decisions. (Their time, moreover, is extremely expensive.)

(b) **As a permanent record and source of reference,** should details need to be confirmed or recalled in the future

(c) **To convey information** or suggestions/ideas to other interested parties (eg in a report for a committee)

Reports and their purpose

6.4 Reports are usually intended to initiate a decision or action by the person or group receiving the report. The decisions or actions might be the following types.

(a) **Control action.** If the report describes what has happened in the past, it might indicate a need for control action, or alternatively it might indicate that there is no need for control action.

(b) **Planning decisions.** Reports that are commissioned to advise on a certain course of action will include a **recommendation** about what decision should be taken.

The report and the report users

6.5 A report is usually prepared by someone who is instructed to do so by a superior.

(a) A special 'one-off' **report will be commissioned by a manager, who will then expect to make a decision on the basis of what the report tells him.** For example, the board of directors of a company might call for a report on the financial viability of a new product or investment, and they will expect to decide whether or not to undertake the product development or the investment on the basis of the report's findings.

(b) **Routine reports,** such as performance reports, might be **required because they are a part of established procedures.** The managers receiving the reports will not have commissioned them specifically, but they will be expected to act on anything out-of-the-ordinary that the report tells them.

(c) **Some reports arise out of a particular event,** on which regulations prescribe the writing of a report. For example, a leaving report must be written following an employee's resignation.

(d) **Individual responsibilities** often include the requirement to write reports. The secretary at a meeting will have to report to members the procedures and decisions taken.

6.6 Whether the report is 'one-off' or routine, there is an **obligation on the part of the person requesting the report to state the use to which it will be put.** In other words, the purpose of the report must be clear to both its writers and its users.

6.7 There is also **an obligation on the part of the report writer to communicate information in an unbiased way.** Information should be communicated impartially, so that the report user can make his own judgements. This has the following implications.

(a) Any assumptions, evaluations and recommendations by the report writer should be clearly 'signalled' as such.

(b) Points should not be over-weighted (or omitted as irrelevant) without honestly evaluating how objective the selection is.

(c) Fact and findings should be balanced against each other.

(d) A firm conclusion should, if possible, be reached. It should be clear how and why it was reached.

Activity 1.7

When writing a report, what can you do to ensure that the particular needs and abilities of the users of your report will be met?

Timeliness

6.8   As with all information, we stress again that a report may be of no use at all if it is not produced **on time**, however well researched and well presented it is. There is no point in presenting a report to influence a decision if the decision has already been made by the time the report is issued. The timescales within which the report user is working must be known, and the time available to produce the report planned accordingly.

Planning a report

Activity 1.8

What basic questions should you ask yourself before writing a report?

6.9   When you then come to plan a report in detail, you can ask yourself questions such as the following.

(a) **What information do I need to provide?** What is relevant to the user's requirements?

(b) **Do I need to follow a line of reasoning?** If so, what is the most logical way in which data can be grouped, and sequenced, to make my reasoning clear?

(c) **Do I need to include my own personal views?** If so, at what point: final recommendation, throughout?

(d) **What can I do to make the report easier to read?**

(i)   Are there suitable sections or sub-headings I can use to indicate effectively each stage of the information/argument?

(ii) Is the subject of the report too technical for the users? What vocabulary should I use to help them understand?

(iii) Do I have a clear introduction to 'ease' the readers in to the subject, and a clear conclusion that will draw everything together for them?

6.10   You could **use the above questions as a checklist for planning your report.** If you can then jot down a 'skeleton' of the headings and sub-headings you have decided to use (with notes of any particular points that occur to you as you go along) you will be ready to write. The formal headings of standard business reports may be useful to help you to organise your thoughts - but may not be necessary, or even advisable, if they simply act as a constraint on what you actually want to say, and how you want to 'shape' it. You should not worry at this stage about having 'Terms of Reference', 'Procedures', 'Findings' (discussed below), unless they provide a relevant framework for your report.

General points on style

6.11 There are certain stylistic requirements in the writing of reports.

(a) **Objectivity and balance.** Even in a report designed to persuade as well as inform, avoid subjective value judgements and emotions: bias can undermine the credibility of the report and its recommendations.

(i) Emotional or otherwise loaded words should be avoided.

(ii) In more formal reports, first person subjects should be replaced with third person:

	It became clear that...
I/we found that...	(Your name) found that...
	Investigation revealed that...

(iii) Colloquialisms and abbreviated forms should be avoided in formal written English: colloquial (informal) 'I've', 'don't' etc should be replaced by 'I have' and 'do not'. You should not use expressions like 'blew his top': formal phrases should be used, such as 'showed considerable irritation'.

(b) **Ease of understanding**

(i) Avoid technical language and complex sentence structures.

(ii) The material will have to be logically organised.

(iii) Relevant themes should be signalled by appropriate headings or highlighted for easy scanning.

(iv) The layout of the report should display data clearly and attractively. Figures and diagrams should be used with discretion. Highlight key figures which appear within large tables of numbers.

6.12 Various **display techniques** may be used to make the content of a report easy to identify and digest. For example, the relative importance of points should be signalled, each point may be referenced, and the body of text should be broken up to be easy on the eye. These aims may be achieved as follows.

(a) **Headings.** Spaced out or enlarged CAPITALS may be used for the main title.

Important headings, such as sections of the report, may be in CAPITALS. Underlining or *Italics* may be used for subheadings.

(b) **References.** Each section or point in a formal report should have a code for easy identification and reference.

Use different labelling for each type of heading	*Alternatively a 'decimal' system may be used:*	
Main section headings		
I,II,III,IV,V etc.	1	Heading 1
A,B,C,D,E etc.	1.1	Subheading 1
Subsections	1.1.1	Subheading 1, Point 1
1,2,3,4,5 etc.	1.1.2	Subheading 1, Point 2
	1.2	Subheading 2
Points and subpoints	1.2.1	(a) Subheading 2, Point 1,
Subpoint (a),		
(a), (b), (c) etc.	2	Heading 2
(i), (ii), (iii) etc.		

(c) **Spacing.** Intelligent use of spacing separates headings from the body of the text for easy scanning, and also makes a large block more attractive and 'digestible'.

Activity 1.9

Rewrite the following sentence so that it is more suitable for inclusion into a report.

'I've had a good hard look but try as I might I've not been able to find out who's been nicking money from the petty cash box. I'd prefer it if you'd take over now.'

The format of reports

6.13 When a **formal request is made by a superior for a report** to be prepared, such as in a formally-worded memorandum or letter, the **format and style of the report** will obviously have to be **formal as well**.

An **informal request** for a report - 'Can you jot down a few ideas for me about...' or 'Let me know what happens, will you?' - **will result in an informal report**, in which the structure will be less rigid, and the style slightly more personal (depending on the relationship perceived to exist between the writer and user).

If in doubt, it is better (more courteous and effective) to be too formal than over-familiar.

6.14 EXAMPLE: SHORT INFORMAL REPORT

REPORT

To: A Manager, Accounts Manager
From: A Student, Senior Accounts Clerk
Date: 17 March 20X1
Subject: Customer complaint by Anne Gre

1 *Background*

I have thoroughly investigated the situation with regard to Ms Gre, and the correspondence provided. Ms Gre is Accounts Clerk for Paunch & Pull who have had an account with us since October 1995: account number 123 xwp. Credit terms were agreed with the firm whereby 10% discount is credited to their account for payment within two weeks of the statement date, payment in any case to be made within 30 days.

I have questioned the Accounts Clerk concerning the Paunch & Pull account for January, and we have together consulted the records. In addition I telephoned the third party, Palls & Sons, to make enquiries about payments received from them.

2 *Findings*

The substance of Ms Gre's complaint was that she had received from us a reminder that an amount of £5,932.60 was outstanding on the Paunch & Pull account for January: according to Ms Gre, a cheque payment for that amount had been sent on the 12th January, ie within 10 days of receiving the statement on 3rd January.

Records show no payment credited to the Paunch & Pull account. However, an amount of £5,932.60 was credited to the account of Palls & Sons on the same day, and payment duly acknowledged. Palls & Sons when consulted admitted to having been puzzled by the acknowledgement of a payment they had never made.

The Accounts Clerk was absent through illness that week, and a temporary Clerk employed.

3 *Conclusion*

It would appear that the temporary Clerk credited the payment to the wrong account. The entries have been duly corrected, and 10% prompt payment discount credited to Paunch & Pull as usual. I am writing an appropriate letter of apology and explanation to Ms Gre.

Obviously this is a matter of some concern in terms of customer relations. I suggest that all clerks be reminded of the need for due care and attention, and that temporary staff in particular be briefed on this matter in the future.

The memorandum report

6.15 In informal reporting situations within an organisation, the 'short informal report' may well be presented in A4 **memorandum** format, which incorporates title headings and can thereafter be laid out at the writer's discretion. An ordinary memorandum or 'memo' may be used for **flexible, informal reports**: aside from the convenient title headings, there are no particular requirements for **structure, headings or layout**. The writer may consider whatever is logical, convenient and attractive for the reader.

BPP PUBLISHING

ASSESSMENT ALERT

When doing assessed work, always make sure that your work is neat and well-presented.

Key learning points

- Costs can be divided into three elements, **materials, labour** and **expenses.**

- A **cost unit** is a unit of product which has costs attached to it.

- A **cost centre** is something that incurs costs. It may be a place, a person, a group of people or an item of equipment.

- A **profit centre** is similar to a cost centre but it is accountable for both costs *and* revenues.

- Costs can be **analysed** in different ways. For example, direct, indirect, fixed, variable.

- Costs can also be analysed according to their **function**. For example, production, distribution and selling, administration and financing costs.

- Cost information is recorded to aid **price setting, decision making, planning** and **budgeting, control** and **reporting**.

- Costing using **standards** is a good way of keeping a business under control.

- The purpose of a **report** must be clear, and certain general principles should be followed in planning and giving structure to a report.

- Stylistic qualities of reports include **objectivity, balance** and **ease of understanding.**

- To keep the main body of the report short enough to hold the reader's interest, detailed explanations, charts and tables of figures should be put into **appendices**. The main body of the report should make cross-reference to the appendices in appropriate places.

Quick quiz

1   What is a cost unit?

2   Which cost elements make up overheads?

3   List five reasons for recording cost information.

4   Why is cost information essential for reporting?

5   List four types of functional cost.

6   How is cost accounting distinguished from financial accounting?

7   Why is it important to space out a report?

8   When should appendices be used in reports?

9   When would a memorandum report be used?

Answers to quick quiz

1   A unit of product or service which incurs cost.

2   Indirect materials, indirect labour and indirect expenses.

3 • Determination of selling prices
   • Decision making
   • Planning and budgeting
   • Control
   • Reporting

4 • Companies need to prepare accounts in order to comply with statute
   • In order to keep a record of VAT due to/due from Customs & Excise
   • For senior management to assess whether targets have been met

5 • Production costs
   • Distribution and selling costs
   • Administration costs
   • Financing costs

6 • Cost information is used internally, whereas financial accounts are for external use
   • Cost information is recorded and presented in a manner which is based on what management require
   • Financial accounts are required by law
   • Financial accounts are an historical record, whereas cost information is an historical record *and* also used as a tool for future planning

7 Intelligent use of spacing separates headings from the body of the text for easy scanning, and also makes a large block more attractive and 'digestible'.

8 Appendices should be used if the report will be too long and detailed to hold the reader's interest.

9 A memorandum would be used for flexible, informal reports.

Answers to activities

Answer 1.1

Labour	*Materials*	*Expenses*
Petrol station staff	Saleable stocks	Heating
Car park attendant	Carrier bags	Lighting
Check-out staff	Other packaging	Telephone
Supervisors	Cleaning materials	Post
Delicatessen staff	Bakery ingredients	Stationery
Bakery staff		Rent
Shelf fillers		Business rates
Warehouse staff		Water rates
Cleaners		Vehicle running costs
Security staff		Advertising
Administrative staff		Discounts
Managers		Bank charges
Delivery staff		Waste disposal
Maintenance staff		

Answer 1.2

(a) Variable
(b) Fixed
(c) Fixed
(d) Fixed
(e) Variable

Answer 1.3

(a) Costs are recorded for the following reasons.

   (i) To set selling prices

(ii)   To aid decision making
(iii)   To help with planning
(iv)   As a means of control
(v)   For inclusion in accounts

(b) If costs are monitored and the results are compared with what was originally planned, a significant difference in a particular area may suggest that area of the business is not being properly managed. The reasons can be investigated and corrective action taken as necessary.

(c) Parties interested in cost information will include the following.

(i)   The manager responsible for the costs
(ii)   The board of directors
(iii)   Shareholders
(iv)   Competitors
(v)   The Inland Revenue and Customs & Excise

Answer 1.4

	Job	Batch	Process
Suit (off the peg)		X	
Suit (tailored)	X		
Soap			X
Yoghurt			X
House decoration	X		
Car alarm		X	
Paper			X
Poster		X	
Audit	X		

Answer 1.5

(a) A **cost unit** is a unit of product (or service) for which costs are ascertained.

(b) A **functional cost** is one that relates to a 'function' or area of operations of a business, for example production, administration, research, distribution and so on.

(c) A **fixed cost** is one that does not increase or decrease when a different number of units are produced.

(d) A **standard cost** is an estimate of what a cost should be on average in the future.

(e) An **indirect cost** is one that cannot be identified with one particular product.

(f) An **overhead** is another name for an indirect cost (as explained in (e)).

(g) A **cost centre** is a location, a function (a person or a department), an activity or a piece of equipment which incurs costs that can be attributed to cost units.

(h) A **variable cost** is one that increases when more units are made and decreases when fewer units are made.

(i) A **budget** is a business's plan for a forthcoming period expressed in money. It shows how many of its products the business expects to sell at what price and how much the costs are expected to be.

(j) A **direct cost** is one that can be traced directly to a unit of product.

Answer 1.6

REPORT

To: Managing Director
From: Cost Accountant
Date: 1 January 20X1
Subject: The need for a costing system and the classification of costs

As requested, this report will outline the need for a costing system and it will provide suggestions for alternative classifications of cost which can assist management decision making, planning and control.

The need for a costing system

The managers of a business need detailed information to help them to plan and control the organisation's resources. The aggregate information provided by the financial accounting system does not provide sufficient control information. Managers need to know the answers to questions such as the following.

(a) What is it costing to make each product?

(b) Is the actual cost of running this department higher or lower than budgeted?

(c) How will the company profit be affected by this proposed course of action?

(d) Is investment in this capital expenditure project worthwhile?

A properly designed costing system can provide the answers to questions like these and it will assist managers in their tasks of decision making, planning and control.

The financial accountant's classification of costs

The financial accountant has classified costs in accordance with the requirements of the Companies Act for external reporting purposes in financial accounts. This classification will not help to answer the type of questions outlined above and a more detailed analysis is needed for internal control purposes.

Alternative classifications of cost

Four alternative classifications of cost which can assist management decision making, planning and control are as follows.

(a) *Classification by element of cost.* Costs can be classified according to whether they are direct materials, direct labour, direct expenses, production overhead, administration overhead or selling and distribution overhead. This further analysis, in particular of cost of sales, will improve control because management will be able to allocate responsibilities more effectively and they will be able to concentrate on the most important and significant elements of cost.

(b) *Direct costs and indirect costs.* A direct cost is a cost which is actually caused by a particular cost unit or cost centre. An indirect cost is a cost which must be shared between several cost units or cost centres because it is not caused by any particular one. This classification is especially useful for decision making and for control purposes. For example if managers know the direct cost of a unit they can assess its individual profitability and the direct cost of a cost centre can help in judging the efficiency and effectiveness of the centre.

(c) *Fixed costs and variable costs.* A fixed cost is a cost which remains constant whatever the level of activity, within the relevant range. A variable cost increases if activity levels rise and it falls if activity levels are reduced. If managers know which costs are fixed and which are variable then they can plan to achieve a desired level of profit and they can determine the breakeven point. A knowledge of cost behaviour will also help them to understand the effect on cost of any proposed changes in activity levels and it will assist in various ad hoc decisions such as dropping a product line and make or buy decisions.

(d) *Controllable costs and uncontrollable costs.* A budgetary control system allocates responsibility for the control of budget centre costs to individual managers. The managers must receive feedback of their actual costs compared with budget costs so that they can take control action to correct any variances. Control reports should provide a separate analysis of the costs which are within the manager's control (the controllable costs) and those over which the manager cannot exercise control (the uncontrollable costs). Highlighting the controllable costs will concentrate management attention on the areas where their control action is likely to be worthwhile. This analysis will also avoid the motivational problems which can arise when managers are held responsible for a cost over which they have no control.

21

Answer 1.7

Avoid 'jargon', overly technical terms and specialist knowledge which the user may not share.

Keep vocabulary, sentence and paragraph structures as simple as possible, for clarity (without patronising an intelligent user).

Bear in mind the type and level of detail that will interest the user and be relevant to his/her purpose.

In a business context, the user may range from senior manager to junior supervisor, to non-managerial employee (such as in the case of minutes of a meeting) to complete layman (customer, press and so on). Vocabulary, syntax and presentation, the amount of detail gone into, the technical matter included and the formality of the report structure should all be influenced by such concerns.

Answer 1.8

(a)   Who is the user?
(b)   What type of report will be most useful to him/her?
(c)   What exactly does he/she need to know, and for what purpose?
(d)   How much information is required, how quickly and at what cost?
(e)   Do you need to give judgements, recommendations etc (or just information)?

Answer 1.9

This is one suggestion as to how the sentence could be rewritten.

'Despite thorough investigations it has been impossible to find an explanation for the differences that have been occurring between petty cash records and the petty cash float. It is clear the investigations should now be carried out at a higher level.'

2 Cost behaviour

Chapter topic list

1 Cost behaviour and levels of activity

2 Cost behaviour patterns

Learning objectives

On completion of this chapter you will be able to:

	Performance criteria	Range statement
• Understand techniques related to cost analysis		16.2
• Explain and illustrate the nature of fixed and variable costs		16.1, 16.2
• Explain and illustrate the nature of direct and indirect costs		16.1, 16.2

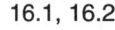

1   COST BEHAVIOUR AND LEVELS OF ACTIVITY

Activity 2.1

The following data relates to expenditure on the estate management (building services, grounds and gardens) of two colleges.

	College Alpha	College Beta
Number of students	4,000	10,000
Total area in cubic metres	877,000	2,800,000

	College Alpha		College Beta	
	Own		Own	
Cost element	workforce	Contractors	workforce	Contractors
	£	£	£	£
Category A				
(work of a periodic nature)				
1 Painting	20,000	-	-	12,000
2 Maintenance	2,000	-	4,000	14,000
Category B				
(irregular work)				
1 Painting	1,500	-	10,800	-
2 Maintenance	7,000	47,000	14,500	13,000
Category C				
(ground and gardens)				
3 General	18,000	3,000	35,000	-
Category D				
(unallocated)				
3 General	10,600	-	70,000	-

Task

Tabulate the above information showing the expenditure per 1,000 cubic metres.

Calculations should be in pounds to two decimal places.

Activity 2.2

Comment briefly on your findings in Activity 2.1

1.1   How would you go about dividing costs into variable costs and fixed costs? Well, you can hopefully remember the general rule which is that **variable costs vary directly with changes in activity levels,** whereas **fixed costs do not vary directly with changes in activity levels.** We are concerned here primarily with the short run - eg a period of one year or less - and therefore with a defined range of activity.

1.2   We can demonstrate the ways in which costs behave by drawing graphs. This chapter aims to examine the different ways in which costs behave (this is known as **cost behaviour** analysis) and to demonstrate this behaviour graphically.

KEY TERM

Cost behaviour is 'the variability of input costs with activity undertaken. A number of cost behaviour patterns are possible, ranging from variable costs whose level varies directly with the level of activity, to fixed costs, where changes in output have no effect upon the cost level'.

CIMA *Official Terminology, 2000*

Level of activity

KEY TERM

The **level of activity** refers to the amount of work done, or the number of events that have occurred.

1.3 Depending on circumstances, the level of activity may refer to the volume of production in a period, or the number of items sold, or the value of items sold, the number of invoices issued, the number of invoices received, the number of units of electricity consumed, the labour turnover and so on.

Basic principles of cost behaviour

1.4 The basic principle of cost behaviour is that **as the level of activity rises, costs will usually rise**. It will cost more to produce 2,000 units of output than it will cost to produce 1,000 units; it will usually cost more to make five telephone calls than to make one call and so on.

1.5 This principle is common sense. The problem for the accountant, however, is to determine for each item of cost the way in which costs rise and by how much as the level of activity increases. For our purposes here, the level of activity for measuring cost will generally be taken to be the volume of production.

2 COST BEHAVIOUR PATTERNS

Fixed costs

2.1 As you probably know, a **fixed cost** is a cost which tends to be unaffected by increases or decreases in the volume of output. Fixed costs are a period charge, in that they relate to a span of time. As the time span increases, so too will the fixed costs (which are sometimes referred to as period costs for this reason).

2.2 A sketch graph of a fixed cost would look like this.

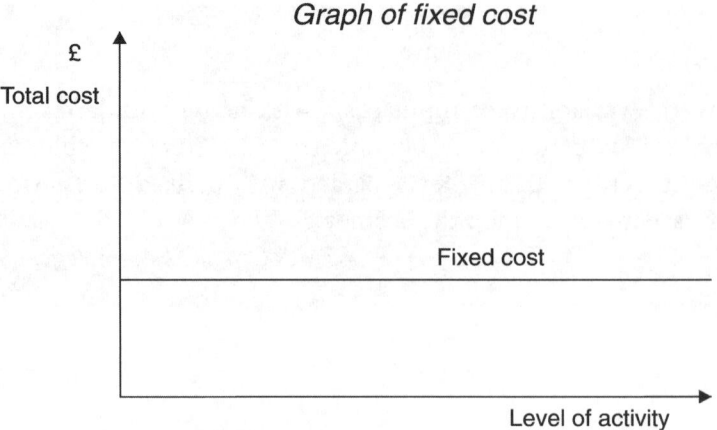

Graph of fixed cost

The following are fixed costs.

(a) The salary of the managing director (per month or per annum)
(b) The rent of a single factory building (per month or per annum)
(c) Straight line depreciation of a single machine (per month or per annum)

Step costs

2.3 Many items of cost are a fixed cost in nature within certain levels of activity. For example the **depreciation of a machine** may be fixed if production remains below 1,000 units per month, but if production exceeds 1,000 units, a second machine may be required, and the cost of depreciation (on two machines) would go up a step.

2.4 A sketch graph of a **step cost** would look as in graph (a) below.

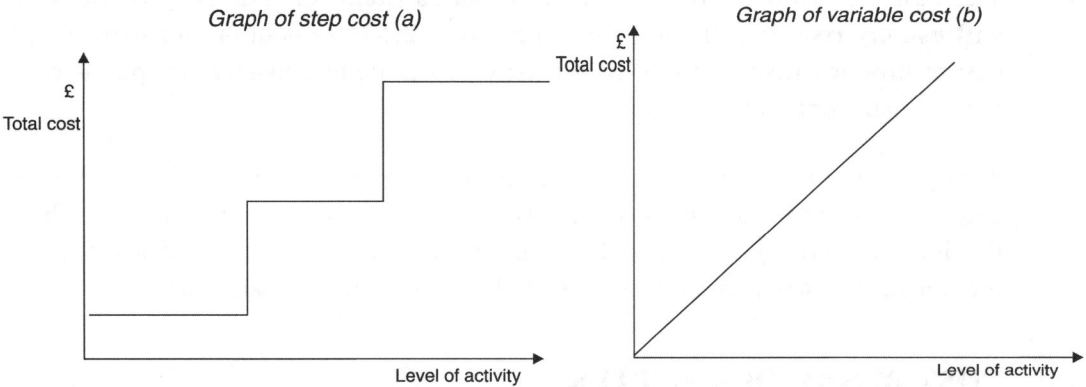

Graph of step cost (a)   *Graph of variable cost (b)*

2.5 **Other examples of step costs**

(a) **Rent,** where accommodation requirements increase as output levels get higher.

(b) **Basic wages**. Basic pay of employees is nowadays usually fixed, but as output rises, more employees (direct workers, supervisors, managers etc) are required.

Variable costs

2.6 A **variable cost** is a cost which tends to vary directly with the volume of output. The variable cost per unit is the same amount for each unit produced whereas *total* variable cost increases as volume of output increases. A sketch graph of variable cost would look as in (b) above.

2.7   A constant variable cost per unit implies that the purchase price per unit of material purchased or cost per labour hour worked and so on is constant, and that the rate of material usage/labour productivity is also constant. In other words, **constant rate and efficiency levels are implied in variable costs.**

(a)   The most important variable cost is the cost of raw materials (where there is no discount for bulk purchasing. Bulk purchase discounts reduce the cost of purchases).

(b)   Direct labour costs are, for very important reasons, classed as a variable cost even though basic wages are usually fixed.

(c)   Sales commission is variable in relation to the volume or value of sales.

Mixed costs (or semi-variable costs or semi-fixed costs)

2.8   **Mixed costs** are cost items which are **part fixed** and **part variable**, and are therefore partly affected by changes in the level of activity.

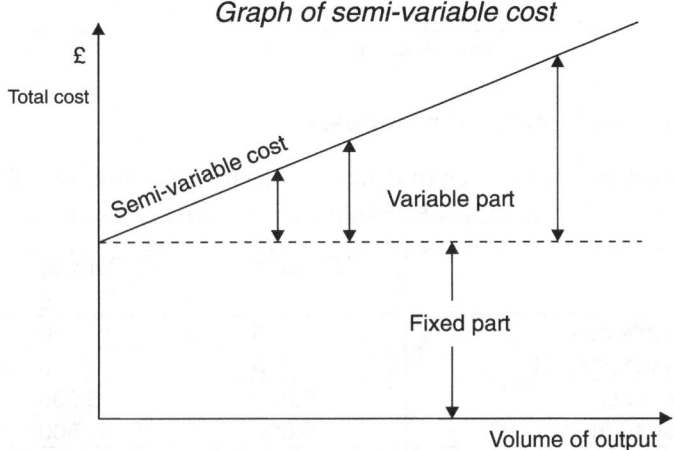

Graph of semi-variable cost

2.9   **Examples** of these costs include electricity and gas bills, both of which are costs where there is normally a standing basic charge plus a variable charge per unit of consumption.

Other cost behaviour patterns

2.10   Other cost behaviour patterns may be appropriate to certain cost items. Graphs (1) and (2) show the behaviour of the cost of materials after deduction of bulk purchase discount.

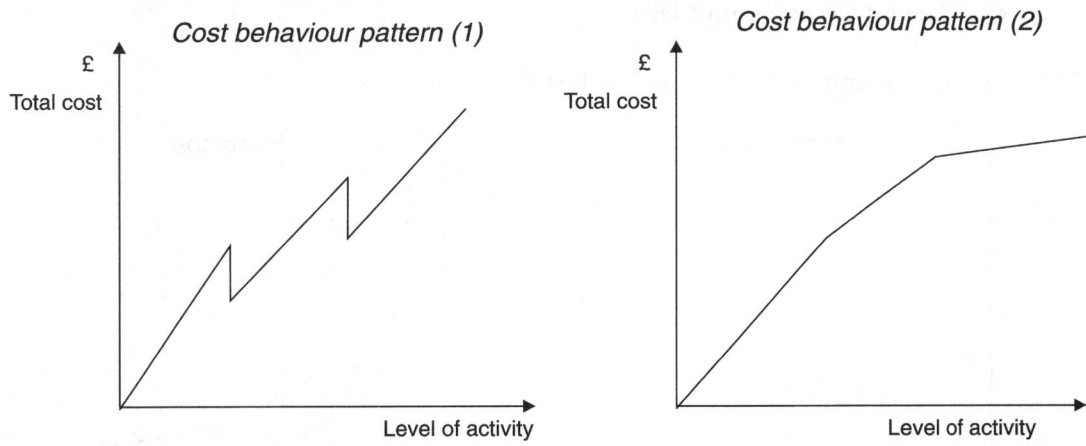

Cost behaviour pattern (1)

Cost behaviour pattern (2)

2.11 In graph (1) the bulk purchase discount applies retrospectively to all units purchased whereas in graph (2) the discount applies only to units purchased in excess of a certain quantity, the earlier units being be paid for at a higher unit cost.

Graph (3) represents an item of cost which is variable with output up to a certain maximum level of cost; graph (4) represents a cost which is variable with output, subject to a minimum (fixed) charge.

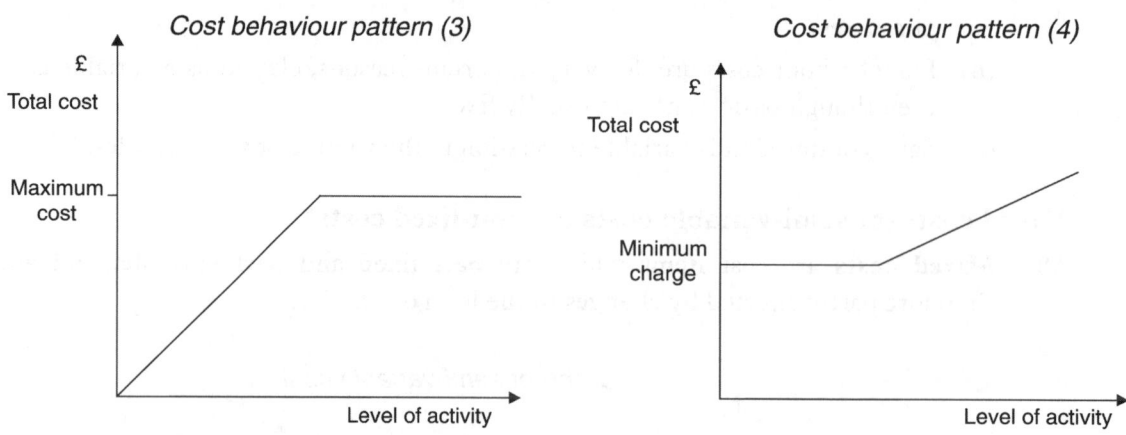

Cost behaviour and total and unit costs

2.12 The following table relates to different levels of production of the Randolph. The variable cost of producing a Randolph is £5. Fixed costs are £5,000.

	1 Randolph £	10 Randolphs £	50 Randolphs £
Total variable cost	5	50	250
Variable cost per unit	5	5	5
Total fixed cost	5,000	5,000	5,000
Fixed cost per unit	5,000	500	100
Total cost (fixed and variable)	5,005	5,050	5,250
Total cost per unit	5,005	505	105

2.13 By studying the table above, you should be able to see how different activity levels have an affect on the variable cost per unit, fixed cost per unit and the total cost per unit of a Randolph.

2.14 In summary, as activity levels rise:

- The variable cost per unit remains constant
- The fixed cost per unit falls
- The total cost per unit falls

2.15 In sketch graph form this may be illustrated as follows.

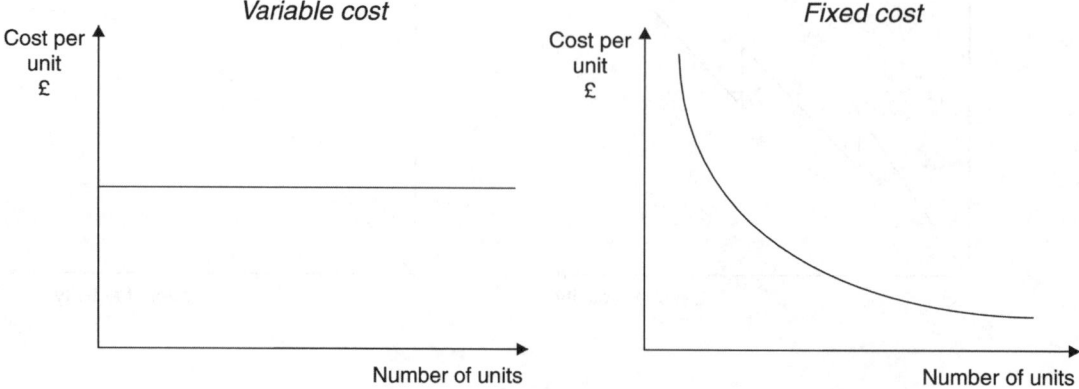

Activity 2.3

Are the following likely to be fixed, variable or mixed costs?

(a) Mobile telephone bill
(b) Annual salary of the chief accountant
(c) The accounting technician's annual membership fee to the AAT (paid by the company)
(d) Cost of materials used to pack 20 units of product X into a box
(e) Wages of warehousemen

Activity 2.4

Draw graphs to illustrate the following cost behaviour patterns.

(a) Variable costs
(b) Fixed costs
(c) Step costs

Key learning points

- **Cost behaviour patterns** demonstrate the way in which costs are affected by changes in the level of activity.

- Costs which are affected by the level of activity are **variable costs.**

- Costs which are not affected by the level of activity are **fixed costs** or **period costs.**

- **Step costs** are costs which are fixed in nature within certain levels of activity.

- **Mixed costs** (semi-variable/semi-fixed costs) are partly fixed and partly variable, and therefore only partly affected by changes in activity levels.

- The basic principle of cost behaviour is that **as the level of activity rises, costs will usually rise**.

- The **level of activity** is the amount of work done or the number of events that have occurred.

- In general, **as activity levels rise**, the variable cost per unit remains constant, the fixed cost per unit falls and the total cost per unit falls.

Quick quiz

1 How do variable costs differ from fixed costs?

2 How would you describe cost behaviour?

3 What does the level of activity refer to?

4 What is the basic principle of cost behaviour?

5 What is a step cost?

6 How do mixed costs behave?

Answers to quick quiz

1   Variable costs vary directly with changes in activity levels, whereas fixed costs do not.

2   The way in which costs vary with the level of activity.

3   The amount of work done or the number of events that have occurred.

4   As the level of activity rises, costs will normally rise.

5   A cost which is fixed in nature within certain levels of activity.

6   They are only partly affected by changes in the level of activity (as they are part fixed and part variable costs).

Answers to activities

Answer 2.1

	College Alpha		College Beta	
	Own workforce	Contractors	Own workforce	Contractors
£ per 1,000 cubic metres	£	£	£	£
Category A				
1 Painting	22.81	-	-	4.29
2 Maintenance	2.28	-	1.43	5.00
Category B				
1 Painting	1.71	-	3.86	-
2 Maintenance	7.98	53.59	5.18	4.64
Category C				
3 General	20.52	3.42	12.50	-
Category D				
3 General	12.09	-	25.00	-
Total	67.39	57.01	47.97	13.93
Total cost per 1,000 cubic metres	£124.40		£61.90	

Answer 2.2

The total cost per cubic metre for college Alpha is approximately double the cost for college Beta. The main difference occurs on category B irregular work. There seems to be an exceptional maintenance job which has been carried out by contractors at college Alpha this period. It is difficult to draw any conclusions without knowing the relative ages of the college buildings.

College Beta covers a much larger area than Alpha but does not necessarily incur proportionately higher fixed costs, particularly in respect of maintaining the grounds and gardens. This seems to be reflected in the lower cost per cubic metre in category C.

Answer 2.3

(a)   Mixed
(b)   Fixed
(c)   Fixed
(d)   Variable
(e)   Variable

Answer 2.4

See the graphs at paragraphs 2.2 and 2.3.

3 Overheads and absorption costing

Chapter topic list

1 What are overheads?

2 What is absorption costing?

3 Overhead apportionment

4 Overhead absorption

5 Over and under absorption

6 Predetermined rates and actual costs

7 Fixed and variable overheads and capacity

8 Non-production overheads

9 Activity based costing

Learning objectives

On completion of this chapter you will be able to:

	Performance criteria	Range statement
• Describe and justify the process of apportioning manufacturing overhead costs incurred in production	16.1	
• Explain and illustrate the apportionment of overheads using appropriate bases	16.1	
• Apply overhead absorption rates using different methods	16.1	

BPP PUBLISHING

1 WHAT ARE OVERHEADS?

KEY TERM

An **overhead** is the cost incurred in the course of making a product, providing a service or running a department, but which cannot be traced directly and in full to the product, service or department.

1.1 **Overheads** are the total of indirect materials, indirect labour and indirect expenses. (Note that in the previous chapter we were looking at **expenses**, and whether they were direct or indirect.)

1.2 Here is one common way of categorising overheads.

KEY TERMS

- **Production (or factory) overhead** includes all indirect material costs, indirect wages and indirect expenses incurred in the factory from receipt of the order until its completion.

- **Administration overhead** is all indirect material costs, wages and expenses incurred in the direction, control and administration of an undertaking.

- **Selling overhead** is all indirect materials costs, wages and expenses incurred in promoting sales and retaining customers.

- **Distribution overhead** is all indirect material costs, wages and expenses incurred in making the packed product ready for despatch and delivering it to the customer.

1.3 **Examples of production overhead**

(a) **Indirect materials** which cannot be traced in the finished product

- Consumable stores, eg material used in negligible amounts

(b) **Indirect wages,** meaning all wages not charged directly to a product

- Salaries and wages of non-productive personnel in the production department, eg foremen

(c) **Indirect expenses** (other than material and labour) not charged directly to production

- Rent, rates and insurance of a factory

- Depreciation, fuel, power, repairs and maintenance of plant, machinery and factory buildings

1.4 **Examples of administration overhead**

(a) **Depreciation** of office administration overhead, buildings and machinery.

(b) **Office salaries,** including salaries of administrative directors, secretaries and accountants.

(c) Rent, rates, insurance, lighting, cleaning and heating of general offices, telephone and postal charges, bank charges, legal charges, audit fees.

1.5 Examples of selling overhead

(a) **Printing** and **stationery**, such as catalogues and price lists

(b) **Salaries** and **commission** of salesmen, representatives and sales department staff

(c) **Advertising** and **sales promotion**, market research

(d) Rent, rates and insurance of sales offices and showrooms, bad debts and collection charges, cash discounts allowed, after sales service

1.6 Examples of distribution overhead

(a) Cost of packing cases

(b) Wages of packers/drivers/despatch clerks

(c) Freight/insurance charges, rent, rates, insurance/depreciation of warehouses, depreciation/running expenses of delivery vehicles

1.7 There are different schools of thought as to the correct method of dealing with overheads. We will be looking at **absorption costing** in detail in this chapter. **Activity based costing** is considered briefly in Section 9 of this chapter while **marginal costing** is examined in the next chapter.

2 WHAT IS ABSORPTION COSTING?

2.1 **The objective of absorption costing is to include in the total cost of a product** (unit or job, say) **an appropriate share of the organisation's total overhead** (ie an amount that reflects the amount of time and effort that has gone into producing a unit or completing a job).

2.2 If an organisation had but one production department and produced identical units then the total overheads would be divided among the total units produced. Life is, of course, never that simple.

> **KEY TERM**
>
> **Absorption costing** is a method of sharing overheads between a number of different products on a fair basis.

The effect of absorption costing

2.3 Before describing the procedures by which overhead costs are shared out among products, it may be useful to consider the reasons why absorption costing is commonly used.

2.4 Suppose that a company makes and sells 100 units of a product each week. The direct cost per unit is £6 and the unit sales price is £10. Production overhead costs £200 per week and administration, selling and distribution overhead costs £150 per week. The weekly profit could be calculated as follows.

	£	£
Sales (100 units × £10)		1,000
Direct costs (100 × £6)	600	
Production overheads	200	
Administration, selling, distribution costs	150	
		950
Profit		50

2.5 In absorption costing, overhead costs will be added to each unit of product manufactured and sold.

	£ per unit
Direct cost per unit	6
Production overhead (£200 per week for 100 units)	2
Full factory cost	8

The weekly profit would be calculated as follows.

	£
Sales	1,000
Less factory cost of sales (100 × £8)	800
Gross profit	200
Less administration, selling, distribution costs	150
Net profit	50

2.6 It may already be apparent that the weekly profit is £50 no matter how the figures have been presented. This being so, how does absorption costing serve any useful purpose in accounting? Is it necessary?

Is absorption costing necessary?

2.7 The reasons for using absorption costing have traditionally been identified as follows.

(a) **Stock valuations**. Stock in hand must be valued for two reasons.

    (i)   For the closing stock figure in the balance sheet

    (ii)   For the cost of sales figure in the profit and loss account. The valuation of stocks will actually affect profitability during a period because of the way in which cost of sales is calculated.

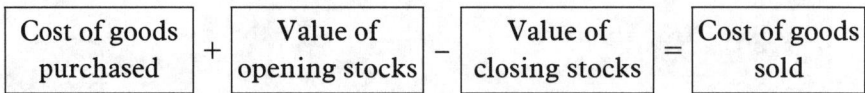

    In our example above, closing stocks could be valued at direct cost (£6), but in absorption costing, they would be valued at a fully absorbed factory cost of £8 per unit.

(b) **Pricing decisions**. Many companies attempt to fix selling prices by calculating the full cost of production or sales of each product, and then adding a margin for profit. In our example, the company might have fixed a gross profit margin at 25% on factory cost, or 20% of the sales price, in order to establish the unit sales price of £10. 'Full cost plus pricing' (discussed later in this Interactive Text) can be particularly useful for companies which do jobbing or contract work, where each job or contract is different, so that a standard unit sales price cannot be fixed. Without using absorption costing, a full cost is difficult to ascertain.

(c) **Establishing the profitability of different products**. This argument in favour of absorption costing is more contentious, but is worthy of mention here. If a company sells more than one product, it will be difficult to judge how profitable each individual product is, unless overhead costs are shared on a fair basis and charged to the cost of sales of each product.

Statement of standard accounting practice 9 (SSAP 9)

2.8 Of these three arguments, the problem of valuing stocks is perhaps the most significant, because **absorption costing is recommended in financial accounting by the Statement of Standard Accounting Practice on Stocks and long-term contracts (SSAP 9)**. SSAP 9 deals with financial accounting systems and not with cost accounting systems. The cost accountant is (in theory) free to value stocks by whatever method seems best, but where companies integrate their financial accounting and cost accounting systems into a single system of accounting records, the valuation of closing stocks will be determined by SSAP 9.

Costing procedures

2.9 The three stages of calculating the costs of overheads to be charged to manufactured output are **allocation, apportionment** and **absorption**. (Absorption costing is the name used since absorption is the ultimate aim of the other two procedures.) **Allocation** is the process of assigning costs to cost centres. We shall now begin our study of absorption costing by looking at the process of **overhead apportionment**.

3 OVERHEAD APPORTIONMENT

KEY TERM

Apportionment is a procedure whereby indirect costs (overheads) are spread fairly between cost centres.

Stage 1: sharing out common costs

3.1 Overhead apportionment follows on from overhead allocation. The first stage of overhead apportionment is to **identify all overhead costs** as production, administration, selling and distribution overhead. This means that the shared costs (such as rent and rates, heat and light and so on) initially allocated to a single cost centre must now be shared out between the other (functional) cost centres.

Bases of apportionment

3.2 It is rarely possible to use only one method of apportioning costs to the various cost centres of an organisation. The bases of apportionment for the most usual cases are given below. (Some overhead costs can be allocated directly to the user cost centre without having to be apportioned, for example indirect wages and consumable supplies, because they relate solely to that cost centre.)

BPP PUBLISHING

Overhead to which the basis applies	Basis
Rent, rates, heating and light, repairs and depreciation of buildings	Floor area occupied by each cost centre
Depreciation, insurance of equipment	Cost or book value of equipment
Personnel office, canteen, welfare, wages and cost offices, first aid	Number of employees, or labour hours worked in each cost centre
Heating, lighting (see above)	Volume of space occupied by each cost centre
Carriage inwards (costs paid for the delivery of material supplies)	Value of material issues to each cost centre

3.4 EXAMPLE: OVERHEAD APPORTIONMENT

Kettle Ltd incurred the following overhead costs.

	£
Depreciation of factory	1,000
Factory repairs and maintenance	600
Factory office costs (treat as production overhead)	1,500
Depreciation of equipment	800
Insurance of equipment	200
Heating	390
Lighting	100
Canteen	900
	5,490

Information relating to the production and service departments in the factory is as follows.

	Department			
	Production A	Production B	Service X	Service Y
Floor space (sq. metres)	1,200	1,600	800	400
Volume (cubic metres)	3,000	6,000	2,400	1,600
Number of employees	30	30	15	15
Book value of equipment	£30,000	£20,000	£10,000	£20,000

How should the overhead costs be apportioned between the four departments?

3.5 SOLUTION

		Total cost	To Department			
Item of cost	*Basis of apportionment*		A	B	X	Y
		£	£	£	£	£
Factory depreciation	(floor area)	1,000	300	400	200	100
Factory repairs	(floor area)	600	180	240	120	60
Factory office	(no. of employees)	1,500	500	500	250	250
Equipment depn	(book value)	800	300	200	100	200
Equipment insurance	(book value)	200	75	50	25	50
Heating	(volume)	390	90	180	72	48
Lighting	(floor area)	100	30	40	20	10
Canteen	(no. of employees)	900	300	300	150	150
Total		5,490	1,775	1,910	937	868

Stage 2: apportioning service cost centre costs to production cost centres

3.6 The second stage of overhead apportionment concerns **the treatment of service cost centres**. A factory is divided into several production cost centres and also many service cost centres, but **only the production cost centres are directly involved in the manufacture of the units**. In order to be able to add production overheads to unit costs, it is necessary to have all the overheads charged to (or located in) the production cost centres. The next stage in absorption costing is therefore to apportion the costs of service cost centres to the production cost centres.

3.7 There are two methods by which the apportionment of service cost centre costs can be done.

(a) Apportion the costs of each service cost centre to production cost centres only.

(b) Apportion the costs of each service cost centre not only to production cost centres, but also to other service cost centres which make use of its services, and eventually apportion all costs to the production cost centres alone by a gradual process of **repeated distribution**.

3.8 Whichever method is used, the basis of apportionment must be fair and a different apportionment basis may be applied for each service cost centre. This is demonstrated in the following table.

Service cost centre	Possible basis of apportionment
Stores	Number or cost value of material requisitions
Maintenance	Hours of maintenance and repair work done for each cost centre
Production planning	Direct labour hours worked for each production cost centre

3.9 EXAMPLE: DIRECT APPORTIONMENT

Maid Marion Ltd incurred the following overhead costs.

	Production departments		Stores	Maintenance
	P	*Q*	*department*	*department*
	£	£	£	£
Allocated costs	6,000	4,000	1,000	2,000
Apportioned costs	2,000	1,000	1,000	500
	8,000	5,000	2,000	2,500

Production department P requisitioned materials to the value of £12,000. Department Q requisitioned £8,000 of materials. The maintenance department provided 500 hours of work for department P and 750 for department Q. What are the total production overhead costs of Departments P and Q?

3.10 SOLUTION

Service department	Basis of apportionment	Total cost	Dept P	Dept Q
		£	£	£
Stores	Value of requisitions	2,000	1,200	800
Maintenance	Direct labour hours	2,500	1,000	1,500
		4,500	2,200	2,300
Previously allocated and apportioned costs		13,000	8,000	5,000
Total overhead		17,500	10,200	7,300

The repeated distribution method

3.11 Apportionment is a procedure whereby indirect costs are spread fairly between cost centres. It could therefore be argued that a fair sharing of service cost centre costs is not possible unless consideration is given to the work done by each service cost centre for other service cost centres.

3.12 For example, suppose a company has two production and two service departments (stores and maintenance). The following information about activity in a recent costing period is available.

	Production departments		Stores	Maintenance
	1	2	department	department
Overhead costs	£10,030	£8,970	£10,000	£8,000
Cost of material requisitions	£30,000	£50,000	-	£20,000
Maintenance hours needed	8,000	1,000	1,000	-

The problem is that the stores department uses the maintenance department, and the maintenance department uses the stores.

(a) If service department overheads were apportioned directly to production departments, the apportionment would be as follows.

Service department	Basis of apportionment	Total cost	1	2
		£	£	£
Stores	(Material requisitions)	10,000	3,750	6,250
Maintenance	(Maintenance hours)	8,000	7,111	889
		18,000	10,861	7,139
Overheads of Department 1 and 2		19,000	10,030	8,970
		37,000	20,891	16,109

(b) If, however, recognition is made of the fact that the stores and maintenance department do work for each other, and the basis of apportionment remains the same, we ought to apportion service department costs as follows.

	Production departments		Stores	Maintenance
	1	2	department	department
Stores (100%)	30%	50%	-	20%
Maintenance (100%)	80%	10%	10%	-

This may be done using the repeated distribution method of apportionment, which is perhaps best explained by means of an example.

3.13 EXAMPLE: REPEATED DISTRIBUTION METHOD OF APPORTIONMENT

	Production departments		Stores	Maintenance
	1	*2*	*department*	*department*
	£	£	£	£
Overhead costs	10,030	8,970	10,000	8,000
Apportion stores (see note (a))	3,000	5,000	(10,000)	2,000
			0	10,000
Apportion maintenance	8,000	1,000	1,000	(10,000)
			1,000	0
Repeat: Apportion stores	300	500	(1,000)	200
Repeat: Apportion maintenance	160	20	20	(200)
Repeat: Apportion stores	6	10	(20)	4
Repeat: Apportion maintenance	4	-	-	(4)
	21,500	15,500	0	0

Notes

(a) The first apportionment could have been the costs of maintenance, rather than stores; there is no difference to the final results.

(b) When the repeated distributions bring service department costs down to small numbers (here £4), the final apportionment to production departments is an approximate rounding.

3.14 You should note the difference in the final overhead apportionments to each production department using the different apportionment methods. Unless the difference is substantial, the first method might be preferred because it is clerically simpler to use.

4 OVERHEAD ABSORPTION

KEY TERM

Overhead absorption is the process whereby overhead costs allocated and apportioned to production cost centres are added to unit, job or process costs. Overhead absorption is sometimes called **overhead recovery.**

4.1 Having allocated and/or apportioned all overheads, the next stage in the costing treatment of overheads is to add them to, or absorb them into, cost units. The cost unit of a business is the thing that it sells. For the biro manufacturer it is the biro, or a box of 100 biros if he only sells them in that quantity. For a solicitor it is an hour of his time and there are as many more examples as there are different types of business. Overheads are usually added to cost units using a **predetermined overhead absorption rate**, which is calculated using figures from the budget.

4.2 An overhead absorption rate for the forthcoming accounting period is calculated as follows.

(a) An **estimate is made of the overhead** likely to be incurred during the coming period.

(b) An **estimate is made of the total hours, units, or direct costs** or whatever it is upon which the overhead absorption rates are to be based (the **activity level**).

(c) The **estimated overhead is divided by the budgeted activity level**. This produces the overhead absorption rate.

4.3 The overhead then gets into the cost unit by **applying** the rate that has been calculated to the information already established for the cost unit. If overhead is absorbed at, say £2 per labour hour, then a cost unit that takes 3 labour hours to produce absorbs $3 \times £2 = £6$ in overheads. Let's look at a very simple example. It might help to make things clearer.

4.4 EXAMPLE: THE BASICS OF ABSORPTION COSTING

Suppose total overhead of Athena Ltd is estimated to be £50,000 and total labour hours are expected to be 100,000 hours. The business makes two products, the Greek and the Roman. Greeks take 2 labour hours each to make and Romans take 5. What is the overhead cost per unit for Greeks and Romans respectively if overheads are absorbed on the basis of labour hours?

4.5 SOLUTION

(a) First calculate the absorption rate.

$$\text{Absorption rate} = \frac{\text{Total estimated overhead}}{\text{Total estimated activity level}} = \frac{£50,000}{100,000 \text{ hrs}}$$

$$= £0.50 \text{ per labour hour}$$

(b) Now apply it to the products.

	Greek	Roman
Labour hours per unit	2	5
Absorption rate per labour hour	£0.50	£0.50
Overhead absorbed per unit	£1	£2.50

Possible bases of absorption

4.6 The different bases of absorption (or 'overhead recovery rates') which can be used are as follows.

- A percentage of direct materials cost
- A percentage of direct labour cost
- A percentage of total direct cost (prime cost)
- A rate per machine hour
- A rate per direct labour hour
- A rate per unit
- A percentage of factory cost (for administration overhead)
- A percentage of sales or factory cost (for selling and distribution overhead)

4.7 Which basis should be used for production overhead depends largely on the organisation concerned. As with apportionment it is a matter of being fair.

4.8   Percentages of materials cost, wages or direct cost should be adopted only where the value of the materials and/or wages is considered to have some relationship with the overhead.

For example, it is safe to assume that the indirect costs for producing brass screws are similar to the indirect costs for producing steel screws, but the cost of brass is very much greater than that of steel. Consequently, the overhead charge for brass screws would be too high and that for steel screws too low, if a percentage of cost of materials rate were to be used.

A similar argument applies if a wages based rate is used since a unit produced by a trained mechanic would be charged with too much overhead whereas one produced by an apprentice would be charged with too little.

4.9   Note in particular that a rate per unit is only effective if all units are identical and therefore give rise to an identical amount of overhead.

4.10   Many factories therefore use the **direct labour hour rate** or **machine hour rate** in preference to a rate based on a percentage of direct materials cost, wages or prime cost. A machine hour rate would be used in departments where production is controlled or dictated by machines. In such a situation, where a small number of workers supervise a process that is performed almost entirely by machine, the distinction between direct and indirect labour may be difficult to identify, and labour costs may not be the principal costs of production. A direct labour hour basis is more appropriate in a labour intensive environment. We shall return to this point at the end of this chapter.

4.11   EXAMPLE: OVERHEAD ABSORPTION RATES

The budgeted production overheads and other budget data of Eiffel Ltd are as follows.

	Production dept X	*Production dept Y*
Budget		
Overhead cost	£36,000	£5,000
Direct materials cost	£32,000	
Direct labour cost	£40,000	
Machine hours	10,000	
Direct labour hours	18,000	
Units of production		1,000

What would the absorption rate be for each department using the various bases of apportionment?

4.12   SOLUTION

(a)   Department X

(i)   % of direct materials cost $\dfrac{£36,000}{£32,000} \times 100\% = 112.5\%$

(ii)   % of direct labour cost $\dfrac{£36,000}{£40,000} \times 100\% = 90\%$

(iii) % of total direct cost $\dfrac{£36,000}{£72,000} \times 100\% = 50\%$

(iv) Rate per machine hour

$$\frac{£36,000}{10,000 \text{ hrs}} = £3.60 \text{ per machine hour}$$

(v) Rate per direct labour hour

$$\frac{£36,000}{18,000 \text{ hrs}} = £2 \text{ per direct labour hour}$$

(b) For department Y the absorption rate will be based on units of output.

$$\frac{£5,000}{1,000 \text{ units}} = £5 \text{ per unit produced}$$

The effect on total cost of applying different bases

4.13 The choice of the basis of absorption is significant in determining the cost of individual units, or jobs, produced. Using the Eiffel Ltd example in Paragraphs 4.11 and 4.12, suppose that in department X an individual product has a materials cost of £80, a labour cost of £85, and requires 36 labour hours and 23 machine hours to complete. The overhead cost of the product would vary, depending on the basis of absorption used by the company for overhead recovery.

(a) As a percentage of direct material cost, the overhead cost would be:

$$112.5\% \times £80 = £90.00$$

(b) As a percentage of direct labour cost, the overhead cost would be:

$$90\% \times £85 = £76.50$$

(c) As a percentage of total direct cost, the overhead cost would be:

$$50\% \times £165 = £82.50$$

(d) Using a machine hour basis of absorption, the overhead cost would be:

$$23 \text{ hrs} \times £3.60 = £82.80$$

(e) Using a labour hour basis, the overhead cost would be: $36 \text{ hrs} \times £2 = £72.00$

4.14 In theory, each basis of absorption would be possible, but the company should choose the most appropriate basis for its own costs. In our example, this choice will be significant in determining the cost of individual products, as the following summary shows, but the total cost of production overheads is the estimated overhead expenditure, no matter what basis of absorption is selected. It is the relative share of overhead costs borne by individual products and jobs which is affected by the choice of overhead absorption basis.

4.15 A summary of the product costs for the example beginning in Paragraph 4.11 is shown as follows.

	Percentage of materials cost	*Percentage of labour cost*	*Percentage of prime cost*	*Machine hours*	*Direct labour hours*
	£	£	£	£	£
Direct material	80	80.0	80.0	80.0	80
Direct labour	85	85.0	85.0	85.0	85
Production overhead	90	76.5	82.5	82.8	72
Full factory cost	255	241.5	247.5	247.8	237

Basis of overhead recovery

The arbitrary nature of absorption costing

4.16 Absorption costing may irritate you because, even if a company is trying to be 'fair', there is a great lack of precision about the way an absorption base is chosen. This arbitrariness is one of the main criticisms of absorption costing, and if absorption costing is to be used (because of its other virtues) then it is important that the methods used are kept under regular review. Changes in working conditions should, if necessary, lead to changes in the way in which work is accounted for.

Activity 3.1

The traditional methods of cost allocation, cost apportionment and absorption into products are being challenged by some writers who claim that much information given to management is misleading when these methods of dealing with fixed overheads are used to determine product costs. You are required to explain what is meant by *cost allocation*, *cost apportionment* and *absorption*.

Blanket absorption rates and separate departmental absorption rates

KEY TERM

A **blanket overhead absorption rate** is an absorption rate used throughout a factory for all jobs and units of output irrespective of the department in which they were produced.

4.17 Consider a factory in which total overheads were £500,000 and there were 250,000 direct machine hours, during the period under consideration. We could calculate a **blanket overhead absorption rate** of £2 per direct machine hour (£500,000 ÷ 250,000). This would mean that all jobs passing through the factory would be charged at the same rate of £2 per direct machine hour.

4.18 If a factory has a number of departments, and jobs do not spend an equal amount of time in each department, then the use of a blanket overhead absorption rate is not really appropriate. The main argument against the use of blanket overhead absorption rates is the fact that some products will absorb a higher overhead charge than is fair. Likewise, other products may absorb less overhead charge than is fair.

4.19 If different departments use separate absorption rates, overheads should be charged to products on a fairer basis than when blanket overhead absorption rates are used. The overhead charged to products should then be representative of the costs of the efforts and resources put into making them.

5 OVER AND UNDER ABSORPTION

5.1 It was stated earlier that the usual method of accounting for overheads is to add overhead costs on the basis of a **predetermined recovery rate**. This rate is a sort of **standard cost** since it is based on figures representing what is supposed to happen (that is, figures from the budget). Using the predetermined absorption rate, the actual cost of production can be established as follows.

Direct materials	+	Direct labour	+	Direct expenses	+	Overheads*	=	Actual cost of production

* based on the predetermined overhead absorption rate

ASSESSMENT ALERT

If you have calculated an overhead absorption rate of £20 per direct labour hour and a product requires 5 direct labour hours, it will absorb £100 (£20 × 5) of overhead.

5.2 Many students become seriously confused about what can appear a very unusual method of costing (actual cost of production including a figure based on the budget). Study the following example to help clarify this tricky point.

5.3 EXAMPLE: USING THE PREDETERMINED RECOVERY RATE

Patrick Ltd budgeted to make 100 units of product called Jasmine at a cost of £3 per unit in direct materials and £4 per unit in direct labour.

The sales price would be £12 per unit, and production overheads were budgeted to amount to £200. A unit basis of overhead recovery is in operation.

During the period 120 units were actually produced and sold (for £12 each) and the actual cost of direct materials was £380 and of direct labour, £450. Overheads incurred came to £210.

What was the cost of sales of product Jasmine, and what was the profit? Ignore administration, selling and distribution overheads.

5.4 SOLUTION

The cost of production and sales is the actual direct cost plus the cost of overheads, absorbed at a predetermined rate as established in the budget. In our example, the overhead recovery rate would be £2 per unit produced (£200 ÷ 100 units).

The actual cost of sales is calculated as follows.

	£
Direct materials (actual)	380
Direct labour (actual)	450
Overheads absorbed (120 units × £2)	240
Full cost of sales, product Jasmine	1,070
Sales of product Jasmine (120 units × £12)	1,440
Profit, product Jasmine	370

5.5 You may already have noticed that the actual overheads incurred, £210, are not the same as the overheads absorbed (that is, included) into the cost of production and hence charged against profit, £240. Nevertheless, in normal absorption costing £240 is the 'correct' cost. The discrepancy between actual overheads incurred, and the overheads absorbed, which is an inevitable feature of absorption costing, is only reconciled at the end of an accounting period, as the **under absorption** or **over absorption** of overhead.

Why does under or over absorption occur?

5.6 The rate of overhead absorption is based on two estimates and so it is quite likely that either one or both of the estimates will not agree with what actually occurs. Overheads incurred will, therefore, probably be either greater than or less than overheads absorbed into the cost of production. Let's consider an example.

5.7 Suppose that the estimated overhead in a production department is £80,000 and the estimated activity is 40,000 direct labour hours. The overhead recovery rate (using a direct labour hour basis) would be £2 per direct labour hour.

Actual overheads in the period are, say £84,000 and 45,000 direct labour hours are worked.

	£
Overhead incurred (actual)	84,000
Overhead absorbed (45,000 × £2)	90,000
Over absorption of overhead	6,000

In this example, the cost of produced units or jobs has been charged with £6,000 more than was actually spent. An adjustment to reconcile the overheads charged to the actual overhead is necessary and the over-absorbed overhead will be written off as an adjustment to the profit and loss account at the end of the accounting period.

5.8 **The overhead absorption rate is predetermined from estimates of overhead cost and the expected volume of activity.** Under or over recovery of overhead will therefore occur in the following circumstances.

(a) Actual overhead costs are different from the estimates.

(b) The actual activity volume is different from the estimated activity volume.

(c) Both actual overhead costs and actual activity volume are different from the estimated costs and volume.

5.9 **EXAMPLE: UNDER/OVER ABSORPTION**

Watkins Ltd has a budgeted production overhead of £50,000 and a budgeted activity of 25,000 direct labour hours and therefore a recovery rate of £2 per direct labour hour. Calculate the under-/over-absorbed overhead, and the reasons for the under/over absorption, in the following circumstances.

(a) Actual overheads cost £47,000 and 25,000 direct labour hours are worked.
(b) Actual overheads cost £50,000 and 21,500 direct labour hours are worked.
(c) Actual overheads cost £47,000 and 21,500 direct labour hours are worked.

5.10 **SOLUTION**

(a)	£
Actual overhead	47,000
Absorbed overhead (25,000 × £2)	50,000
Over-absorbed overhead	3,000

Here there is over absorption because although the actual and estimated direct labour hours are the same, actual overheads cost *less* than expected and so too much overhead has been charged against profit.

(b)

	£
Actual overhead	50,000
Absorbed overhead (21,500 × £2)	43,000
Under-absorbed overhead	7,000

Here there is under absorption because although estimated and actual overhead costs were the same, fewer direct labour hours were worked than expected and hence insufficient overheads have been charged against profit.

(c)

	£
Actual overhead	47,000
Absorbed overhead (21,500 × £2)	43,000
Under-absorbed overhead	4,000

The reason for the under absorption is a combination of the reasons in (a) and (b).

5.11 If you are still unsure about when the overhead is under absorbed and when it is over absorbed try looking at it from a different point of view.

(a) If the actual absorption rate that would have been calculated if the actual figures had been known turns out to be less than the estimated one used for absorption then too much overhead will have been absorbed and there will have been **over absorption**.

(b) If the actual rate is more than the estimated one then too little overhead will have been absorbed and there will have been **under absorption**.

The occurrence of under- and over-absorbed overheads can be summarised as follows.

Actual rate	*Absorption of overheads*
Less	Over
More	Under

Activity 3.2

Brave & Hart Ltd has a budgeted production overhead of £214,981 and a budgeted activity of 35,950 hours of direct labour. Before settling on these estimates the company's accountant had a number of other possibilities for each figure, as shown below. Determine (preferably by inspection rather than full calculation) whether overheads will be over or under absorbed in each case if the alternatives turn out to be the actual figures.

		Over or under?
(a)	$\dfrac{215,892}{35,950}$	☐
(b)	$\dfrac{214,981}{36,005}$	☐
(c)	$\dfrac{213,894}{36,271}$	☐
(d)	$\dfrac{215,602}{35,440}$	☐

---

6 PREDETERMINED RATES AND ACTUAL COSTS

6.1 Using a **predetermined overhead absorption rate** more often than not leads to under or over absorption of overheads because actual output and overhead expenditure will turn out to be different from estimated output and expenditure. You might well wonder why the complications of under or over absorption are necessary. Surely it would be better to use actual costs and outputs, both to avoid under or over absorption entirely and to obtain more 'accurate' costs of production?

6.2 Suppose that a company draws up a budget (a plan based on estimates) to make 1,200 units of a product in the first half of 20X7. Budgeted production overhead costs, all fixed costs, are £12,000. Due to seasonal demand for the company's product, the volume of production varies from month to month. Actual overhead costs are £2,000 per month. Actual monthly production in the first half of 20X7 is listed below, and total actual production in the period is 1,080 units.

The table below shows the production overhead cost per unit using the following.

(a) A predetermined absorption rate of $\dfrac{£12,000}{1,200} = £10$ per unit

(b) An actual overhead cost per unit each month

(c) An actual overhead cost per unit based on actual six-monthly expenditure of £12,000 and actual six-monthly output of 1,080 units = £11.11 per unit

			Overhead cost per unit		
			(a)	*(b)*	*(c)*
			Predetermined	*Actual cost*	*Average actual cost*
	Expenditure	*Output*	*unit rate*	*each month*	*in the six months*
Month	*(A)*	*(B)*		*(A) ÷ (B)*	
	£	Units	£	£	£
January	2,000	100	10	20.00	11.11
February	2,000	120	10	16.67	11.11
March	2,000	140	10	14.29	11.11
April	2,000	160	10	12.50	11.11
May	2,000	320	10	6.25	11.11
June	2,000	240	10	8.33	11.11
	12,000	1,080			

6.3 Methods (a) and (c) give a constant overhead cost per unit each month, regardless of seasonal variations in output. Method (b) gives variable unit overhead costs, depending on the time of the year. For this reason, it is argued that method (a) or (c) would provide more useful (long-term) costing information.

6.4 If prices are based on full cost with a percentage mark-up for profit, method (b) would give seasonal variations in selling prices, with high prices in low-season and low prices in high-season. Methods (a) and (c) would give a constant price based on 'cost plus'.

6.5 With method (a), overhead costs per unit are known throughout the period, and cost statements can be prepared at any time. This is because **predetermined overhead rates are known in advance**. With method (c), overhead costs cannot be established until after the end of the accounting period. For example, overhead costs of output in January 20X7 cannot be established until actual costs and output for the period are known, which will be not until after the end of June 20X7.

6.6 For the reasons given above, **predetermined overhead rates are preferable to actual overhead costs**, in spite of being estimates of costs and in spite of the need to write off under-or over-absorbed overhead costs to the profit and loss account.

7 FIXED AND VARIABLE OVERHEADS AND CAPACITY

7.1 When an organisation has estimated fixed and variable production overheads, it may calculate a separate absorption rate for each.

(a) A **fixed overhead absorption rate** is intended to share out a fixed cost for a given time period between items of production (or other activities).

(b) A **variable overhead absorption rate** is intended to charge a variable cost to the item of production (or other activity) that is responsible for incurring the cost. Extra activity adds to the total variable overhead cost, and the variable overhead absorption rate is intended to recognise this fact.

7.2 For example, suppose that a company expects its fixed overhead costs in period 9 to be £12,000 and its variable overhead costs to be £1 per direct labour hour.

(a) If the budget is for 4,000 direct labour hours, the absorption rate per hour would be as follows.

	£
Fixed overhead (£12,000 ÷ 4,000)	3
Variable overhead	1
Total	4

(b) If the budget is for 5,000 direct labour hours, the absorption rate per hour would be as follows.

	£
Fixed overhead (£12,000 ÷ 5,000)	2.4
Variable overhead	1.0
Total	3.4

The absorption rate, and so the fully absorbed cost of production, comes down as the budgeted volume of activity rises, but only for fixed overheads, not variable overheads. This is because the (constant) fixed overheads are being shared between a greater number of hours whereas the total variable overhead continues to rise with the volume of activity.

7.3 **The importance of the volume of activity in absorption costing cannot be overstated,** not only because large differences between budgeted and actual volume create large amounts of under- or over-absorbed overheads, but also because higher budgeted output reduces absorption rates and costs.

Full capacity, practical capacity and budgeted capacity

7.4 In connection with capacity you may come across a number of terms, as follows.

> **KEY TERMS**
>
> - **Full capacity** is the maximum number of hours that could be worked in ideal conditions.
>
> - **Practical capacity** is full capacity less an allowance for hours lost unavoidably because conditions are not ideal.
>
> - **Budgeted capacity** is the number of hours that a business plans to work.

As a simple example, budgeted capacity would be 60% of practical capacity if a business planned to work a 3 day week rather than a 5 day week. Full capacity would be a 7 day week.

8 NON-PRODUCTION OVERHEADS

8.1 For **external reporting** (eg statutory accounts) it is not necessary to allocate non-production overheads to products.

8.2 For **internal reporting** purposes and for a number of industries which base the selling price of their product on estimates of *total* cost or even actual cost (such industries usually use a job costing system), a total cost per unit of output may be required. Builders, law firms and garages often charge for their services by adding a percentage profit margin to actual cost. For product pricing purposes and for internal management reports it may therefore be appropriate to allocate non-production overheads to units of output.

Bases for apportioning non-production overheads

8.3 A number of non-production overheads such as delivery costs or salespersons' salaries are clearly identified with particular products and can therefore be classified as direct costs. The majority of non-production overheads, however, cannot be directly allocated to particular units of output.

8.4 Two possible methods of allocating such non-production overheads are as follows.

Method 1

8.5 **Choose a basis for the overhead absorption rate** which most closely matches the non-production overhead such as direct labour hours, direct machine hours and so on. The problem with such a method is that most non-production overheads are unaffected in the short term by changes in the level of output and tend to be fixed costs.

Method 2

8.6 **Allocate non-production overheads on the ability of the products to bear such costs**. One possible approach is to use the production cost as the basis for allocating non-production costs to products.

The **overhead absorption rate** is calculated as follows.

$$\text{Overhead absorption rate} = \frac{\text{Estimated non-production overheads}}{\text{Estimated production costs}}$$

8.7 If, for example, budgeted distribution overheads are £200,000 and budgeted production costs are £800,000, the predetermined distribution overhead absorption rate will be 25% of production cost.

8.8 Other bases for absorbing overheads are as follows.

Types of overhead	Possible absorption base
Selling and marketing	Sales value
Research and development	Consumer cost (= production cost minus cost of direct materials) or added value (= sales value of product minus cost of bought in materials and services)
Distribution	Sales values
Administration	Consumer cost or added value

Administration overheads

8.9 The administration overhead usually consists of the following.

- Executive salaries
- Office rent and rates
- Lighting
- Heating and cleaning the offices

In cost accounting, administration overheads are regarded as periodic charges which are charged against the gross costing profit for the year (as in financial accounting).

Selling and distribution overheads

8.10 **Selling and distribution overheads** are often considered collectively as one type of overhead but they are actually quite different forms of expense.

(a) **Selling costs** are incurred in order to obtain sales.

(b) **Distribution costs** begin as soon as the finished goods are put into the warehouse and continue until the goods are despatched or delivered to the customer.

8.11 **Selling overhead** is therefore often absorbed on the basis of sales value so that the more profitable product lines take a large proportion of overhead.

8.12 **Distribution overhead** is more closely linked to production than sales and from one point of view could be regarded as an extra cost of production. It is, however, more usual to regard production cost as ending on the factory floor and to deal with distribution overhead separately. It is generally absorbed on a percentage of production cost but special circumstances, such as size and weight of products affecting the delivery charges, may cause a different basis of absorption to be used.

Activity 3.3

You are the cost accountant of an industrial concern and have been given the following budgeted information regarding the four cost centres within your organisation.

	Dept 1 £	Dept 2 £	Maintenance dept £	Canteen £	Total £
Indirect labour	60,000	70,000	25,000	15,000	170,000
Consumables	12,000	16,000	3,000	10,000	41,000
Heating and lighting					12,000
Rent and rates					18,000
Depreciation					30,000
Supervision					24,000
Power					20,000
					315,000

You are also given the following information.

	Dept 1	Dept 2	Maintenance dept	Canteen	Total
Floor space in square metres	10,000	12,000	5,000	3,000	30,000
Book value of machinery (£)	150,000	120,000	20,000	10,000	300,000
Number of employees	40	30	10		80
Kilowatt hours	4,500	4,000	1,000	500	10,000

You are also told the following.

(a) The canteen staff are outside contractors.

(b) Departments 1 and 2 are production cost centres and the maintenance department and canteen are service cost centres.

(c) The maintenance department provides 4,000 service hours to Department 1 and 3,000 service hours to Department 2.

(d) That Department 1 is machine intensive and Department 2 is labour intensive.

(e) That 6,320 machine hours and 7,850 labour hours are budgeted for Departments 1 and 2 respectively for 20X4.

Tasks

(a) Provide an overhead cost statement showing the allocation and apportionment of overhead to the four cost centres for 20X4, clearly showing the basis of apportionment.

(b) Calculate the overhead absorption rates for Department 1 on the basis of the machine hours and department 2 on the basis of labour hours.

(c) On the basis that for 20X4 actual overheads for Department 1 turn out to be £155,000 and machine hours worked 6,000, whilst actual overheads for Department 2 turn out to be £156,000 and labour hours worked 7,900, calculate the under or over recovery of overheads for each department.

Activity 3.4

This activity continues the scenario given in Activity 3.3.

The managing director of your organisation suggests to you that one blanket rate rather than separate overhead absorption rates for Departments 1 and 2 based on machine hours and labour hours respectively would be more beneficial for future years.

Draft a reply, in the form of a memorandum, to this assertion.

9 ACTIVITY BASED COSTING

9.1 **Absorption costing** appears to be a relatively straightforward way of adding overhead costs to units of production using, more often than not, a volume-related

absorption basis (such as direct labour hours or direct machine hours). Absorption costing assumes that all overheads are related primarily to production volume. This system was developed in a time when most organisations produced only a narrow range of products and when overhead costs were only a very small fraction of total costs, direct labour and direct material costs accounting for the largest proportion of the costs. Errors made in adding overheads to products were therefore not too significant.

9.2 Nowadays, however, with the advent of **advanced manufacturing technology**, overheads are likely to be far more important and in fact direct labour may account for as little as 5% of a product's cost. Moreover, there has been an increase in the costs of service support functions, such as setting-up, production scheduling, first item inspection and data processing, which assist the efficient manufacture of a wide range of products. These overheads are not, in general, affected by changes in production volume. They tend to vary in the long term according to the range and complexity of the products manufactured rather than the volume of output.

9.3 Because absorption costing tends to allocate too great a proportion of overheads to high volume products (which cause relatively little diversity), and too small a proportion of overheads to low volume products (which cause greater diversity and therefore use more support services), alternative methods of costing have been developed. **Activity based costing (ABC)** is one such development.

9.4 The major ideas behind **activity based costing** are as follows.

(a) **Activities cause costs**. Activities include ordering, materials handling, machining, assembly, production scheduling and despatching.

(b) **Products create demand for the activities.**

(c) **Costs are assigned to products on the basis of a product's consumption of the activities.**

Outline of an ABC system

9.5 An ABC costing system operates as follows.

Step 1 Identify an organisation's major activities.

Step 2 Identify the factors which determine the size of the costs of an activity/cause the costs of an activity. These are known as **cost drivers**. Look at the following examples.

Activity	Cost driver
Ordering	Number of orders
Materials handling	Number of production runs
Production scheduling	Number of production runs
Despatching	Number of despatches

Step 3 Collect the costs of each activity into what are known as **cost pools** (equivalent to cost centres under more traditional costing methods).

Step 4 Charge support overheads to products on the basis of their usage of the activity. A product's usage of an activity is measured by the

number of the activity's cost driver it generates.

Suppose, for example, that the cost pool for the ordering activity totalled £100,000 and that there were 10,000 orders (the cost driver). Each product would therefore be charged with £10 for each order it required. A batch requiring five orders would therefore be charged with £50.

9.6 **Absorption costing** and **ABC** have many similarities. In both systems, **direct costs go straight to the product and overheads are allocated to production cost centres/cost pools.** The main difference is as follows.

(a) **Absorption costing** uses usually two **absorption bases** (labour hours and/or machine hours) to charge overheads to products.

(b) **ABC** uses many **cost drivers** as absorption bases (number of orders, number of despatches and so on) to charge overheads to products.

9.7 In summary, ABC has absorption rates which are more closely linked to the cause of the overheads.

Cost drivers

9.8 **The principal idea of ABC is to identify cost drivers**. A **cost driver** is an activity which generates costs. Examples of cost drivers are:

- Sales levels, as these **drive** the costs of sales commission
- Miles travelled, as these **drive** the fuel costs
- Hours worked, as these **drive** the costs of labour

9.9 There are no clear-cut rules for selecting cost drivers, just as there are no rules for what to use as the basis for absorbing costs in absorption costing.

9.10 Consider the following.

(a) **Overheads which vary with output** should be traced to products using volume-related cost drivers, eg direct labour hours or direct machine hours.

(b) **Overheads which do not vary with output** should be traced to products using transaction based cost drivers, eg number of production runs or number of orders received.

9.11 The following example illustrates the point that traditional cost accounting techniques result in a misleading division of costs between low-volume and high-volume products, and that ABC can provide a more meaningful allocation of costs.

9.12 EXAMPLE: ABC

Suppose that Cooplan Ltd manufactures four products, W, X, Y and Z. Output and cost data for the period just ended are as follows.

BPP PUBLISHING

	Output	Number of production runs in the period	Material cost per unit	Direct labour hours per unit	Machine hours per unit
	Units		£		
W	10	2	20	1	1
X	10	2	80	3	3
Y	100	5	20	1	1
Z	100	5	80	3	3
		14			

Direct labour cost per hour is £5. Overhead costs are as follows.

	£
Short run variable costs	3,080
Set-up costs	10,920
Expediting and scheduling costs	9,100
Materials handling costs	7,700
	30,800

Required

Calculate product costs using the following approaches.

(a) Absorption costing

(b) ABC

9.13 SOLUTION

(a) Using a conventional absorption costing approach and an absorption rate for overheads based on either direct labour hours or machine hours, the product costs would be as follows.

	W	X	Y	Z	Total
	£	£	£	£	£
Direct material	200	800	2,000	8,000	11,000
Direct labour	50	150	500	1,500	2,200
Overheads *	700	2,100	7,000	21,000	30,800
	950	3,050	9,500	30,500	44,000
Units produced	10	10	100	100	
Cost per unit	£95	£305	£95	£305	

* £30,800 ÷ 440 hours = £70 per direct labour or machine hour.

(b) Using activity based costing and assuming that the number of production runs is the cost driver for set-up costs, expediting and scheduling costs and materials handling costs and that machine hours are the cost driver for short-run variable costs, unit costs would be as follows.

	W	X	Y	Z	Total
	£	£	£	£	£
Direct material	200	800	2,000	8,000	11,000
Direct labour	50	150	500	1,500	2,200
Short-run variable overheads (W1)	70	210	700	2,100	3,080
Set-up costs (W2)	1,560	1,560	3,900	3,900	10,920
Expediting, scheduling costs (W3)	1,300	1,300	3,250	3,250	9,100
Materials handling costs (W4)	1,100	1,100	2,750	2,750	7,700
	4,280	5,120	13,100	21,500	44,000

	W	X	Y	Z
Units produced	10	10	100	100
Cost per unit	£428	£512	£131	£215

Workings

1	£3,080 ÷ 440 machine hours	=	£7 per machine hour
2	£10,920 ÷ 14 production runs	=	£780 per run
3	£9,100 ÷ 14 production runs	=	£650 per run
4	£7,700 ÷ 14 production runs	=	£550 per run

Summary

Product	Conventional costing Unit cost £	ABC Unit cost £	Difference £
W	95	428	+ 333
X	305	512	+ 207
Y	95	131	+ 36
Z	305	215	− 90

Activity 3.5

Having attended an AAT course on activity based costing (ABC), you decide to experiment by applying the principles of ABC to the four products currently made and sold by your company. Details of the four products and relevant information are given below for one period.

Product	A	B	C	D
Output in units	120	100	80	120
Costs per unit:	£	£	£	£
Direct material	40	50	30	60
Direct labour	28	21	14	21

The four products are similar and are usually produced in production runs of 20 units.

The total of the production overhead for the period has been analysed as follows.

	£
Set up costs	5,250
Stores receiving	3,600
Inspection/quality control	2,100
Materials handling and despatch	4,620

You have ascertained that the 'cost drivers' to be used are as listed below for the overhead costs shown.

Cost	Cost driver
Set up costs	Number of production runs
Stores receiving	Requisitions raised
Inspection/quality control	Number of production runs
Materials handling and despatch	Orders executed

The number of requisitions raised on the stores was 20 for each product and the number of orders executed was 42, each order being for a batch of 10 of a product.

Task

Calculate the total costs for each product using activity based costing.

Key learning points

- **Overhead** is the cost incurred in the course of making a product, providing a service or running a department, but which cannot be traced directly and in full to the product, service or department.

- The four main types of overhead are **production, administration, selling** and **distribution.**

- Overheads may be dealt with by **absorption** costing, **activity based** costing or **marginal** costing.

- The main reasons for using absorption costing are for **stock valuations, pricing decisions** and **establishing the profitability of different products.**

- **Allocation, apportionment** and **absorption** are the three stages of calculating the costs of overheads to be charged to manufactured output.

- **Apportionment** is a procedure whereby indirect costs (overheads) are spread fairly between cost centres.

- Service cost centres costs may be apportioned to production cost centres by the **repeated distribution method.**

- Overhead absorption is the process whereby costs of cost centres are added to unit, job or process costs. Overhead absorption is sometimes called **overhead recovery.**

- **Predetermined overhead absorption** rates are calculated using budgeted figures.

- A **blanket overhead absorption rate** is an absorption rate used throughout a factory for all jobs and units of output irrespective of the department in which they were produced.

- The actual cost of production is made up of the following.

  ° Direct materials
  ° Direct labour
  ° Direct expenses
  ° Overheads (based on the predetermined overhead absorption rate)

- **Under** or **over absorption** of overheads occurs because the predetermined overhead absorption rates are based on forecasts (estimates).

- If an organisation has estimated fixed and variable production overheads, it may calculate a **separate absorption rate** for each.

- The three main types of capacity are **full** capacity, **practical** capacity and **budgeted** capacity.

- **Non-production overheads** may be allocated by choosing a basis for the overhead absorption rate which most closely matches the non-production overhead, or on the basis of a product's ability to bear costs.

- **Activity based costing** is an alternative to absorption costing. It involves the identification of the factors (**cost drivers**) which cause the costs of an organisation's major activities.

Quick quiz

1 What are the three main ways of dealing with overheads?

2 What is the main objective of absorption costing?

3 What are the three stages in charging overheads to units of output?

4 What is overhead apportionment?

5 What are the two stages of overhead apportionment?

6 What are the two methods by which the costs of service cost centres can be apportioned?

7 What is overhead absorption?

8 What is the main argument against the use of blanket overhead absorption rates?

9   What makes up the actual cost of production?

10   In which circumstances will under or over absorption of overheads occur?

11   What are the three types of capacity that you are likely to encounter in absorption costing, and how would you define them?

12   Suggest two possible methods for allocating non-production overheads to products.

13   What are the major ideas behind activity based costing?

Answers to quick quiz

1   Absorption costing, activity based costing and marginal costing.

2   To include an appropriate share of the organisation's total overhead in the total cost of a product.

3   Allocation, apportionment and absorption.

4   A procedure whereby indirect costs (overheads) are spread fairly between cost centres.

5   Sharing out common costs and apportioning service cost centre costs to production cost centres.

6   • To production cost centres only

        • To production cost centres *and* service cost centres which make use of its services using the repeated distribution method

7   The process whereby costs of cost centres are added to unit, job or process costs.

8   The fact that some products will absorb a higher or lower overhead charge than is fair.

9   Direct materials, direct labour, direct expenses and overheads (based on the predetermined overhead absorption rate).

10   • If actual overhead costs are different from estimates

        • If actual activity volume is different from estimated activity volume

        • If both actual overhead costs and actual activity volume are different from estimated costs and volume

11   • *Full capacity:* the maximum number of hours that could be worked in ideal conditions

        • *Practical capacity:* full capacity less an allowance for hours lost unavoidably because conditions are not ideal

        • *Budgeted capacity:* the number of hours that a business plans to work

12   By choosing a basis for the overhead absorption rate which most closely matches the non-production overhead or by allocating the non-production overheads on the product's ability to bear such costs.

13   • Activities cause costs.

        • Products create demand for activities.

        • Costs are assigned to products on the basis of a product's consumption of the activities.

Answers to activities

Answer 3.1

The terms requiring explanation are the three stages of calculating the costs of overheads to be charged to output.

(a)   Cost allocation is the process by which whole (discrete and identifiable) cost items are charged directly to a cost unit or cost centre. In the case of overhead costs, overhead cost items are charged direct to various overhead cost centres.

(b)   Cost apportionment is the process by which cost items, or cost centre costs, are divided between several cost centres in a 'fair' proportion based on the estimated benefit received.

(c)   Absorption is the process whereby costs of cost centres are added to unit, job or process costs.

In the past it has been common for costs to be absorbed into products on the basis of the number of direct labour hours it takes to make that product. It has been held that direct labour hours is the best measure of the levels of activity required.

However, it is no longer the case that direct labour hours is the most significant factor in production cost. With advanced manufacturing technology this is not the case: perhaps only 5% of a product's cost will be direct labour, the majority of the remainder being made up of overheads.

Some overheads are still determined by volume of activity as measured by the number of direct labour or machine hours. Other overheads, however, are not so much related to the volume of output as to the activities or transactions in the departments where the overhead is incurred.

Answer 3.2

You could try to answer this activity by considering how the value of a simple fraction like 4 divided by 2 would increase or decrease as the value of the denominator or numerator varied. Remember that if the actual rate is more than the estimated rate there will be under absorption and *vice versa*.

(a)   Under (because actual production overheads are higher than standard)
(b)   Over (because actual hours are higher than standard)
(c)   Over (because actual production overheads are lower than standard)
(d)   Under (because actual hours are lower than standard)

If you find it difficult to do this by inspection, there is nothing wrong with calculating the estimated rate (£5.98) and then the actual rate in each case (£6.00; £5.97; £5.90; £6.08), but having done this make sure that you can explain in non-numerical terms what has happened. For example, in (c) lower overheads and a higher number of active hours have led to over absorption.

Answer 3.3

	Basis	Dept 1 £	Dept 2 £	Maintenance dept £	Canteen £	Total £
Indirect labour	-	60,000	70,000	25,000	15,000	170,000
Consumables	-	12,000	16,000	3,000	10,000	41,000
Heat and light	Space	4,000	4,800	2,000	1,200	12,000
Rent and rates	Space	6,000	7,200	3,000	1,800	18,000
Depreciation	Book value	15,000	12,000	2,000	1,000	30,000
Supervision	Employees	12,000	9,000	3,000	-	24,000
Power	Kilowatt hours	9,000	8,000	2,000	1,000	20,000
		118,000	127,000	40,000	30,000	315,000
Canteen	Employees	15,000	11,250	3,750	(30,000)	-
		133,000	138,250	43,750	-	315,000
Maintenance	Service hours	25,000	18,750	(43,750)		-
		158,000	157,000	-		315,000

Overhead absorption rates

Dept 1

$$\frac{\text{Overhead} \quad £158,000}{\text{Machine hours} \quad 6,320} = £25 \text{ per machine hour}$$

Dept 2

$$\frac{\text{Overhead} \quad £157,000}{\text{Labour hours} \quad 7,850} = £20 \text{ per labour hour}$$

	Dept 1	Dept 2
Machine hours/labour hours	6,000	7,900
Absorption rate (per (b))	× £25	× £20
Overhead absorbed	£150,000	£158,000
Actual overhead	£155,000	£156,000
(Under)/over absorbed	£(5,000)	£2,000

Answer 3.4

MEMORANDUM

To:	Managing Director
From:	Management Accountant
Date:	1 January 20X5
Subject:	Overhead absorption rates

CIMA Official Terminology defines the term 'absorption rate' as a 'rate charged to a cost unit intended to account for the overhead at a predetermined level of activity'. The idea is to include a proportion of overheads in the cost which is attributed to individual units of production. The implication is that the amount of overheads incurred depends upon the level of activity.

Given that Department 1 is machine-intensive and Department 2 labour-intensive, machine hours and labour hours respectively most accurately measure the level of activity within each department. (This would show up more clearly if we were to examine the *direct* costs of each department.) It is therefore far more probable that these bases will result in a *fair* apportionment of costs than it is that a blanket rate will do.

Answer 3.5

	A	B	C	D
	£	£	£	£
Direct material	4,800	5,000	2,400	7,200
Direct labour	3,360	2,100	1,120	2,520
Production overhead (W):				
Set up costs	1,500	1,250	1,000	1,500
Stores receiving	900	900	900	900
Inspection/quality control	600	500	400	600
Material handling and despatch	1,320	1,100	880	1,320
Total cost	12,480	10,850	6,700	14,040

Working

Overhead costs will be divided in the following ratios, depending upon the number of production runs, requisitions or orders per product.

	A	B	C	D
Production runs	6	5	4	6
Requisitions raised	20	20	20	20
Orders executed	12	10	8	12

4 Marginal costing and absorption costing

Chapter topic list

1   Marginal cost and marginal costing

2   The principles of marginal costing

3   The contribution/sales ratio

4   Marginal costing and absorption costing and the calculation of profit

5   Reconciling the profit figures given by the two methods

6   Marginal costing versus absorption costing - which is better?

Learning objectives

On completion of this chapter you will be able to:

	Performance criteria	Range statement
• Explain and evaluate the impact of absorption and marginal costing on stock valuation and profit measurement	16.1, 16.2	16.2.3
• Reconcile the profits reported by absorption and marginal costing	16.1, 16.2	16.2.3

BPP PUBLISHING

1 MARGINAL COST AND MARGINAL COSTING

> **KEY TERMS**
>
> **Marginal costing** is an alternative method of costing to absorption costing. In marginal costing, only variable costs are charged as a cost of sale and a contribution is calculated which is sales revenue minus the variable cost of sales. Closing stocks of work in progress or finished goods are valued at marginal (variable) production cost. Fixed costs are treated as a period cost, and are charged in full to the profit and loss account of the accounting period in which they are incurred.
>
> **Marginal cost** is the cost of a unit of a product or service which would be avoided if that unit were not produced or provided.

1.1 The marginal production cost per unit of an item usually consists of **direct materials, direct labour** and **variable production overheads**.

1.2 Direct labour costs might be excluded from marginal costs when the work force is a given number of employees on a fixed wage or salary. Even so, it is not uncommon for direct labour to be treated as a variable cost, even when employees are paid a basic wage for a fixed working week. If in doubt, you should treat direct labour as a variable cost unless given clear indications to the contrary.

1.3 The **marginal cost of sales** usually consists of the marginal cost of production adjusted for stock movements plus the variable selling costs, which would include items such as sales commission, and possibly some variable distribution costs.

> **KEY TERM**
>
> **Contribution** is the difference between sales value and the marginal cost of sales.

Contribution is of fundamental importance in marginal costing, and the term 'contribution' is really short for 'contribution towards covering fixed overheads and making a profit'.

2 THE PRINCIPLES OF MARGINAL COSTING

2.1 The principles of marginal costing are as follows.

(a) Period fixed costs are the same, for any volume of sales and production (provided that the level of activity is within the 'relevant range'). Therefore, by selling an extra item of product or service the following will happen.

 (i) Revenue will increase by the sales value of the item sold.

 (ii) Costs will increase by the variable cost per unit.

 (iii) Profit will increase by the amount of contribution earned from the extra item.

(b) Similarly, if the volume of sales falls by one item, the profit will fall by the amount of contribution earned from the item.

(c) Profit measurement should therefore be based on an analysis of total contribution. Since fixed costs relate to a period of time, and do not change with increases or decreases in sales volume, it is misleading to charge units of sale with a share of fixed costs. Absorption costing is therefore misleading, and it is more appropriate to deduct fixed costs from total contribution for the period to derive a profit figure.

(d) When a unit of product is made, the extra costs incurred in its manufacture are the **variable production costs**. Fixed costs are unaffected, and no extra fixed costs are incurred when output is increased. It is therefore argued that the valuation of closing stocks should be at variable production cost (direct materials, direct labour, direct expenses (if any) and variable production overhead) because these are the only costs properly attributable to the product.

Before explaining marginal costing principles any further, it will be helpful to look at a numerical example.

2.2 EXAMPLE: MARGINAL COSTING PRINCIPLES

Bain Painkillers Ltd makes a drug called 'Relief', which has a variable production cost of £6 per unit and a sales price of £10 per unit. At the beginning of June 20X1, there were no opening stocks and production during the month was 20,000 units. Fixed costs for the month were £45,000 (production, administration, sales and distribution). There were no variable marketing costs.

Required

Calculate the contribution and profit for June 20X1, using marginal costing principles, if sales were as follows.

(a) 10,000 Reliefs
(b) 15,000 Reliefs
(c) 20,000 Reliefs

2.3 SOLUTION

The first stage in the profit calculation must be to identify the variable cost of sales, and then the contribution. Fixed costs are deducted from the total contribution to derive the profit. All closing stocks are valued at marginal production cost (£6 per unit).

	10,000 Reliefs		*15,000 Reliefs*		*20,000 Reliefs*	
	£	£	£	£	£	£
Sales (at £10)		100,000		150,000		200,000
Opening stock	0		0		0	
Variable production cost	120,000		120,000		120,000	
	120,000		120,000		120,000	
Less value of closing stock (at marginal cost)	60,000		30,000		-	
Variable cost of sales		60,000		90,000		120,000
Contribution		40,000		60,000		80,000
Less fixed costs		45,000		45,000		45,000
Profit/(loss)		(5,000)		15,000		35,000
Profit/(loss) per unit		£(0.50)		£1		£1.75
Contribution per unit		£4		£4		£4

2.4 The conclusions which may be drawn from this example are as follows.

(a) The **profit per unit varies** at differing levels of sales, because the average fixed overhead cost per unit changes with the volume of output and sales.

(b) The **contribution per unit is constant** at all levels of output and sales. Total contribution, which is the contribution per unit multiplied by the number of units sold, increases in direct proportion to the volume of sales.

(c) Since the **contribution per unit does not change**, the most effective way of calculating the expected profit at any level of output and sales would be as follows.

(i)   First calculate the total contribution

(ii) Then deduct fixed costs as a period charge in order to find the profit

(d) In our example the expected profit from the sale of 17,000 Reliefs would be as follows.

	£
Total contribution (17,000 × £4)	68,000
Less fixed costs	45,000
Profit	23,000

2.5 (a) If total contribution **exceeds fixed costs**, a profit is made.

(b) If total contribution **exactly equals fixed costs**, no profit and no loss is made. This is known as the **breakeven point**.

(c) If total contribution is **less than fixed costs**, there will be a loss.

Activity 4.1

WPR Ltd makes two products, the Ping and the Pong. Information relating to each of these products for May 20X1 is as follows.

	Ping	Pong
Opening stock	nil	nil
Production (units)	15,000	6,000
Sales (units)	10,000	5,000
Sales price per unit	£20	£30
Unit costs	£	£
Direct materials	8	14
Direct labour	4	2
Variable production overhead	2	1
Variable sales overhead	2	3

Fixed costs for the month	£
Production costs	40,000
Administration costs	15,000
Sales and distribution costs	25,000

(a) Using marginal costing principles and the method in 2.4(d) above, calculate the profit in May 20X1.

(b) Calculate the profit if sales had been 15,000 units of Ping and 6,000 units of Pong.

Profit or contribution information

2.6 The main advantage of **contribution information** (rather than profit information) is that it allows an easy calculation of profit if sales increase or decrease from a certain level. By comparing total contribution with fixed overheads, it is possible to determine whether profits or losses will be made at certain sales levels. **Profit information,** on the other hand, does not lend itself to easy manipulation.

3 THE CONTRIBUTION/SALES RATIO

3.1 Since the contribution per unit is the same at all sales volumes, given no change in the unit sales price, there must be a consistent relationship between contribution and sales; ie the contribution earned per £1 of sales revenue must be constant. The **contribution/sales (C/S) ratio** (sometimes called the profit/volume (P/V) ratio or the contribution margin ratio) can be important in marginal costing calculations for this reason.

3.2 EXAMPLE: C/S RATIO

Argot Slang Ltd makes two products, the Drawl and the Twang. Information relating to each of these products for April 20X1 is as follows.

	Drawl	*Twang*
Opening stock	nil	nil
Production (units)	15,000	6,000
Sales (units)	10,000	5,000
	£	£
Sales price per unit	20	30
Unit costs		
Direct material	8	14
Direct labour	4	2
Variable production overhead	2	1
Variable sales overhead	2	3

Fixed costs for the month	£
Production costs	40,000
Administration costs	15,000
Sales and distribution costs	25,000

Tasks

(a) Using marginal costing principles, calculate the profit in April 20X1.

(b) Calculate the contribution/sales ratio for each product.

(c) Determine what the profit would have been if sales had been 15,000 units of Drawl and 6,000 units of Twang.

(d) Ascertain the contribution/sales ratios for each product at these higher levels of output.

BPP PUBLISHING

3.3 SOLUTION

(a) ARGOT SLANG LIMITED
PROFIT AND LOSS ACCOUNT FOR APRIL 20X1

		Drawl		Twang	Total
		£		£	£
Variable production cost (15,000 units)			(6,000 units)		
Direct materials		120,000		84,000	204,000
Direct labour		60,000		12,000	72,000
Variable overhead		30,000		6,000	36,000
		210,000		102,000	312,000
Less closing stock (5,000 units)			(1,000 units)		
values (1/3)		70,000	(1/6)	17,000	87,000
Variable production					
cost of sales		140,000		85,000	225,000
Variable sales overhead					
(varying with sales volume)		20,000		15,000	35,000
Variable cost of sales		160,000		100,000	260,000
Sales (10,000 units)		200,000	(5,000 units)	150,000	350,000
Contribution		40,000		50,000	90,000
Less fixed costs (total)					80,000
Profit					10,000

Notes

(i) Variable costs of selling and distribution vary with the volume of sales, not the volume of production.

(ii) A quicker calculation of profit would be as follows.

	£
Contribution from Drawls (unit contribution = £20 − £16 = £4 × 10,000)	40,000
Contribution from Twangs (unit contribution = £30 − £20 = £10 × 5,000)	50,000
Total contribution	90,000
Fixed costs for the period	80,000
Profit	10,000

(b) Contribution/sales ratios at this volume of sales are as follows.

Drawl $\dfrac{£20-16}{£20} = \dfrac{£4}{£20} = 20\%$ (or $\dfrac{£40,000}{£200,000} \times 100\%$)

Twang $\dfrac{£30-20}{£30} = \dfrac{£10}{£30} = 33^1/_3\%$ (or $\dfrac{£50,000}{£150,000} \times 100\%$)

(c) At a higher volume of sales, profit would be as follows.

	£
Contribution from sales of 15,000 Drawls (× £4)	60,000
Contribution from sales of 6,000 Twangs (× £10)	60,000
Total contribution	120,000
Less fixed costs	80,000
Profit	40,000

(d) The contribution/sales ratio of each product is the same at all levels of output and sales (given no changes in the sales price or variable cost per unit). Profit increases from £30,000 at the lower volume by the amount of extra contribution earned.

	£
5,000 extra units of Drawl (5,000 × £4)	20,000
1,000 extra units of Twang (1,000 × £10)	10,000
Increase in contribution and profit	30,000

4 MARGINAL COSTING AND ABSORPTION COSTING AND THE CALCULATION OF PROFIT

4.1 **Marginal costing** as a cost accounting system is significantly different from absorption costing. It is an *alternative* method of accounting for costs and profit, which rejects the principles of absorbing fixed overheads into unit costs.

(a) **In marginal costing**

(i) Closing stocks are valued at marginal production cost.

(ii) Fixed costs are charged in full against the profit of the period in which they are incurred.

(b) **In absorption costing** (sometimes referred to as **full costing**)

(i) Closing stocks are valued at full production cost, and include a share of fixed production costs.

(ii) This means that the cost of sales in a period will include some fixed overhead incurred in a previous period (in opening stock values) and will exclude some fixed overhead incurred in the current period but carried forward in closing stock values as a charge to a subsequent accounting period.

4.2 In **marginal costing,** it is necessary to identify **variable costs, contribution** and **fixed costs**.

In **absorption costing** it is not necessary to distinguish variable costs from fixed costs.

4.3 EXAMPLE: MARGINAL AND ABSORPTION COSTING COMPARED

Look back at the information contained in Activity 4.1. Suppose that the budgeted production for May 20X1 was 15,000 units of Ping and 6,000 units of Pong, and production overhead is absorbed on the basis of budgeted direct labour costs.

Task

Calculate the profit if production was as budgeted, and sales were as follows.

(a) 10,000 units of Ping and 5,000 units of Pong
(b) 15,000 units of Ping and 6,000 units of Pong

Administration, sales and distribution costs should be charged as a period cost against profit.

4.4 SOLUTION

Budgeted production overhead is calculated as follows.

		£
Fixed		40,000
Variable:	Pings (15,000 × £2)	30,000
	Pongs (6,000 × £1)	6,000
Total		76,000

The production overhead absorption rate would be calculated as follows.

$$\frac{\text{Budgeted production overhead}}{\text{Budgeted direct labour cost}} = \frac{£76,000}{(15,000 \times £4) + (6,000 \times £2)} \times 100\%$$

$$= 105.56\% \text{ of direct labour cost}$$

(a) If sales are 10,000 units of Ping and 5,000 units of Pong, profit would be as follows.

Absorption costing

	Pings	Pongs	Total
	£	£	£
Costs of production			
Direct materials	120,000	84,000	204,000
Direct labour	60,000	12,000	72,000
Overhead (105.56% of labour)	63,333	12,667	76,000
	243,333	108,667	352,000
Less closing stocks	(1/3) 81,111	(1/6) 18,111	99,222
Production cost of sales	162,222	90,556	252,778
Administration costs			15,000
Sales and distribution costs			
Variable			35,000
Fixed			25,000
Total cost of sales			327,778
Sales	200,000	150,000	350,000
Profit			22,222

Note. There is no under/over absorption of overhead, since actual production is the same as budgeted production.

The profit derived using absorption costing techniques is different from the profit (£10,000) using marginal costing techniques at this volume of sales (see Activity 4.1).

(b) If production and sales are exactly the same (15,000 units of Ping and 6,000 units of Pong), profit would be £40,000.

	£
Sales (300,000 + 180,000)	480,000
Cost of sales (352,000* + 15,000 + 48,000 + 25,000)	440,000
Profit	40,000

* No closing stock if sales and production are equal.

This is the same as the profit calculated by marginal costing techniques in the earlier question.

4.5 Conclusions from this example

(a) Marginal costing and absorption costing are different techniques for assessing profit in a period.

(b) If there are changes in stocks during a period, so that opening stock or closing stock values are different, marginal costing and absorption costing give different results for profit obtained.

(c) If the opening and closing stock volumes and values are the same, marginal costing and absorption costing will give the same profit figure. This is because the total cost of sales during the period would be the same, no matter how calculated.

The long-run effect on profit

4.6 **In the long run, total profit for a company will be the same whether marginal costing or absorption costing is used.** Different accounting conventions merely affect the profit of individual accounting periods.

4.7 EXAMPLE: COMPARISON OF TOTAL PROFITS

To illustrate this point, let us suppose that a company makes and sells a single product. At the beginning of period 1, there are no opening stocks of the product, for which the variable production cost is £4 and the sales price £6 per unit. Fixed costs are £2,000 per period, of which £1,500 are fixed production costs.

	Period 1	Period 2
Sales	1,200 units	1,800 units
Production	1,500 units	1,500 units

Task

Determine the profit in each period using the following methods of costing.

(a) Absorption costing (Assume normal output is 1,500 units per period)
(b) Marginal costing

4.8 SOLUTION

It is important to notice that although production and sales volumes in each period are different (and therefore the profit for each period by absorption costing will be different from the profit by marginal costing), over the full period, total production equals sales volume, the total cost of sales is the same, and therefore the profit is the same by either method of accounting.

(a) **Absorption costing.** The absorption rate for fixed production overhead is:

$$\frac{£1,500}{1,500 \text{ units}} = £1 \text{ per unit}$$

	Period 1		Period 2		Total	
	£	£	£	£	£	£
Sales		7,200		10,800		18,000
Production costs						
Variable	6,000		6,000		12,000	
Fixed	1,500		1,500		3,000	
	7,500		7,500		15,000	
Add opening stock b/f	-		1,500			
	7,500		9,000			
Less closing stock c/f	1,500		-		-	
Production cost of sales	6,000		9,000		15,000	
Other costs	500		500		1,000	
Total cost of sales		6,500		9,500		16,000
Unadjusted profit		700		1,300		2,000
(Under-)/over-absorbed overhead		-		-		-
Profit		700		1,300		2,000

(b) **Marginal costing**

	Period 1		Period 2		Total	
	£	£	£	£	£	£
Sales		7,200		10,800		18,000
Variable production cost	6,000		6,000		12,000	
Add opening stock b/f	-		1,200			
	6,000		7,200			
Less closing stock c/f	1,200		-		-	
Variable production cost						
of sales		4,800		7,200		12,000
Contribution		2,400		3,600		6,000
Fixed costs		2,000		2,000		4,000
Profit		400		1,600		2,000

Notes

(a) The total profit over the two periods is the same for each method of costing, but the profit in each period is different.

(b) In absorption costing, fixed production overhead of £300 is carried forward from period 1 into period 2 in stock values, and becomes a charge to profit in period 2. In marginal costing all fixed costs are charged in the period they are incurred, therefore the profit in period 1 is £300 lower and in period 2 is £300 higher than the absorption costing profit.

Activity 4.2

The following budgeted information relates to a company that sells one product.

	January 20X5	February 20X5
Sales	18,000	32,000
Production	25,000	25,000

	£
Selling price per unit	16
Cost per unit: Material	5
Direct labour	3
Variable production cost	2
Fixed production costs - £75,000 per month	

There is no opening stock and company policy is to absorb fixed overheads on the basis of direct labour cost.

Tasks

(a) Prepare profit and loss statements for the months of January and February on the basis of the following.

    (i)   Marginal costing
    (ii)   Absorption costing

(b) Account for the differences in profit figures between the two methods.

---

5 RECONCILING THE PROFIT FIGURES GIVEN BY THE TWO METHODS

5.1 **The difference in profits reported under the two costing systems is due to the different stock valuation methods used.**

(a) **If stock levels increase** between the beginning and end of a period, absorption costing will report the higher profit. This is because some of the fixed production overhead incurred during the period will be carried forward in closing stock (which reduces cost of sales) to be set against sales revenue in the following period instead of being written off in full against profit in the period concerned.

(b) **If stock levels decrease**, absorption costing will report the lower profit because as well as the fixed overhead incurred, fixed production overhead which had been carried forward in opening stock is released and is also included in cost of sales.

5.2 EXAMPLE: RECONCILING PROFITS

The profits reported under absorption costing and marginal costing for period 1 in the example in Paragraph 4.7 would be reconciled as follows.

	£
Marginal costing profit [(£2 × 1,200) − (2,000)]	400
Adjust for fixed overhead in stock:	
Stock increase of 300 units × £1 per unit	300
Absorption costing profit	700

ASSESSMENT ALERT

If you have trouble reconciling the different profits reported under absorption costing and marginal costing, remember the following formula.

Marginal costing profit	X
Increase/(decrease) in stock units × fixed production overhead absorption rate	Y
Absorption costing profit	Z

Activity 4.3

Reconcile the profits reported under the two systems for period 2 of the example in Paragraph 4.7.

Activity 4.4

Martel Ltd manufactures one product only which is sold for £100 each. There is given below a budgeted profit and loss statement for one year based on sales and production at a normal level of activity.

Profit and loss statement

		£'000	£'000
Sales			1,000
Costs:			
Direct material		300	
Direct wages		200	
Production overhead:	variable	50	
fixed		200	
Administration overhead:	fixed	100	
Selling overhead:	fixed	50	
			900
Net profit			100

BPP PUBLISHING

Budgets have been prepared for year ending 30 June 20X1 and year ending 30 June 20X2. In the budget to 30 June 20X1 sales have been shown as only 80% of the normal level of activity while production has been included at the normal level of activity. In the budget for year ending 30 June 20X2 sales have been shown as achieving the normal level of activity while production has been reduced to 80% of the normal level of activity to utilise stock made previously.

Tasks

(a) Prepare a budgeted profit and loss statement for each of the years ending 30 June 20X1 and 20X2 based on a system of:

    (i)   Absorption costing
    (ii)   Marginal costing

(b) Discuss briefly the effect on profit of these *two* different systems.

---

6 MARGINAL COSTING VERSUS ABSORPTION COSTING - WHICH IS BETTER?

6.1 There are accountants who favour each costing method.

(a) Absorption costing lends itself to relatively easy manipulation, in that profits in any particular year can be boosted by increasing production without having to increase sales.

Arguments in favour of absorption costing

(i) Fixed production costs are incurred in order to make output; it is therefore 'fair' to charge all output with a share of these costs.

(ii) Closing stock values, by including a share of fixed production overhead, will be valued on the principle required for the financial accounting valuation of stocks by SSAP 9.

The explanatory notes to SSAP 9 (paragraph 3) state that 'in order to match costs and revenue, 'costs' of stocks and work in progress should comprise that expenditure which has been incurred in the normal course of business in bringing the product or service to its present location and condition. Such costs will include all related production overheads, even though these may accrue on a time basis'.

(iii) A problem with calculating the contribution of various products made by a company is that it may not be clear whether the contribution earned by each product is enough to cover fixed costs, whereas by charging fixed overhead to a product we can decide whether it is profitable or not.

(iv) Where stock building is necessary, such as in fireworks manufacture, fixed costs should be included in stock valuations otherwise a series of losses will be shown in earlier periods, to be offset eventually by excessive profits when the goods are sold.

(b) **Arguments in favour of marginal costing**

(i) It is simple to operate.

(ii) There are no apportionments, which are frequently done on an arbitrary basis, of fixed costs. Many costs, eg the managing director's salary, are indivisible.

(iii)   Fixed costs will be the same regardless of the volume of output, being period costs. It makes sense, therefore, to charge them in full as a cost to the period.

(iv)   The cost to produce an extra unit is the variable production cost. It is realistic to value closing stock items at this directly attributable cost.

(v)   As we have seen, the size of total contribution varies directly with sales volume at a constant rate per unit. For management purposes, better information about expected profit is obtained from the use of variable costs and contribution in the accounting system.

(vi)   It is also argued that absorption costing gives managers the wrong signals. Goods are produced, not to meet market demand, but to absorb allocated overheads. Production in excess of demand in fact increases the overheads (for example warehousing) the organisation must bear.

(vii)   Under or over absorption of overheads is avoided.

(viii)   It is a useful aid to decision making, especially when a particular resource is limited. Absorption costing information is not really appropriate for decision making.

Activity 4.5

(a)   Distinguish between absorption costing and marginal costing.

(b)   Discuss the effect of both costing methods on short-term results where sales and production are not equal.

Key learning points

- **Absorption costing** is most often used for routine profit reporting and must be used for financial accounting purposes. **Marginal costing** provides better management information for planning and decision making.

- **Marginal cost** is the variable cost of one unit of product or service.

- **Contribution** is an important measure in marginal costing, and it is calculated as the difference between sales value and marginal or variable cost.

- **In marginal costing, fixed production costs are treated as period costs** and are written off as they are incurred. **In absorption costing, fixed production costs are absorbed into the cost of units** and are carried forward in stock to be charged against sales for the next period. Stock values using absorption costing are therefore greater than those calculated using marginal costing.

- **Reported profit figures** using marginal costing or absorption costing will differ if there is any change in the level of stocks in the period. If production is equal to sales, there will be no difference in calculated profits using these costing methods.

- **SSAP 9** recommends the use of absorption costing for the valuation of stocks in financial accounts.

- There are a number of arguments both for and against each of the costing systems.

BPP PUBLISHING

Quick quiz

1   What is marginal costing?

2   What is a period cost in marginal costing?

3   Define contribution.

4   What is a breakeven point?

5   What is the main difference between marginal costing and absorption costing?

6   If opening and closing stock volumes and values are the same, does absorption costing or marginal costing give the higher profit?

7   What are the arguments in favour of marginal costing?

Answers to quick quiz

1   An alternative method of costing to absorption costing in which a contribution is calculated (that is, sales revenue minus the *variable* cost of sales), since only variable costs are charged as a cost of sales.

2   Fixed costs.

3   Contribution is the difference between sales value and the marginal cost of sales.

4   It is the point at which total contribution exactly equals fixed costs, and when no profit and no loss is made.

5   Marginal costing does not absorb fixed overheads into unit costs, unlike absorption costing.

6   Neither. Both methods give the same profit figure.

7
   - It is simple to operate.
   - There are no apportionments.
   - Fixed costs are charged in full to the period.
   - Closing stock is realistically valued at its variable production cost.
   - By using variable costs and contribution in the accounting system, the information obtained for management purposes is more meaningful.
   - Under or over absorption of overheads is avoided.

Answers to activities

Answer 4.1

(a)

	£
Contribution from Pings (unit contribution = £20 − £(8 + 4 + 2 + 2) = £4 × 10,000)	40,000
Contribution from Pongs (unit contribution = £30 − £(14 + 2 + 1 + 3) = £10 × 5,000)	50,000
Total contribution	90,000
Fixed costs for the period (£40,000 + £15,000 + £25,000)	80,000
Profit	10,000

(b)   At a higher volume of sales, profit would be as follows.

	£
Contribution from sales of 15,000 Pings (× £4)	60,000
Contribution from sales of 6,000 Pongs (× £10)	60,000
Total contribution	120,000
Less fixed costs	80,000
Profit	40,000

Answer 4.2

(a) and (b)

| | Marginal costing | | | | Absorption costing | | | |
| | January | | February | | January | | February | |
	£'000	£'000	£'000	£'000	£'000	£'000	£'000	£'000
Sales		288		512		288		512
Opening stock	-		70		-		91	
Materials	125		125		125		125	
Labour	75		75		75		75	
Variable costs	50		50		50		50	
Fixed costs (W1)	-		-		75		75	
	250		320		325		416	
Closing stock								
(W2)	(70)		-		(91)		-	
		(180)		(320)		(234)		(416)
		108		192		54		96
Fixed costs		(75)		(75)		-		-
Profit		33		117		54		96

Workings

1   *Overhead absorption rate*

$$\frac{\text{Overhead}}{\text{Labour costs}} \times 100\% = \frac{£75,000}{£75,000} \times 100\% = 100\%$$

Overheads are absorbed at 100% of direct labour costs, that is, £75,000 in each month.

2   *Closing stock*

	Units
January production	25,000
January sales	(18,000)
Closing stock - January	7,000
February production	25,000
February sales	(32,000)
Closing stock - February	nil

	Marginal costing	Absorption costing
Cost of production - January (25,000 units)	£250,000	£325,000
Closing stock - January (7,000 units)	£70,000	£91,000
Stock valuation per unit	£10	£13

The overall profit for the two months is the same (£150,000). The differences are explained by the difference in stock valuation. Absorption costing includes fixed production overheads of £3 per unit in closing stock and therefore there is a difference of 7,000 × £3 = £21,000 in the January profit figures. This difference is exactly reversed in February when all stocks are sold.

Answer 4.3

	£
Marginal costing profit	1,600
Adjust for fixed overhead in stock:	
Stock decrease of 300 units × £1 per unit	(300)
Absorption costing profit	1,300

Answer 4.4

(a) (i) PROFIT AND LOSS STATEMENT
YEARS ENDED 30 JUNE 20X1 AND 20X2

	20X2		20X1	
	£'000	£'000	£'000	£'000
Sales		1,000		800
Opening stock	150		-	
Production costs absorbed:				
10,000 units @ £75 *(Working)*			750	
8,000 units @ £75	600			
	750		750	
Less: closing stock				
2,000 units @ £75	-		150	
	750		600	
Under absorbed overhead				
2,000 @ £20	40		-	
		790		600
Gross profit		210		200
Administration overhead	100		100	
Selling overhead	50		50	
		150		150
		60		50

(ii) PROFIT AND LOSS STATEMENT
YEARS ENDED 30 JUNE 20X1 AND 20X2

	20X2		20X1	
	£'000	£'000	£'000	£'000
Sales		1,000		800
Opening stock	110		-	
Variable production cost:				
10,000 units @ £55 (W)			550	
8,000 units @ £55	440			
	550		550	
Less: closing stock				
2,000 units @ £55	-		110	
Variable cost of sales		550		440
Contribution		450		360
Fixed production overhead	200		200	
Administration overhead	100		100	
Selling overhead	50		50	
		350		350
		100		10

Working

Since the product selling price is £100, the profit and loss statement shown must represent sales of 10,000 units. We can therefore deduce the following:

	£
Standard product cost	
Materials	30
Direct wages	20
Variable production overhead	5
Variable production cost	55
Fixed production overhead	20
Standard production cost	75
Standard profit	25
Selling price	100

(b) Over the two year period there has been no change in the level of stock held, stock being nil both at 1 July 20X0 and at 30 June 20X2. As a result both costing methods produce the same total profit for the period of £110,000.

The effect of the difference in methods can be seen by looking at the position on 30 June 20X1. At this date there are stocks of 2,000 units valued as follows:

	£'000
Marginal costing (@ £55)	110
Absorption costing (@ £75)	150
Difference	40

The 20X1 profit is £40,000 greater under the absorption method because of this. In 20X2 the position reverses: the higher cost of opening stock leads to a higher cost of sales and hence a lower profit under the absorption method.

Answer 4.5

(a) Absorption costing is the costing principle whereby all cost units are valued at full cost, including absorbed fixed overhead. No distinction is made between fixed and variable costs in absorption costing statements.

Marginal costing is the costing principle whereby all cost units are valued at variable cost only, and fixed costs are written off in full each period in the costing profit and loss account. Marginal costing statements distinguish between fixed and variable costs in order to highlight the contribution for the period.

(b) Each costing method will have a different effect on short-term reported profits when sales and production are not equal.

   (i) *When sales exceed production.* Stocks are being reduced and with absorption costing some fixed overheads will be released from stock and charged against sales for the period. Reported profits will therefore be lower with absorption costing than with marginal costing.

   (ii) *When production exceeds sales.* Stocks are being increased and with absorption costing some fixed overheads will be carried forward in stock to be matched against the sales revenues of future periods. Reported profits will therefore be higher with absorption costing than with marginal costing.

Part B

Decision making and capital expenditure appraisal

5 Decision making

Chapter topic list

1   Cost behaviour and decision making

2   Absorption costing, marginal costing and decision making

3   Relevant and non-relevant costs

4   Limiting budget factors and opportunity costs

5   Make or buy decisions

6   Shutdown decisions

Learning objectives

On completion of this chapter you will be able to:

	Performance criteria	Range statement
• Analyse total costs into their fixed and variable elements	16.2	
• Describe the relationship between fixed and variable costs and the time horizon under consideration	16.2	
• Explain the advantages and limitations of using a marginal costing approach for decision making and analyse problems involved in decision making	16.2	16.2.3
• Describe the concept of relevant costs and its importance for decision making	16.2	
• Describe and explain project costs using an opportunity cost approach	16.2	
• Use an opportunity cost approach to solve make or buy type decisions and describe the qualitative factors which may influence decisions to make or buy	16.2	16.2.1
• Prepare reports making recommendations for management action in connection with make or buy and other decisions	16.2	16.2.1

1 COST BEHAVIOUR AND DECISION MAKING

1.1 Conventional cost and management accounting data collection systems accumulate costs by product to meet the financial accounting requirements of allocating production costs incurred during a period between cost of sales and stock. This type of data collection system is not designed to accumulate product costs for decision-making purposes. **Costs derived from the cost accumulation system should not, therefore, be used for decision making.**

1.2 The management accountant must understand cost behaviour so as to be able to evaluate different courses of action open to an organisation. Examples of decisions that require information on how costs and revenues vary at different levels of activity include the following.

- What should the planned activity level be for the next period?

- Should the selling price be reduced in order to sell more units?

- Should sales staff be paid by a straight salary, a straight commission or a combination of the two?

- Should additional plant be purchased so that an expansion of output is possible?

- Should a particular component be manufactured internally or bought in?

- Should a contract be undertaken?

1.3 For each of the above decisions, management require estimates of costs at different levels of activity for alternative courses of action. A company might decide to tender for a contract without understanding that the extra work will mean buying a new factory, a factor not taken into account when calculating the tender price. Fulfilling the contract at the tender price is therefore likely to result in an overall loss to the company.

Activity 5.1

This Activity is designed to refresh your memory on cost behaviour.

(a) What is a fixed cost?
(b) What type of cost tends to vary directly with the volume of output?
(c) Is the monthly salary of a managing director likely to be a fixed cost or a variable cost?
(d) The cost of raw materials is a fixed cost. True or false?
(e) What is a mixed cost?
(f) Why might the cost of electricity be a semi-variable cost?

Determining the fixed and variable elements of semi-variable costs

1.4 It is often possible to assume that within the normal range of output, costs are either variable, fixed or semi-variable. For this reason management accountants usually treat all costs as fixed or variable for decision-making purposes, and semi-variable costs are divided into their variable and fixed elements.

1.5 There are several ways in which the fixed cost element and variable cost element within a semi-variable cost may be ascertained. Each method only gives an estimate, and can therefore give differing results from the other methods. One of the principal methods is the high-low method.

High-low method

1.6 (a) To estimate the fixed and variable elements of semi-variable costs, records of costs in previous periods are reviewed and the **costs of the following two periods are selected.**

(i) **The period with the highest volume of output**
(ii) **The period with the lowest volume of output**

(*Note.* The periods with the highest/lowest output may not be the periods with the highest/lowest cost.)

(b) The **difference** between the total cost of the high output and the total cost of the low output **will be the variable cost of the difference in output levels** (since the same fixed cost is included in each total cost).

(c) The **variable cost per unit** may be calculated from this (**difference in total costs ÷ difference in output levels**), and the **fixed cost** may then also be determined (**total cost at either output level – variable cost for output level chosen**).

1.7 EXAMPLE: THE HIGH-LOW METHOD

The costs of operating the maintenance department of a computer manufacturer, Sillick and Chips Ltd, for the last four months have been as follows.

Month	Cost	Production volume
	£	Units
1	110,000	7,000
2	115,000	8,000
3	111,000	7,700
4	97,000	6,000

Task

Calculate the costs that should be expected in month five when output is expected to be 7,500 units. Ignore inflation.

1.8 SOLUTION

(a)

	Units		£
High output	8,000	total cost	115,000
Low output	6,000	total cost	97,000
Variable cost of	2,000		18,000
Variable cost per unit	£18,000/2,000 =		£9

(b) Substituting in either the high or low volume cost:

		High		Low
		£		£
Total cost		115,000		97,000
Variable costs	(8,000 × £9)	72,000	(6,000 × £9)	54,000
Fixed costs		43,000		43,000

(c) Estimated costs of 7,500 units of output:

	£
Fixed costs	43,000
Variable costs (7,500 × £9)	67,500
Total costs	110,500

Activity 5.2

Using the high-low method and the following information, determine the cost of electricity in July if 2,750 units of electricity are consumed.

Month	Cost	Electricity consumed
	£	Units
January	204	2,600
February	212	2,800
March	200	2,500
April	220	3,000
May	184	2,100
June	188	2,200

Cost behaviour and time

1.9 We looked at cost behaviour in Chapter 2 of this Study Text. Costs must be categorised as either fixed or variable in relation to the span of time under consideration. Over a sufficiently **long period of time of several years, virtually all costs are variable** because all costs that are normally considered fixed could, in fact, increase or decrease in line with long-term changes in activity level. Salaried employees could be released and even land and buildings could be sold if demand dropped. Additional managers could be appointed and land and buildings acquired if demand increased.

1.10 **Within shorter time periods, costs will be either fixed or variable in relation to changes in activity level.** The shorter the time period, the greater the probability that a cost will be fixed. Over a time period of one year, costs associated with providing an organisation's operating capacity (such as depreciation and the salaries of senior managers) will probably be fixed in relation to changes in activity level.

1.11 **Relationship between cost behaviour and time: summary**

(a) Over a given short time period, such as one year, costs will be fixed, variable or semi-variable.

(b) Over longer time periods of several years, all costs will tend to change in response to large changes in activity level.

1.12 Because fixed costs do not remain fixed in the long term, they are sometimes described as **long-term variable costs**.

2 ABSORPTION COSTING, MARGINAL COSTING AND DECISION MAKING

2.1 Because **marginal costing** separates fixed and variable costs and hence focuses on those costs that are likely to change as a result of a decision (variable costs and stepped fixed costs), it **provides better decision-making information than absorption costing.**

(a) Attention is focused on activity-related variable costs and so management can see how costs and profit will be affected by changes in sales volume.

(b) Focusing on marginal costs may aid pricing decisions because a mark-up on variable costs will often be a convenient price (for example in the retail industry).

(c) Marginal costing information is better when making short-term decisions about whether or not to make a few extra units of a product. In such circumstances fixed costs will not change and, providing selling price exceeds variable costs, a contribution towards profit will be made. If absorption costing is used, however, extra fixed costs will be absorbed and it may appear that the few extra units are making a negative contribution towards profit.

2.2 Most organisations use absorption costing systems for internal and external reporting, and so do not have marginal costing information readily available. But there is no reason why an absorption costing system cannot be used for reporting purposes, and costs can be analysed into their fixed and variable elements for decision making.

2.3 The following example illustrates why the **absorption of fixed overheads is irrelevant when making decisions.**

2.4 EXAMPLE: DECISION ACCOUNTING AND OVERHEAD ABSORPTION

Glebe Dibbling Ltd manufactures a product from three components, which are made in two departments. The draft budget for 20X3 is as follows.

		A	B	C
Component		£	£	£
Prime costs per unit				
Direct materials:	Dept X	4	8	6
Direct labour:	Dept X	4	2	12
	Dept Y	8	6	4
		16	16	22
Production time per unit:				
Machine time per unit:	Dept X	2 hrs	1½ hrs	3 hrs
Labour time per unit:	Dept Y	4 hrs	3 hrs	2 hrs

	Dept X	Dept Y
	£	£
Variable overheads	14,500	10,500
Fixed overheads	43,500	73,500
	58,000	84,000

Machine time available and required, Dept X	29,000 hrs	
Labour time available and required, Dept Y		42,000 hrs

The absorption rate for overheads is based on machine hours in department X and direct labour hours in department Y. Variable overheads are also incurred in proportion to machine hours worked in department X and labour hours worked in department Y.

Tasks

(a) Calculate the full cost of manufacture of components, A, B and C.

(b) Another firm has offered to supply next year's budgeted quantities of the above components at the following prices.

> Component A   £35
> Component B   £24
> Component C   £30

On the basis of costs alone, recommend whether Glebe Dibbling Ltd should sub-contract any production work to this firm. There are no alternative uses for the spare capacity which would be made available 'in-house' and fixed cost expenditure would be unchanged as a result of any sub-contracting done.

(c) Comment briefly on the purpose of calculating a full cost of production for component A, B and C.

2.5 SOLUTION

(a) The overhead absorption rates are as follows.

	Dept X	*Dept Y*
Budgeted overheads	£58,000	£84,000
Budgeted activity	29,000 machine hrs	42,000 labour hrs
Absorption rate	£2 per machine hr	£2 per direct labour hr

(b) The variable cost per unit may be calculated by adding variable overheads to prime cost, at the rate of £0.50 per machine hour in department X and £0.25 per direct labour hour in department Y.

	A £	*B* £	*C* £
Unit variable cost			
Prime cost	16	16.00	22.00
Variable overhead:			
Department X	1	0.75	1.50
Department Y	1	0.75	0.50
	18	17.50	24.00

(c) The full cost per unit is calculated by adding total overheads on to component prime costs, without the need to distinguish between fixed and variable overheads.

	A £	*B* £	*C* £
Full cost per unit			
Prime cost	16	16	22
Overhead:			
Dept X (£2 per machine hour)	4	3	6
Dept Y (£2 per labour hour)	8	6	4
	28	25	32

2.6 The other company has offered a unit price of £35 for component A, £24 for component B and £30 for component C. If we look at the full costs of production, it would appear that it would be cheaper to sub-contract products B and C. However, this would be an incorrect decision.

2.7 The full costs of in-house manufacture include a share of fixed costs which would not be saved if components were sub-contracted. The only saving would be in the variable costs of production:

	A	*B*	*C*
	£	£	£
Variable cost of production	18	17.50	24
Variable cost of purchase	35	24.00	30
Extra cost of purchasing	17	6.50	6

It would cost the company money to sub-contract any work, therefore all components should be manufactured internally.

2.8 The **full cost per unit** is not intended to be used for decision making. The purposes of calculating a full cost are as follows.

(a) To calculate a full cost of finished products, in order perhaps to fix a selling price

(b) To evaluate closing stocks of components and finished goods, in order to determine balance sheet stock values, and the cost of sales and profit for an accounting period

3 RELEVANT AND NON-RELEVANT COSTS

3.1 The costs which should be used for decision making are often referred to as **relevant costs**.

KEY TERM

A **relevant cost** is a future cash flow arising as a direct consequence of a decision.

3.2 (a) **Relevant costs are future costs**.

  (i) A decision is about the future. It cannot alter what has been done already. A cost that has been incurred in the past is totally irrelevant to any decision that is being made 'now'.

  (ii) Costs that have been incurred include not only costs that have already been paid, but also costs that are the subject of legally binding contracts, even if payments due under the contract have not yet been made. (These are known as **committed costs**.)

(b) **Relevant costs are cash flows**.

  (i) Reported profits and cash flow are not the same in any period for various reasons, such as the timing differences caused by giving credit and the accounting treatment of depreciation. In the long run, however, a profit that is earned will eventually produce a net inflow of an equal amount of cash. Hence when accounting for decision making we look at **cash flow** as a means of measuring profits.

  (ii) Only cash flow information is required. This means that costs or charges which do not reflect additional cash spending should be ignored for the purpose of decision making. These include the following.

    (1) Depreciation, as a fixed overhead incurred

    (2) Notional rent or interest, as a fixed overhead incurred

(3) All overheads absorbed. (Fixed overhead absorption is always irrelevant since it is overheads to be incurred which affect decisions.)

(c) **Relevant costs are incremental costs**.

A relevant cost is one which arises as a direct consequence of a decision. Thus, only costs which will differ under some or all of the available opportunities should be considered; relevant costs are therefore sometimes referred to as incremental costs. For example, if an employee is expected to have no other work to do during the next week, but will be paid his basic wage (of, say, £100 per week) for attending work and doing nothing, his manager might decide to give him a job which earns only £40. The net gain is £40 and the £100 is irrelevant to the decision because although it is a future cash flow, it will be incurred anyway whether the employee is given work or not.

Relevant costs are therefore future, incremental cash flows.

3.3 Other terms can be used to describe relevant costs.

> **KEY TERM**
>
> **Avoidable costs** are costs which would not be incurred if the activity to which they relate did not exist.

(a) One of the situations in which it is necessary to identify the avoidable costs is in deciding whether or not to discontinue a product. The only costs which would be saved are the avoidable costs, which are usually the variable costs and sometimes some specific fixed costs. Costs which would be incurred whether or not the product is discontinued are known as unavoidable costs.

> **KEY TERM**
>
> **Differential cost** is the difference in total cost between alternatives.

(b) Sometimes the term **differential costs** is used to compare the differences in cost between **two** alternative courses of action, while **incremental costs** is used to state the relevant costs when **two or more** options are compared. If option A will cost an extra £300 and option B will cost an extra £360, the differential cost is £60, with option B being more expensive. A differential cost is the difference between the relevant costs of each option.

> **KEY TERM**
>
> **Opportunity cost** is the benefit which could have been earned, but which has been given up, by choosing one option instead of another.

(c) Suppose for example that there are three mutually exclusive options, A, B and C. The net profit from each would be £80, £100 and £70 respectively. Since only one option can be selected, option B would be chosen because it offers the greatest benefit.

	£
Profit from option B	100
Less opportunity cost (ie the benefit from the most profitable alternative, A)	80
Differential benefit of option B	20

The decision to choose option B would not be taken simply because it offers a profit of £100, but because it offers a differential profit of £20 in excess of the next best alternative.

Opportunity costs will never appear in a set of double entry cost accounts.

Non-relevant costs

3.4   A number of terms are used to describe costs that are **irrelevant for decision making** because they are either not future cash flows or they are costs which will be incurred anyway, regardless of the decision that is taken.

> ### KEY TERM
>
> A **sunk cost** is a cost which has already been incurred and hence should not be taken account of in decision making.

(a)   The principle underlying decision accounting is that 'bygones are bygones'. What has happened in the past is done, and cannot be undone. Management decisions can only affect the future. In decision making, managers therefore require information about future costs and revenues which would be affected by the decision under review, and they must not be misled by events, costs and revenues in the past, about which they can do nothing.

> ### KEY TERM
>
> A **committed cost** is a future cash outflow that will be incurred anyway, whatever decision is taken now about alternative opportunities.

(b)   Committed costs may exist because of contracts already entered into by the organisation, which it cannot get out of.

> ### KEY TERM
>
> A **notional cost** or **imputed cost** is a hypothetical accounting cost to reflect the use of a benefit for which no actual cash expense is incurred.

(c)   Examples in cost accounting systems include the following.

   (i)   Notional rent, such as that charged to a subsidiary, cost centre or profit centre of an organisation for the use of accommodation which the organisation owns.

   (ii)   Notional interest charges on capital employed, sometimes made against a profit centre or cost centre.

(d) Although **historical costs** are irrelevant for decision making, historical cost data will often provide the best available basis for predicting future costs.

Fixed and variable costs

3.5 Unless you are given an indication to the contrary, you should assume the following.

- **Variable costs will be relevant costs.**
- **Fixed costs are irrelevant to a decision.**

This need not be the case, however, and you should analyse variable and fixed cost data carefully. Do not forget that 'fixed' costs may only be fixed in the short term.

Attributable fixed costs

3.6 There might be occasions when a fixed cost is a relevant cost, and you must be aware of the distinction between 'specific' or 'directly attributable' fixed costs, and general fixed overheads.

(a) **Directly attributable fixed costs** are those costs which, although fixed within a relevant range of activity level, or regarded as fixed because management has set a budgeted expenditure level (for example advertising costs are often treated as fixed), would, in fact, do one of two things.

   (i) **Increase if certain extra activities were undertaken**

   (ii) **Decrease/be eliminated entirely if a decision were taken either to reduce the scale of operations or shut down entirely**

(b) **General fixed overheads** are those fixed overheads which will be **unaffected by decisions to increase or decrease the scale of operations**, perhaps because they are an apportioned share of the fixed costs of items which would be completely unaffected by the decisions. An apportioned share of head office charges is an example of general fixed overheads for a local office or department.

3.7 You should appreciate that whereas **directly attributable fixed costs will be relevant** to a decision in hand, **general fixed overheads will not be**.

Activity 5.3

The World History Museum stages exhibitions using its own premises. The managers are currently deciding whether to stage an exhibition of ancient Australian artefacts. The exhibition will run for three months and you have collected together the following data, which may or may not be relevant to a decision to proceed with the exhibition.

(a) Display cabinets will be built and installed at a cost of £1,700. In addition, it will be possible to use cabinets which were originally built for another exhibition at a cost of £500. Repair costs of £150 will be incurred if these extra cabinets are used.

(b) Extra security staff will be employed at a total cost of £6,500 for the three month period. In addition, two of the permanent full-time security staff can be redeployed from other areas, without the need to replace them. The salary costs for these two people will be £5,000 for the three month period.

(c) The exhibition will utilise 400 square metres of space. The museum's policy is to charge all departments £5 per square metre per month to cover the fixed costs of central administration, rates, etc. The museum owns the premises; therefore no rental costs are incurred.

(d) If the space is not used for this exhibition, it will be possible to rent it to another organisation as storage space, for a price of £6 per square metre per month.

(e) Posters and handbills will be printed to advertise the exhibition. These will cost a total of £750, consisting of £450 for the costs of the posters and handbills (paper, ink and power etc), £200 for design and £100 for the apportioned fixed costs of the printing department.

(f) Other costs to be incurred directly as a result of this exhibition will amount to £1,200.

(g) It is anticipated that 4,000 people will attend the exhibition, paying an average admission fee of £4 each. In addition, it is expected that each person will spend an average of £2 in the museum's cafeteria after their visit. The museum makes a gross margin of 50% on all cafeteria sales.

Task

The general manager, Chris Brooks, has asked you to present a statement which shows the financial effect of staging this exhibition. In notes beneath your statement you should indicate the reasons for your treatment of each cost and revenue.

Identifying the relevant cost of materials

3.8 The relevant cost of raw materials is generally their **current replacement cost**. The exception to this rule occurs if materials have already been purchased but will not be replaced.

The relevant cost of using them will be the higher of:

- **Their current resale value**
- **The value they would obtain if they were put to an alternative use**

If the materials have no resale value and no other possible use, then the relevant cost of using them for the opportunity under consideration would be nil.

Test your knowledge of the relevant cost of materials by attempting the following activity.

Activity 5.4

Darwin Ltd has been approached by a customer who would like a special job to be done for him, and who is willing to pay £22,000 for it. The job would require the following materials.

Material	Total units required	Units already in stock	Book value of units in stock £/unit	Realisable value £/unit	Replacement cost £/unit
A	1,000	0	-	-	6.00
B	1,000	600	2.00	2.50	5.00
C	1,000	700	3.00	2.50	4.00
D	200	200	4.00	6.00	9.00

Material B is used regularly by Darwin Ltd, and if units of B are required for this job, they would need to be replaced to meet other production demand.

Materials C and D are in stock as the result of previous over buying, and they have a restricted use. No other use could be found for material C, but the units of material D could be used in another job as substitute for 300 units of material E, which currently costs £5 per unit (and of which the company has no units in stock at the moment).

Task

Calculate the relevant costs of material for deciding whether or not to accept the contract.

The relevant cost of using machines

3.9   Using machinery will involve some incremental **user costs**. These include repair costs arising from use, hire charges and any fall in resale value of owned assets which results from their use. **Depreciation is *not* a relevant cost.**

3.10 EXAMPLE: USER COSTS

Sydney Ltd is considering whether to undertake some contract work for a customer. The machinery required for the contract would be as follows.

(a) A special cutting machine will have to be hired for three months for the work (the length of the contract). Hire charges for this machine are £75 per month, with a minimum hire charge of £300.

(b) All other machinery required in the production for the contract has already been purchased by the organisation on hire purchase terms. The monthly hire purchase payments for this machinery are £500. This consists of £450 for capital repayment and £50 as an interest charge. The last hire purchase payment is to be made in two months' time.

(c) The cash price of this machinery was £9,000 two years ago. It is being depreciated on a straight line basis at the rate of £200 per month. However, it still has a useful life which will enable it to be operated for another 36 months.

(d) The machinery is highly specialised and is unlikely to be required for other, more profitable jobs over the period during which the contract work would be carried out. Although there is no immediate market for selling this machine, it is expected that a customer might be found in the future. It is further estimated that the machine would lose £200 in its eventual sale value if it is used for the contract work.

Task

Calculate the relevant cost of machinery for the contract.

3.11 SOLUTION

(a) The cutting machine will incur an incremental cost of £300, the minimum hire charge.

(b) The historical cost of the other machinery is irrelevant as a past cost; depreciation is irrelevant as a non-cash cost; and future hire purchase repayments are irrelevant because they are committed costs. The only relevant cost is the loss of resale value of the machinery, estimated at £200 through use. This user cost will not arise until the machinery is eventually resold and the £200 should be discounted to allow for the time value of money. However, discounting is ignored here.

(c) *Summary of relevant costs*

	£
	£
Incremental hire costs	300
User cost of other machinery	200
	500

Activity 5.5

A machine which originally cost £12,000 has an estimated life of ten years and is depreciated at the rate of £1,200 a year. It has been unused for some time, however, as expected production orders did not materialise. A special order has now been received which would require the use of the machine for two months.

The current net realisable value of the machine is £8,000. If it is used for the job, its value is expected to fall to £7,500. The net book value of the machine is £8,400. Routine maintenance of the machine currently costs £40 a month. With use, the cost of maintenance and repairs would increase to £60 a month.

Task

Determine the cost of using the machine for the order.

Relevant costs with joint products

3.12 We need to be especially careful when decision making problems involve **joint products**.

> **KEY TERM**
>
> **Joint products** are two or more products which are output from the same processing operation.

3.13 For example, suppose that X and Y are joint products in a weight ratio 2:1 from a process using raw materials A and B. Thus, for every 2kg of X produced, 1 kg of Y is also produced. Suppose that we are considering increasing production of X by 2,000 kg because of a new order from a customer.

3.14 Because X and Y are joint products, we need to look also at the effect of additional production of Y. An extra 1,000 kg of Y will be produced. If we can sell this extra Y, there will be additional revenue. If we cannot, we will need to dispose of it, and the disposal may result in extra costs being incurred.

3.15 **Relevant cash flows** will be:

(a) **Cash inflow**: revenue from sale of 2,000 kg of X

(b) **Cash outflows**: materials costs (for A and B) plus any additional labour or other costs incurred as a result of the increased production

(c) **Cash inflow/outflow**: sales revenue *or* disposal costs for additional 1,000 kg of Y produced.

ASSESSMENT ALERT

You could be presented with a joint products problem in a devolved assessment simulation. In such problems, you need to be clear in your mind about the relevant costs and revenues of decisions. Unlike process costing problems, which you may have met elsewhere, decision making problems to do with joint products are not normally concerned with allocating costs between joint products. Since both products are produced together, whether we need them both or not, changes in production levels of each cannot be separated for decision making purposes.

The relevant cost of scarce resources

3.16 When a decision maker is faced with an opportunity which would call for the use of a **scarce resource** (a resource such as materials or labour which is in short supply), the total **incremental cost of using the resource will be higher than the direct cash cost of purchasing it**. This is because the resource could be used for other purposes, and so by using it in one way, the benefits obtainable from using it another way must be forgone.

3.17 A numerical example may help to clarify this point. Suppose that a customer has asked whether your company would be willing to undertake a contract for him. The work would involve the use of certain equipment for five hours and its running costs would be £2 per hour. However, your company faces heavy demand for usage of the equipment which earns a contribution of £7 per hour from this other work. If the contract is undertaken, some of this work would have to be forgone.

3.18 The **contribution obtainable from putting the scarce resource to its alternative use is its opportunity cost (sometimes referred to as its 'internal' opportunity cost)**. Quite simply, since the equipment can earn £7 per hour in an alternative use, the contract under consideration should also be expected to earn at least the same amount. This can be accounted for by charging the £7 per hour as an opportunity cost to the contract and the total relevant cost of 5 hours of equipment time would be as follows.

	£
Running costs (5 × £2)	10
Internal opportunity cost (5 × £7)	35
Relevant cost	45

It is important to notice that the variable running costs of the equipment are included in the total relevant cost.

3.19 A rule for identifying the relevant cost of a scarce resource is that the **total relevant cost** of the resource, consists of the following.

(a) The **contribution/incremental profit forgone** from the next-best opportunity for using the scarce resource *and*

(b) The **variable cost of the scarce resource**, that is, the cash expenditure to purchase the resource

3.20 We can now look at how to cost products and projects using this **opportunity cost approach**.

3.21 EXAMPLE: RELEVANT COST OF SCARCE RESOURCES

Gloria Ltd has been offered £21,000 by a prospective customer to make some purpose-built equipment. The extra costs of the machine would be £3,000 for materials. There would also be a requirement for 2,000 labour hours. Labour wages are £4 per hour, variable overhead is £2 per hour and fixed overhead is absorbed at the rate of £4 per hour.

Labour, however, is in limited supply, and if the job is accepted, men would have to be diverted from other work which is expected to earn a contribution of £5 per hour towards fixed overheads and profit.

Task

Assess whether the contract should be undertaken.

3.22 SOLUTION

The relevant costs of the scarce resource, labour, are the sum of the following.

(a) The variable costs of the labour and associated variable overheads
(b) The contribution forgone from not being able to put it to its alternative use

Fixed costs are ignored because there is no incremental fixed cost expenditure.

	£
Materials	3,000
Labour (2,000 hours at £4 per hour)	8,000
Variable overhead (2,000 hours at £2 per hour)	4,000
	15,000
Opportunity cost:	
Contribution forgone from other work (2,000 hours × £5 per hour)	10,000
Total costs	25,000
Revenue	21,000
Net loss on contract	(4,000)

The contract should not be undertaken.

3.23 It is worth thinking carefully about **labour costs**. The labour force will be paid £8,000 for 2,000 hours work, and variable overheads of £4,000 will be incurred no matter whether the men are employed on the new job or on other work. Relevant costs are future cash flows arising as a direct consequence of a decision, and the decision here will not affect the total wages paid. If this money is going to be spent anyway, should it not therefore be ignored as an irrelevant cost?

3.24 The answer to this crucial question is 'No'. The labour wages and variable overheads are relevant costs even though they will be incurred whatever happens. The reason for this is that the other work earns a contribution of £5 per hour *after having covered* labour and variable overhead costs. Work on the purpose-built equipment ought therefore to do at least the same.

3.25 If we can suppose that the other work costs, say, £1 per hour in materials, the contribution of £5 per hour would mean that this other work earned £5 contribution after covering the variable costs of materials (£1), labour (£4) and variable overheads (£2) so that revenue would be £12 per hour worked.

	£	£
(Hypothetical) revenue per hour		12
(Hypothetical) materials cost per hour	1	
Labour cost per hour	4	
Variable overhead cost per hour	2	
Variable costs per hour in total		7
Contribution per hour		5

(a) In the 2,000 hours of labour time we are thinking of diverting to the purpose-built equipment, the contribution forgone from other work would be £10,000 after covering labour and variable overhead costs, as follows.

	£	£
Revenue (2,000 × £12)		24,000
Variable costs:		
Materials (2,000 × £1)	2,000	
Labour (2,000 × £4)	8,000	
Variable overhead (2,000 × £2)	4,000	
		14,000
Contribution		10,000

(b) In 2,000 hours on the other contract, to make the purpose-built equipment, contribution measured in similar terms would be calculated as follows.

	£	£
Contract revenue		21,000
Variable costs:		
Materials	3,000	
Labour	8,000	
Variable overhead	4,000	
		15,000
Contribution		6,000

(c) Since the other work earns a greater contribution by £4,000, it is more profitable. The option to make the purpose-built equipment should be rejected.

Activity 5.6

Farro Ltd has been making a machine to order for a customer, but the customer has since gone into liquidation, and there is no prospect that any money will be obtained from the winding up of the company.

Costs incurred to date in manufacturing the machine are £50,000 and progress payments of £15,000 had been received from the customer prior to the liquidation.

The company's sales department has found another customer willing to buy the machine for £34,000 once it has been completed.

To complete the work, the following costs would be incurred.

(a) Materials: these have been bought at a cost of £6,000. They have no other use, and if the machine is not finished, they would be sold for scrap for £2,000.

(b) Further labour costs would be £8,000. Labour is in short supply, and if the machine is not finished, the work force would be switched to another job, which would earn £30,000 in revenue, and incur direct costs of £12,000 and absorbed (fixed) overhead of £8,000.

(c) Consultancy fees £4,000. If the work is not completed, the consultant's contract would be cancelled at a cost of £1,500.

(d) General overheads of £8,000 would be added to the cost of the additional work.

Task

Assess whether the new customer's offer should be accepted.

The assumptions in relevant costing

3.26 **Relevant costs are future costs**. Whenever anyone tries to predict what will happen in the future, the **predictions could well be wrong**. Management accountants have to make the best forecasts of relevant income and costs that they can, and at the same time recognise the assumptions on which their estimates are based.

3.27 Some of the **assumptions** that are typically made in using relevant costing are as follows.

(a) **Cost behaviour patterns are known** (If a department closes down, for example, the attributable fixed cost savings would be known.)

(b) The **amount** of fixed costs, unit variable costs, sales price and sales demand are **known with certainty**.

(c) The **objective** of decision making in the short run is to **maximise** 'satisfaction', which is **often regarded as 'short-term profit'**.

(d) The **information** on which a decision is based is **complete and reliable**.

ASSESSMENT ALERT

In assessed work, it is a good idea to make clear to the assessor any assumptions you are making by explaining them.

4 LIMITING BUDGET FACTORS AND OPPORTUNITY COSTS

4.1 One common type of decision making problems is a budgeting decision in a situation where there are not enough resources to meet the potential sales demand, and so a decision has to be made about using what resources there are as effectively as possible.

KEY TERM

A **limiting factor** or **key factor** is anything which limits activity. An enterprise seeks to optimise the benefit it obtains from the limiting factor.

4.2 The **limiting factor** may change from time to time for the same entity or product. Thus when raw materials are in short supply, performance or profit may be expressed as per kilogramme of material, or, in a restricted skilled labour market, as per skilled labour hour. Alternatively, the limiting factor may be one critical process in a chain.

4.3 There might be just one limiting factor (other than maximum sales demand) but there might also be several scarce resources, with two or more of them putting an effective limit on the level of activity that can be achieved. Here, however, we will concentrate on single limiting factor problems and a technique for resolving these.

Situations in which there are two or more limiting factors (other than sales demand) call for the application of an operational research technique known as **linear programming**, which will not be explained further here.

Limiting factor examples

4.4   Examples of limiting factors are as follows.

Limiting factor	Explanation
(a) Sales	There may be a limit to sales demand.
(b) Labour (either of total quantity or of particular skills)	There may be insufficient labour to produce enough to satisfy sales demand.
(c) Materials	There may be insufficient materials available to produce enough units to satisfy sales demand.
(d) Manufacturing capacity	There may not be sufficient machine capacity to produce enough.
(e) Financial resources	There may not be enough cash to pay for the production demanded.

Limiting factor decisions

4.5   If **sales demand** is the factor which restricts greater production output, profit will be maximised by making exactly the amount required for sales (and no more) provided that each product sold earns a positive contribution. If **labour supply**, **materials availability, machine capacity** or **cash availability** limits production to less than the volume which could be sold, management is faced with the problem of deciding what to produce and what should not be produced because there are insufficient resources to make everything.

4.6   It is assumed in limiting factor accounting that management wishes to maximise profit and that profit will be maximised when contribution is maximised (given no change in fixed cost expenditure incurred). In other words, **marginal costing** ideas are applied.

(a)   Contribution will be maximised by earning the biggest possible contribution per unit of scarce resource. Thus if Grade A labour is the limiting factor, contribution will be maximised by earning the biggest contribution per hour of Grade A labour worked. Similarly, if machine time is in short supply, profit will be maximised by earning the biggest contribution per machine hour worked.

(b)   The limiting factor decision therefore involves the determination of the contribution earned by each different product per unit of scarce resource.

4.7   In limiting factor decisions, we generally assume that fixed costs are the same whatever production mix is selected, so that the only relevant costs are **variable costs.**

4.8 EXAMPLE: LIMITING FACTOR (1)

Desperate Dan Ltd makes two products, the Biff and the Snoot.

Unit variable costs are as follows.

	Biff £	Snoot £
Direct materials	1	3
Direct labour (£3 per hour)	6	3
Variable overhead	1	1
	8	7

The sales price per unit is £14 per Biff and £11 per Snoot. During July 20X2 the available direct labour is limited to 8,000 hours. Sales demand in July is expected to be as follows.

Biffs	3,000 units
Snoots	5,000 units

Task

What production budget will maximise profit, assuming that fixed costs per month are £20,000, and that there are no opening stocks of finished goods or work in progress?

4.9 SOLUTION

(a) The first step in the solution is to confirm that the limiting factor is something other than sales demand.

	Biffs	Snoots	Total
Labour hours per unit	2 hrs	1 hr	
Sales demand	3,000 units	5,000 units	
Labour hours needed	6,000 hrs	5,000 hrs	11,000 hrs
Labour hours available			8,000 hrs
Shortfall			3,000 hrs

Labour is the limiting factor on production.

(b) The second step is to identify the contribution earned by each product per unit of scarce resource, ie per labour hour worked.

	Biffs £	Snoots £
Sales price	14	11
Variable cost	8	7
Unit contribution	6	4
Labour hours per unit	2 hrs	1 hr
Contribution per labour hour (= unit of limiting factor)	£3	£4

Although Biffs have a higher unit contribution than Snoots, two Snoots can be made in the time it takes to make one Biff. Because labour is in short supply it is more profitable to make Snoots than Biffs.

(c) The final stage in the solution is to work out the budgeted production and sales. Sufficient Snoots will be made to meet the full sales demand, and the remaining labour hours available will then be used to make Biffs.

(i)

	Demand Units	Hours required	Hours available	Priority for manufacture
Snoots	5,000	5,000	5,000	1st
Biffs	3,000	6,000	3,000 (bal)	2nd
		11,000	8,000	

(ii)

	Units	Hours	Contribution per unit £	Total contribution £
Snoots	5,000	5,000	4	20,000
Biffs (balance)	1,500	3,000	6	9,000
		8,000		29,000
Less fixed costs				20,000
Profit				9,000

(d) Note that it is not more profitable to begin by making as many units as possible with the bigger unit contribution. We could make 3,000 units of Biff in 6,000 hours and 2,000 units of Snoot (£4 per unit) in the remaining 2,000 hours. However, contribution would be £(3,000 × £6) plus £(2,000 × £4) = £26,000, and profit would be only £6,000. Unit contribution is not the correct way to decide priorities, because it takes two hours to earn £6 from a Biff and one hour to earn £4 from a Snoot. Snoots make more profitable use of the scarce resource, labour hours.

Opportunity costs with a limiting factor

4.10 When there is a limiting factor, an organisation has to make a choice about what it is going to do with the scarce resources. There are alternative courses of action, and each alternative means that the benefits of another option must be sacrificed.

The **opportunity costs** in this situation are the contribution per unit of limiting factor for each product. In the previous example, the contribution per labour hour was £3 per hour per unit of Biff and £4 per hour per unit of Snoot.

If the organisation chooses to make Snoots in preference to making Biffs it will make £4 contribution per hour from Snoots, but it will also forgo making some Biffs, at £3 contribution per hour. This £3 per hour forgone is an opportunity cost of not making Biffs.

	£	
Contribution from Snoots	4	
Contribution forgone from Biffs	3	(opportunity cost)
Differential contribution	1	(differential benefit)

In the example, the budget includes the manufacture of some Biffs, but not as many as could be sold; therefore some potential contribution from Biffs is forgone and there is an opportunity cost.

4.11 EXAMPLE: LIMITING FACTOR (2)

Sparrow Ltd makes four products, P, Q, R and S from the same materials. The sales price and variable costs per unit are as follows.

		P £	*Q* £	*R* £	*S* £
Materials:	A	6	4	3	8
	B	4	8	10	2
Direct labour		5	10	10	8
Variable overhead		2	2	3	2
Sales price		25	23	31	32
Sales demand (units)		4,000	5,000	8,000	6,000

Most production resources are in sufficient supply, but there will only be 6,500 kg of material A available in the period. Material A costs £12 per kilogram.

Task

Calculate the production quantities of each product which will maximise profit in the period.

4.12 SOLUTION

(a) There is a shortage of material A.

Product	Demand Units	Demand kg of A
P	4,000	2,000
Q	5,000	1,667
R	8,000	2,000
S	6,000	4,000
		9,667
Available		6,500
Shortfall		3,167

(b) We now calculate the contribution earned by each product per kilogram of material A consumed.

	P £	*Q* £	*R* £	*S* £
Sales price per unit	25	23	31	32
Variable cost per unit	17	24	26	20
Contribution per unit	8	(1)	5	12
Quantity of material A per unit	½ kg	$^1/_3$ kg	¼ kg	$^2/_3$ kg
Contribution per kg of material A	£16	–	£20	£18
Priority for manufacture	3rd	–	1st	2nd

Because product Q does not earn a positive contribution (its marginal cost exceeds its sales value) it should not be made at all.

(c) Even so, there is still a shortfall in the quantities of material A by 1,500 kilograms.

Products in in order of priority	Demand units	Material A required kg	Cumulative requirements kg
R	8,000 (× ¼)	2,000	2,000
S	6,000 (× $^2/_3$)	4,000	6,000
P	4,000 (× ½)	2,000	8,000

Since only 6,500 kg of material A is available it may be seen that there is sufficient material to satisfy demand for R and S in full, leaving 500 kg left over to make some P.

Product	Material A needs kg	Units produced	Contribution per unit £	Total Contribution £
R	2,000	8,000	5	40,000
S	4,000	6,000	12	72,000
P (balance)	500	1,000	8	8,000
	6,500			120,000

4.13 Management may wish to consider **other factors** before finalising the budget.

- Are the estimates of sales demand reliable?
- Can any production work be sub-contracted to make up the shortfall?
- What will be the effect on customer goodwill of failing to supply enough units of P?
- Is sales demand for R and S dependent on sales of P?

Recognising a limiting factor situation

ASSESSMENT ALERT

You might be presented with a situation in which there is a limiting factor, without specifically being told that this is so, and you will have the task of recognising what the situation is. You may be given a hint with the wording of the task.

(a) 'It is possible that the main raw material used in manufacturing the products will be difficult to obtain in the next year.'

(b) 'The company employs a fixed number of employees who work a maximum overtime of eight hours on top of their basic 36 hour week. The company has also agreed that no more staff will be recruited next year.'

In (a) there is a hint that raw materials might be a limiting factor. In (b), perhaps less obviously, a maximum limit is placed on the available labour hours, and so the possibility should occur to you that perhaps labour is a limiting factor.

4.14 If you suspect the existence of a limiting factor in an assessment problem, some quick computations should confirm your suspicions.

(a) Calculate the amount of the scarce resource (material quantities, labour hours, machine hours and so on) needed to meet the potential sales demand

(b) Calculate the amount of the scarce resource available (for example number of employees multiplied by maximum working hours per employee)

(c) Compare the two figures: obviously, if the resources needed exceed the resources available, there is a limiting factor on output and sales

Advantages and limitations of using opportunity costs for decision making

4.15 **The main argument in favour of opportunity costing** is that management is made more aware of how well they are using resources to make products, and whether resources could be used better in other ways, to make bigger profits or produce more valuable output.

4.16 **The main drawback to opportunity costing** is a practical one. It is not always easy to recognise alternative uses for certain resources, nor to put an accurate value on opportunity cost. It is only likely to be accurate in situations where resources have an alternative use which can be valued at an external market price.

5 MAKE OR BUY DECISIONS

5.1 A **make or buy problem** involves a decision by an organisation about whether it should make a product or whether it should pay another organisation to do so. Here are some examples of make or buy decisions.

(a) Whether a company should manufacture its own components, or else buy the components from an outside supplier

(b) Whether a construction company should do some work with its own employees, or whether it should sub-contract the work to another company

(c) Whether a **service** should be carried out by an internal department or whether an external organisation should be employed

5.2 The 'make' option should give management more direct control over the work, but the 'buy' option often has the benefit that the external organisation has a specialist skill and expertise in the work. Make or buy decisions should certainly **not be based exclusively on cost considerations**.

5.3 EXAMPLE: MAKE OR BUY

Starfish Ltd makes four components, W, X, Y and Z, for which costs in the forthcoming year are expected to be as follows.

	W	X	Y	Z
Production (units)	1,000	2,000	4,000	3,000
Unit marginal costs	£	£	£	£
Direct materials	4	5	2	4
Direct labour	8	9	4	6
Variable production overheads	2	3	1	2
	14	17	7	12

Directly attributable fixed costs per annum and committed fixed costs are as follows.

	£
Incurred as a direct consequence of making W	1,000
Incurred as a direct consequence of making X	5,000
Incurred as a direct consequence of making Y	6,000
Incurred as a direct consequence of making Z	8,000
Other fixed costs (committed)	30,000
	50,000

A sub-contractor has offered to supply units of W, X, Y and Z for £12, £21, £10 and £14 respectively.

Task

Decide whether Starfish Ltd should make or buy the components.

5.4 SOLUTION

The **relevant costs are the differential costs between making and buying,** and they consist of differences in unit variable costs plus differences in directly attributable fixed costs.

	W	X	Y	Z
	£	£	£	£
Unit variable cost of making	14	17	7	12
Unit variable cost of buying	12	21	10	14
	(2)	4	3	2
Annual requirements (units)	1,000	2,000	4,000	3,000
	£	£	£	£
Extra variable cost of buying (per annum)	(2,000)	8,000	12,000	6,000
Fixed costs saved by buying	(1,000)	(5,000)	(6,000)	(8,000)
Extra total cost of buying	(3,000)	3,000	6,000	(2,000)

5.5 The company would save £3,000 pa by sub-contracting component W (where the purchase cost would be less than the marginal cost per unit to make internally) and would save £2,000 pa by sub-contracting component Z (because of the saving in fixed costs of £8,000). In this example, relevant costs are the variable costs of in-house manufacture, the variable costs of sub-contracted units, and the saving in fixed costs.

Qualitative factors to consider

5.6 Important further considerations would be as follows.

(a) If components W and Z are sub-contracted, the company will have spare capacity. **How should that spare capacity be profitably used?** Are there hidden benefits to be obtained from sub-contracting? Would the **company's workforce resent the loss of work to an outside sub-contractor,** and might such a decision cause an industrial dispute?

(b) **Would the sub-contractor be reliable with delivery times,** and would he supply components of the **same quality** as those manufactured internally?

(c) Does the company wish to be **flexible and maintain better control** over operations **by making everything itself?**

(d) **Are the estimates of fixed cost savings reliable?** In the case of Product W, buying is clearly cheaper than making in-house. In the case of Product Z, the decision to buy rather than make would only be financially beneficial if it is feasible that the fixed cost savings of £8,000 will really be 'delivered' by management. All too often in practice, promised savings fail to materialise!

Make or buy decisions and scarce resources

5.7 A company might want to do more things than it has the resources for, and so its choice would be:

(a) To make the best use of the resources it has got, and ignore the opportunities to buy help from outside

(b) To combine internal resources with buying externally so as to do more and increase profitability further

5.8 Buying help from outside is justifiable if it adds to profits. However, a further decision is then how to split the work between internal and external effort. What parts of the work should be given to suppliers or sub-contractors so as to maximise profitability?

5.9 In a situation where a company must sub-contract work to make up a shortfall in its own in-house capabilities, its total costs will be minimised if those units bought have the lowest extra variable cost of buying per unit of scarce resource saved by buying of all the products in question. This basic principle can be illustrated with a simple example.

5.10 EXAMPLE: MAKE OR BUY DECISION WITH SCARCE RESOURCES

Seaman Ltd manufactures three components, S, A and T using the same machines for each. The budget for the next year calls for the production and assembly of 4,000 of each component. The variable production cost per unit of the final product is:

	Machine hours	Variable cost
		£
1 unit of S	3	20
1 unit of A	2	36
1 unit of T	4	24
Assembly		20
		100

Only 24,000 hours of machine time will be available during the year, and a sub-contractor has quoted the following unit prices for supplying components: S £29; A £40; T £34.

Task

Advise Seaman Ltd.

5.11 DISCUSSION AND SOLUTION

The company's budget calls for 36,000 hours of machine time, if all the components are to be produced in-house. Only 24,000 hours are available, and so there is a shortfall of 12,000 hours of machine time, which is therefore a limiting factor. The shortage can be overcome by subcontracting the equivalent of 12,000 machine hours' output to the subcontractor. The assembly costs are not relevant costs because they are unaffected by the decision.

5.12 *Incorrect conclusion:* the company should minimise its internal costs first, and sub-contract what it cannot make itself. In this example, the temptation might be to decide that the variable cost of making each product is:

Product	Variable cost	Machine hours per unit	Variable cost per machine hour
	£		£
S	20	3	6.67
A	36	2	18.00
T	24	4	6.00

and so in-house production would be cheapest by concentrating on T first, then S and finally A, giving a production and buying schedule as follows:

Product		Units	Hours		Variable costs £
Make:	T	4,000	16,000		96,000
	S	2,666	8,000	(balance)	53,320
			24,000		149,320
Buy:	S	1,334		(× £29)	38,686
	A	4,000		(× £40)	160,000
Total costs (excluding assembly)					348,006

5.13 **This is not the cheapest option**. Costs can be reduced still further by minimising the extra variable costs of sub-contracting per unit of scarce resource saved (that is, per machine hour saved).

	S £	A £	T £
Variable cost of making	20	36	24
Variable cost of buying	29	40	34
Extra variable cost of buying	9	4	10
Machine hours saved by buying	3 hrs	2 hrs	4 hrs
Extra variable cost of buying per hour saved	£3	£2	£2.50

5.14 **Correct conclusion**: it is cheaper to buy A than to buy T and it is most expensive to buy S. The priority for **making** the components in-house will be in the reverse order: S, then T, then A. There are enough machine hours to make all 4,000 units of S (12,000 hours) and to produce 3,000 units of T (another 12,000 hours). 12,000 hours' production of T and A must be sub-contracted.

The cost-minimising and so profit-maximising make and buy schedule is as follows:

	Component	Machine hours used/saved	Number of units	Unit variable cost £	Total variable cost £
Make:	S	12,000	4,000	20	80,000
	T	12,000	3,000	24	72,000
		24,000			152,000
Buy:	T	4,000	1,000	34	34,000
	A	8,000	4,000	40	160,000
500		12,000			
Total variable cost of components, excluding assembly costs					346,000

ASSESSMENT ALERT

In an assessment you could be required to write a report making recommendations for management action in connection with a make or buy decision. We covered report writing in Chapter 1 and you now know how to deal with make or buy decisions so you should be well equipped to deal with the following activity.

Activity 5.7

The JK Company has recently signed a long-term lease for premises which will be used to house the manufacturing facilities for component P. The component is used in all of the company's products. No other suitable premises are available.

Since signing the lease, JK has been approached by a reputable manufacturer who has offered to supply all of JK's requirements for component P at a very competitive price.

If the manufacturer's offer is accepted, the directors are undecided whether to continue with the lease. Although JK would not need the premises itself, there is a possibility of sub-letting to another company for an annual rent of £3,400.

JK has made an initial down-payment of £1,500 to the leasing company and, additionally, the annual rent under the lease will be £3,000. JK can cancel the lease completely, but it would be unable to recover the down-payment of £1,500.

Information on the internal costs associated with manufacturing component P is as follows.

	£ per annum
Variable costs	25,000
Fixed costs	
Lease payment (as above)	3,000
Other	8,000
	36,000

The 'other fixed costs' of £8,000 are general salaries and other apportioned costs which are unlikely to be saved if the component is not manufactured internally.

You have been asked to collect data which will assist the decision whether or not to accept the manufacturer's offer to supply component P.

(a) Present a statement of the *relevant* annual cost of manufacturing component P internally. State clearly any assumptions which you make.

(b) In the context of this decision, explain the meaning of the following costs and give an example of each:

(i) A sunk or past cost
(ii) An opportunity cost

---

6 SHUTDOWN DECISIONS

6.1 Shutdown decisions may relate to the problem of closing down a department or factory, or of ceasing to make and to sell an item of product.

6.2 EXAMPLE: SHUTDOWN DECISIONS

Abandon Ship Ltd makes four products, A, B, C and D. The budget for the forthcoming year is as follows. Should production of any product cease?

	A	B	C	D	Total
	£	£	£	£	£
Direct materials	5,000	6,000	4,000	8,000	23,000
Direct labour	4,000	8,000	6,000	4,000	22,000
Variable overheads	1,000	2,000	1,500	1,000	5,500
	10,000	16,000	11,500	13,000	50,500
Sales	20,000	15,000	14,000	20,000	69,000
Contribution	10,000	(1,000)	2,500	7,000	18,500
Share of fixed costs	6,000	4,000	4,000	2,000	16,000
Profit/(loss)	4,000	(5,000)	(1,500)	5,000	2,500

6.3 SOLUTION

(a) Manufacture of product B should cease, because revenue does not cover variable costs and the contribution is negative.

(b) Product C makes a positive contribution, but fails to cover its share of fixed costs.

(i)   If fixed costs of £2,500 or more (ie equal to or greater than the contribution earned) could be saved by ceasing to make product C, the product should be closed down.

(ii)   If the saving in fixed costs from shutdown of product C is less than £2,500 it will remain profitable to continue to make the product until a more profitable alternative use arises for the production resources.

6.4   If we suppose that fixed costs are not stepped costs, and will remain at £16,000 if any products are closed down, then product B only should be abandoned. Profits will then increase by £1,000 as follows.

	A	C	D	Total
	£	£	£	£
Direct materials	5,000	4,000	8,000	17,000
Direct labour	4,000	6,000	4,000	14,000
Variable overheads	1,000	1,500	1,000	3,500
	10,000	11,500	13,000	34,500
Sales	20,000	14,000	20,000	54,000
Contribution	10,000	2,500	7,000	19,500
Fixed costs (new apportionment unknown)				16,000
Profit				3,500

6.5   The company now has spare capacity from the shutdown of product B. It is therefore recommended that management look for an alternative use for the available resources that would earn a positive contribution and thereby increase profit still further.

Key learning points

- The **high-low method** can be used to determine the fixed and variable elements of semi-variable costs.

- The relationship between **cost behaviour and time** can be summarised as follows.

    ° Over a given short time period, costs will be fixed, variable or semi-variable.

    ° Over longer periods of several years, all costs will tend to change in response to large changes in activity level.

- **Marginal costing** provides more useful decision-making information than **absorption costing**.

- **Relevant costs** are future incremental cash flows.

- **Avoidable costs, differential costs** and **opportunity costs** are all relevant costs.

- Non-relevant costs include **sunk costs, committed costs** and **notional (imputed) costs**.

- **Directly attributable fixed costs** are relevant costs, general fixed overheads are not.

- The total relevant cost of a **scarce resource** consists of the following.

    ° The contribution/incremental profit foregone from the next-best opportunity for using the scarce resource

    ° The variable cost of the scarce resource

- Where a **limiting factor** exists, the course of action must be that which gives the maximum possible contribution per unit of limiting factor.

- In a **make or buy situation with no scarce resources,** the relevant costs are the differences in unit variable costs plus differences in directly attributable fixed costs.

- In a situation where a **company must subcontract work to make up a shortfall in its own in-house capabilities,** its total costs will be minimised if those units bought have the lowest extra variable cost of buying per unit of scarce resource saved by buying of all the products in question.

- In a **shutdown decision,** only those costs which would actually be saved by a shutdown are relevant.

Quick quiz

1 Which two periods are selected when using the high-low method to determine the fixed and variable elements of semi-variable costs?

2 Over a sufficiently long period of time, virtually all costs are fixed. True or false?

3 Define opportunity cost.

4 Should you assume that variable costs are relevant costs or non-relevant costs?

5 If materials have already been purchased but will not be replaced, what is their relevant cost?

6 List four assumptions typically made in relevant costing.

7 What is a *limiting factor*? Give five examples of possible limiting factors.

8 What is the rule for maximising profit in cases where a limiting factor is present?

Answers to quick quiz

1 The periods with the highest and lowest volumes of output.

2 False. Virtually all costs are variable.

3 Opportunity cost is the benefit which could have been earned, but which has been given up, by choosing one option instead of another.

4 Relevant costs.

5 The relevant cost will be the higher of their current resale value and the value they would obtain if they were put to an alternative use.

6 Some of the assumptions that are typically made in relevant costing are as follows.

   (a) Cost behaviour patterns are known; if a department closes down, for example, the attributable fixed cost savings would be known.

   (b) The amount of fixed costs, unit variable costs, sales price and sales demand are known with certainty.

   (c) The objective of decision making in the short run is to maximise 'satisfaction', which is often regarded as 'short-term profit'.

   (d) The information on which a decision is based is complete and reliable.

7 Anything which limits activity, eg sales, labour, materials, manufacturing capacity, financial resources.

8 Maximise contribution: ie apply marginal costing principles.

Answers to activities

Answer 5.1

(a)   A fixed cost is a cost which tends to be unaffected by increases or decreases in the volume of output.

(b)   A variable cost.

(c)   A fixed cost.

(d)   False. It is a variable cost.

(e)   A mixed cost (also called a semi-fixed or semi-variable cost) is a cost which contains both fixed and variable components and it is partly affected by changes in the level of activity.

(f)   The standing charge is a fixed cost and the charge per unit of electricity used is a variable cost.

Answer 5.2

	Units		£
High units	3,000	total cost =	220
Low units	2,100	total cost =	184
	900		36

$$\text{Variable cost per unit} = \frac{£36}{900} = £0.04$$

Substituting:

	£
Total cost of 3,000 units	220
Variable costs (3,000 × £0.04)	120
Fixed cost	100

Total cost in July = £(100 + (2,750 × 0.04)) =   £210

Answer 5.3

The financial effect of staging the exhibition

	Notes	£	£
Display cabinets	1		1,700
Repair costs	2		150
Security staff	3		6,500
Rental income forgone	4		7,200
Posters and handbills	5		650
Other costs	6		1,200
			17,400
Revenue from visitors	7	16,000	
Gross margin on cafeteria sales	8	4,000	
			20,000
Net gain from the exhibition			2,600

Notes

1   This is an incremental cost and is therefore relevant to the decision.

2   The original cost of the cabinets is sunk and not relevant.

3   The salaries of the redeployed security staff would be incurred anyway and are not relevant.

4   The central administration costs would be incurred anyway and are not relevant. The opportunity cost of the rental income forgone is relevant and should be included.

5   Only the incremental costs of printing are relevant. The fixed costs would be incurred anyway.

6   These are the incremental costs and are therefore relevant.

7   This is the incremental revenue which will be earned from visitors.

8   An average gross margin of £1 per person will be earned.

Answer 5.4

(a)   *Material A* is not yet owned. It would have to be bought in full at the replacement cost of £6 per unit.

(b)   *Material B* is used regularly by the company. There are existing stocks (600 units) but if these are used on the contract under review a further 600 units would be bought to replace them. Relevant costs are therefore 1,000 units at the replacement cost of £5 per unit.

(c)   1,000 units of *material C* are needed and 700 are already in stock. If used for the contract, a further 300 units must be bought at £4 each. The existing stocks of 700 will not be replaced. If they are used for the contract, they could not be sold at £2.50 each. The realisable value of these 700 units is an opportunity cost of sales revenue forgone.

(d)   The required units of *material D* are already in stock and will not be replaced. There is an opportunity cost of using D in the contract because there are alternative opportunities either to sell the existing stocks for £6 per unit (£1,200 in total) or avoid other purchases (of material E), which would cost 300 x £5 = £1,500. Since substitution for E is more beneficial, £1,500 is the opportunity cost.

(e)   *Summary of relevant costs*

	£
Material A (1,000 × £6)	6,000
Material B (1,000 × £5)	5,000
Material C (300 × £4) plus (700 × £2.50)	2,950
Material D	1,500
Total	15,450

Answer 5.5

Loss in net realisable value of the machine through using it on the order £(8,000 – 7,500)
Costs in excess of existing routine maintenance costs £(120 – 80)
Total marginal user cost

Answer 5.6

(a)   Costs incurred in the past, or revenue received in the past are not relevant because they cannot affect a decision about what is best for the future. Costs incurred to date of £50,000 and revenue received of £15,000 are 'water under the bridge' and should be ignored.

(b)   Similarly, the price paid in the past for the materials is irrelevant. The only relevant cost of materials affecting the decision is the opportunity cost of the revenue from scrap which would be forgone - £2,000.

(c)   *Labour costs*

	£
Labour costs required to complete work	8,000
Opportunity costs: contribution forgone by losing other work £(30,000 – 12,000)	18,000
Relevant cost of labour	26,000

(d)   The incremental cost of consultancy from completing the work is £2,500.

	£
Cost of completing work	4,000
Cost of cancelling contract	1,500
Incremental cost of completing work	2,500

(e)   Absorbed overhead is a notional accounting cost and should be ignored. Actual overhead incurred is the only overhead cost to consider. General overhead costs (and the absorbed overhead of the alternative work for the labour force) should be ignored.

(f)   Relevant costs may be summarised as follows.

	£	£
Revenue from completing work		34,000
Relevant costs		
Materials: opportunity cost	2,000	
Labour: basic pay	8,000	
opportunity cost	18,000	
Incremental cost of consultant	2,500	
		30,500
Extra profit to be earned by accepting the completion order		3,500

Answer 5.7

(a)   *Relevant annual cost of internal manufacture*

	£
Variable costs	25,000
Premises: forgone rent	3,400
	28,400

Assumptions

(i)   'Other fixed costs' would be incurred anyway.

(ii)   Variable costs are all incremental costs which would be saved if the manufacturer's offer was accepted.

(ii)   The premises would be sub-let if not used for manufacturing.

(b)   (i)   A sunk cost is a cost which has already been incurred and which cannot now be recovered. In this situation the down payment of £1,500 is a sunk cost. It cannot be recovered and is not a relevant cost of the decision to continue internal manufacture.

(ii)   An opportunity cost is a benefit forgone as the result of selecting one course of action in preference to another. If JK decides to manufacture the component internally, they will lose the opportunity to sub-let the premises for £3,400. The relevant cost of using the premises for internal manufacture is therefore the full opportunity cost of £3,400.

6 Breakeven analysis

Chapter topic list

1   The breakeven point

2   The margin of safety

3   Breakeven arithmetic

4   Breakeven charts

5   Profit/volume charts

6   Limitations and advantages of breakeven analysis

Learning objectives

On completion of this chapter you will be able to:

	Performance criteria	Range statement
• Calculate and explain the breakeven point	16.2.1	
• Analyse the effect on the breakeven point of changes in sales price and costs	16.2.1	
• Prepare and explain breakeven charts and profit/volume charts	16.2.1	
• Describe the advantages and limitations of breakeven analysis for management decision making	16.2.5	
• Use techniques related to the identification of fixed, variable and semi-fixed costs and their correct use in cost analysis		16.2.3

BPP PUBLISHING

1   THE BREAKEVEN POINT

> ### KEY TERM
>
> **Cost-volume-profit (CVP)/breakeven analysis** is the study of the interrelationships between costs, volume and profit at various levels of activity.

1.1   The management of an organisation usually wishes to know not only the profit likely to be made if the aimed-for production and sales for the year are achieved but also the following.

- The activity level at which there is neither profit nor loss
- The **amount** by which actual **sales can fall** below anticipated sales, **without** a **loss** being incurred

> ### KEY TERM
>
> The **breakeven point** is the activity level at which there is neither profit nor loss.

1.2   The breakeven point (BEP) can be calculated arithmetically.

$$\text{Breakeven point} = \frac{\text{Total fixed costs}}{\text{Contribution per unit}}$$

$$= \frac{\text{Contribution required to break even}}{\text{Contribution per unit}}$$

= Number of units of sale required to break even.

The contribution required to break even is the amount which exactly equals total fixed costs.

1.3   EXAMPLE: BREAKEVEN POINT

Expected sales	10,000 units at £8 = £80,000
Variable cost	£5 per unit
Fixed costs	£21,000

Compute the breakeven point.

1.4   SOLUTION

The contribution per unit is £(8 – 5)	=	£3
Contribution required to break even	=	fixed costs = £21,000
Breakeven point (BEP)	=	21,000 ÷ 3
	=	7,000 units
In revenue, BEP	=	(7,000 × £8) = £56,000

Sales above £56,000 will result in profit of £3 per unit of additional sales and sales below £56,000 will mean a loss of £3 per unit for each unit by which sales fall short of 7,000 units. In other words, profit will improve or worsen by the amount of contribution per unit.

	7,000 units	7,001 units
	£	£
Revenue	56,000	56,008
Less variable costs	35,000	35,005
Contribution	21,000	21,003
Less fixed costs	21,000	21,000
Profit	0 (= breakeven)	3

Breakeven point and the C/S ratio

1.5 Another way of calculating the breakeven point to give an answer in terms of sales revenue is as follows.

$$\frac{\text{Required contribution} \left(= \text{fixed costs}\right)}{\text{C/S ratio}} = \text{Sales revenue at breakeven point}$$

(The **C/S (contribution/sales)** ratio (which we looked at in Chapter 4) is also sometimes called a **profit/volume or P/V ratio.**)

1.6 In the example in Paragraph 1.3 the C/S ratio is $\dfrac{£3}{£8} = 37.5\%$

Breakeven is where sales revenue equals $\dfrac{£21,000}{37.5\%}$

$$= £56,000$$

At a price of £8 per unit, this represents 7,000 units of sales.

The contribution/sales ratio is a measure of how much contribution is earned from each £1 of sales. The C/S ratio of 37.5% in the above example means that for every £1 of sales, a contribution of 37.5p is earned. Thus, in order to earn a total contribution of £21,000 and if contribution increases by 37.5p per £1 of sales, sales must be:

$$\frac{£1}{37.5p} \times £21,000 = £56,000$$

Activity 6.1

The C/S ratio of product A is 20%. AB Ltd, the manufacturer of product A, wishes to make a contribution of £50,000 towards fixed costs. How many units of product A must be sold if the selling price is £10 per unit?

Activity 6.2

Maria manufactures commemorative medals. The following data relates to the year 20X0.

	Medal
	£
Selling price	50
Variable production cost	(30)
Variable selling cost	(5)
Contribution per medal	15
Fixed production cost, based on annual sales of 20,000 medals	(5)
Fixed selling costs, based on annual sales of 20,000 medals	(1)
Profit per medal	9

Tasks

(a) Calculate the level of production needed for Maria to break even.

(b) Maria is thinking of doubling her production. To do so, she will have to occupy additional premises at an annual rent of £210,000. Calculate the new breakeven point and the margin of safety.

2 THE MARGIN OF SAFETY

KEY TERM

The **margin of safety** is the difference in units between the budgeted sales volume and the breakeven sales volume and it is sometimes expressed as a percentage of the budgeted sales volume.

2.1 The margin of safety may also be expressed as the difference between the budgeted sales revenue and breakeven sales revenue, expressed as a percentage of the budgeted sales revenue.

2.2 EXAMPLE: MARGIN OF SAFETY

Homer Ltd makes and sells a product which has a variable cost of £30 and which sells for £40. Budgeted fixed costs are £70,000 and budgeted sales are 8,000 units. Calculate the breakeven point and the margin of safety.

2.3 SOLUTION

(a) Breakeven point $= \dfrac{\text{Total fixed costs}}{\text{Contribution per unit}} = \dfrac{£70,000}{£(40-30)}$

$= 7,000$ units

(b) Margin of safety $= 8,000 - 7,000$ units $= 1,000$ units

which may be expressed as $\dfrac{1,000 \text{ units}}{8,000 \text{ units}} \times 100\% = 12\frac{1}{2}\%$ of budget

(c) The margin of safety indicates to management that actual sales can fall short of budget by 1,000 units or 12½% before the breakeven point is reached and no profit at all is made.

Activity 6.3

The margin of safety on the production of product L is 200 units and the breakeven point is 400 units. What is the budgeted level of sales?

Activity 6.4

Dragon, a transport company, operates with one vehicle only, and has produced the following forecast for next year.

Estimated operating kilometres	30,000
	£
Revenue	30,000
Total wages cost	10,000
Total standing cost	6,000
Total vehicle running costs	12,000

Revenue and vehicle running costs are directly variable with operating kilometres.

Tasks

(a) Calculate the breakeven point and margin of safety in kilometres for the forecast period.

(b) Prepare a table showing Dragon's profit or loss at the following levels of activity.

    (i)   20,000 kilometres
    (ii)   30,000 kilometres
    (iii) 40,000 kilometres

(c) Calculate Dragon's breakeven point in kilometres if the operating kilometres were forecast to be only 28,500 kilometres and the annual wage cost was cut to £8,000.

3 BREAKEVEN ARITHMETIC

3.1 At the **breakeven point,** sales revenue equals total costs and there is no profit.

$$S = V + F$$

where	S	=	Sales revenue
	V	=	Total variable costs
	F	=	Total fixed costs

Subtracting   V from each side of the equation, we get:

$S - V = F$, that is, **total contribution = fixed costs**

3.2 EXAMPLE: BREAKEVEN ARITHMETIC

Bluebell Ltd makes a product which has a variable cost of £7 per unit. If fixed costs are £63,000 per annum, calculate the selling price per unit if the company wishes to break even with a sales volume of 12,000 units.

3.3 SOLUTION

Contribution required to break even (= Fixed costs)	=	£63,000		
Volume of sales	=	12,000 units		
				£
Required contribution per unit (S – V)	=	£63,000 ÷ 12,000 =		5.25
Variable cost per unit (V)	=			7.00
Required sales price per unit (S)	=			12.25

Target profits

3.4 A similar formula may be applied where a company wishes to **achieve a certain profit** during a period. To achieve this profit, **sales must cover all costs and leave the required profit**.

The target profit is achieved when: $S = V + F + P,$
    where P = required profit

Subtracting V from each side of the equation, we get:

S – V   = F + P, so
Total contribution required   = F + P

3.5 EXAMPLE: TARGET PROFITS (1)

Whippy Ltd makes and sells a single product, for which variable costs are as follows.

	£
Direct materials	10
Direct labour	8
Variable production overhead	6
	24

The sales price is £30 per unit, and fixed costs per annum are £68,000. The company wishes to make a profit of £16,000 per annum. You are required to determine the sales required to achieve this profit.

3.6 SOLUTION

Required contribution = fixed costs + profit
= £68,000 + £16,000 = £84,000

Required sales can be calculated in one of two ways.

(a) $\dfrac{\text{Required contribution}}{\text{Contribution per unit}}$ = $\dfrac{£84,000}{£(30 - 24)}$

= 14,000 units, or £420,000 in revenue

(b) $\dfrac{\text{Required contribution}}{\text{C / S ratio}}$ = $\dfrac{£84,000}{20\%}$

= £420,000 of revenue, or 14,000 units.

Activity 6.5

Grumpy Ltd wishes to sell 14,000 units of its product, which has a variable cost of £15 to make and sell. Fixed costs are £47,000 and the required profit is £23,000. Calculate the sales price per unit.

3.7 EXAMPLE: TARGET PROFITS (2)

Flash Ltd makes and sells three products, Bang, Crash and Wallop. The selling price per unit and costs are as follows.

	Bang	*Crash*	*Wallop*
Selling price per unit	£80	£50	£70
Variable cost per unit	£50	£10	£20
Fixed costs per month = £160,000			

The maximum sales demand per month is 2,000 units of each product and the minimum sales demand is 1,000 of each.

Tasks

(a) Comment on the potential profitability of the company.

(b) Suppose that there is a fixed demand for Bangs and Crashes of 1,500 units per month, which will not be exceeded, but for which firm orders have been received. Determine how many Wallops would have to be sold to achieve a profit of at least £25,000 per month.

3.8 SOLUTION

(a) When there is no indication about whether marginal or absorption costing is in use, it is simpler (and more informative too) to assess profitability with contribution analysis and marginal costing. This is the requirement in part (a) of the problem. The obvious analysis to make is a calculation of the worst possible and best possible results.

		Best possible			*Worst possible*	
	Sales units	*Contrib'n per unit*	*Total cont'n*	*Sales units*	*Contrib'n per unit*	*Total cont'n*
		£	£		£	£
Bangs	2,000	30	60,000	1,000	30	30,000
Crashes	2,000	40	80,000	1,000	40	40,000
Wallops	2,000	50	100,000	1,000	50	50,000
Total contribution			240,000			120,000
Fixed costs			160,000			160,000
Profit/(loss)			80,000			(40,000)

The company's potential profitability ranges from a profit of £80,000 to a loss of £40,000 per month.

(b) The second part of the problem is a variation of a 'target profit' calculation.

	£	£
Required (minimum) profit per month		25,000
Fixed costs per month		160,000
Required contribution per month		185,000
Contribution to be earned from:		
product Bang 1,500 × £30	45,000	
product Crash 1,500 × £40	60,000	
		105,000
Contribution required from product Wallop		80,000
Contribution per unit of Wallop		£50
Minimum required sales of Wallops per month in units		1,600

Decisions to change sales price or costs

3.9 You may come across a problem in which you will be expected to analyse the effect of altering the selling price, variable cost per unit or fixed cost. These problems are slight variations on basic breakeven arithmetic, as shown in the following examples.

3.10 EXAMPLE: CHANGE IN SELLING PRICE

Fairy Ltd bake and sell a single type of cake. The variable cost of production is 15p and the current sales price is 25p. Fixed costs are £2,600 per month, and the annual profit for the company at current sales volume is £36,000. The volume of sales demand is constant throughout the year.

The sales manager, Mr Currant, wishes to raise the sales price to 29p per cake, but considers that a price rise will result in some loss of sales. Your task is to ascertain the minimum volume of sales required each month to justify a rise in price to 29p.

3.11 SOLUTION

The minimum volume of demand which would justify a price of 29p is one which would leave total profit at least the same as before, ie £3,000 per month. Required profit should be converted into required contribution, as follows.

	£
Monthly fixed costs	2,600
Monthly profit, minimum required	3,000
Current monthly contribution	5,600
Contribution per unit (25p – 15p)	10p
Current monthly sales	56,000 cakes

The minimum volume of sales required after the price rise will be an amount which earns a contribution of £5,600 per month, no worse than at the moment. The contribution per cake at a sales price of 29p would be 14p.

$$\text{Required sales} \quad = \quad \frac{\text{required contribution}}{\text{contribution per unit}} \quad = \quad \frac{£5,600}{14p}$$

$$= \quad 40,000 \text{ cakes per month.}$$

3.12 EXAMPLE: CHANGE IN PRODUCTION COSTS

Brickhill Ltd makes a product which has a variable production cost of £8 and a variable sales cost of £2 per unit. Fixed costs are £40,000 per annum, the sales price per unit is £18, and the current volume of output and sales is 6,000 units. The company is considering whether to have an improved machine for production. Annual hire costs would be £10,000 and it is expected that the variable cost of production would fall to £6 per unit.

Tasks

(a) Determine the number of units that must be produced and sold to achieve the same profit as is currently earned, if the machine is hired.

(b) Calculate the annual profit with the machine if output and sales remain at 6,000 units per annum.

3.13 SOLUTION

The current unit contribution is £(18 – (8+2)) = £8

		£
(a)	Current contribution (6,000 × £8)	48,000
	Less current fixed costs	40,000
	Current profit	8,000

With the new machine fixed costs will go up by £10,000 to £50,000 per annum. The variable cost per unit will fall to £(6 + 2) = £8, and the contribution per unit will be £10.

	£
Required profit (as currently earned)	8,000
Fixed costs	50,000
Required contribution	58,000

Contribution per unit		£10
Sales required to earn £8,000 profit		5,800 units

(b) *If sales are 6,000 units*

	£	£
Sales (6,000 × £18)		108,000
Variable costs: production (6,000 × £6)	36,000	
sales (6,000 × £2)	12,000	
		48,000
Contribution (6,000 × £10)		60,000
Less fixed costs		50,000
Profit		10,000

	£
Alternative calculation	
Profit at 5,800 units of sale (see (a))	8,000
Contribution from sale of extra 200 units (× £10)	2,000
Profit at 6,000 units of sale	10,000

Activity 6.6

The following details relate to a shop which currently sells 25,000 pairs of shoes annually.

Selling price per pair of shoes	£40
Purchase cost per pair of shoes	£25

Total annual fixed costs

	£
Salaries	100,000
Advertising	40,000
Other fixed expenses	100,000

Tasks

Answer each part independently of data contained in other parts of the requirement.

(a) Calculate the breakeven point and margin of safety in number of pairs of shoes sold.

(b) Assume that 20,000 pairs of shoes were sold in a year. Calculate the shop's net income (or loss).

(c) If a selling commission of £2 per pair of shoes sold was to be introduced, calculate the number of pairs of shoes which would need to be sold in a year in order to earn a net income of £10,000.

(d) Assume that for next year an additional advertising campaign costing £20,000 is proposed, whilst at the same time selling prices are to be increased by 12%. Calculate the breakeven point in number of pairs of shoes.

Guidance note

When performing the calculations you will find that the quickest method is to calculate the contribution first and then deduct the fixed costs.

4 BREAKEVEN CHARTS

Breakeven charts

4.1 The breakeven point can also be determined graphically using a **breakeven chart.**

> ### KEY TERM
>
> A **breakeven chart** is a chart which shows approximate levels of profit or loss at different sales volume levels within a limited range.

4.2   A breakeven chart has the following axes.

- A **horizontal** axis showing the **sales/output** (in value or units).
- A **vertical axis** showing £ for **sales revenues** and **costs**

The following lines are drawn on the breakeven chart.

(a)   The **sales line**

(i)   Starts at the origin

(ii)   Ends at the point signifying expected sales

(b)   The **fixed costs line**

(i)   Runs parallel to the horizontal axis

(ii)   Meets the vertical axis at a point which represents total fixed costs

(c)   The **total costs line**

(i)   Starts where the fixed costs line meets the vertical axis

(ii)   Ends at the point which represents the following

- Anticipated sales on the horizontal axis
- Total costs of anticipated sales on the vertical axis

4.3   The **breakeven point** is the **intersection** of the **sales line** and the **total costs line**.

Activity 6.7

Use breakeven arithmetic to show why the breakeven point can be found at the intersection of the sales line and the total costs line.

4.4   The **distance between the breakeven point** and the **expected (or budgeted) sales**, in units, indicates the **margin of safety**.

4.5   EXAMPLE: A BREAKEVEN CHART

The budgeted annual output of a factory is 120,000 units. The fixed overheads amount to £40,000 and the variable costs are 50p per unit. The sales price is £1 per unit. You are required to construct a breakeven chart showing the current breakeven point and profit earned up to the present maximum capacity.

4.6   SOLUTION

We begin by calculating the profit at the budgeted annual output.

	£
Sales (120,000 units)	120,000
Variable costs	60,000
Contribution	60,000
Fixed costs	40,000
Profit	20,000

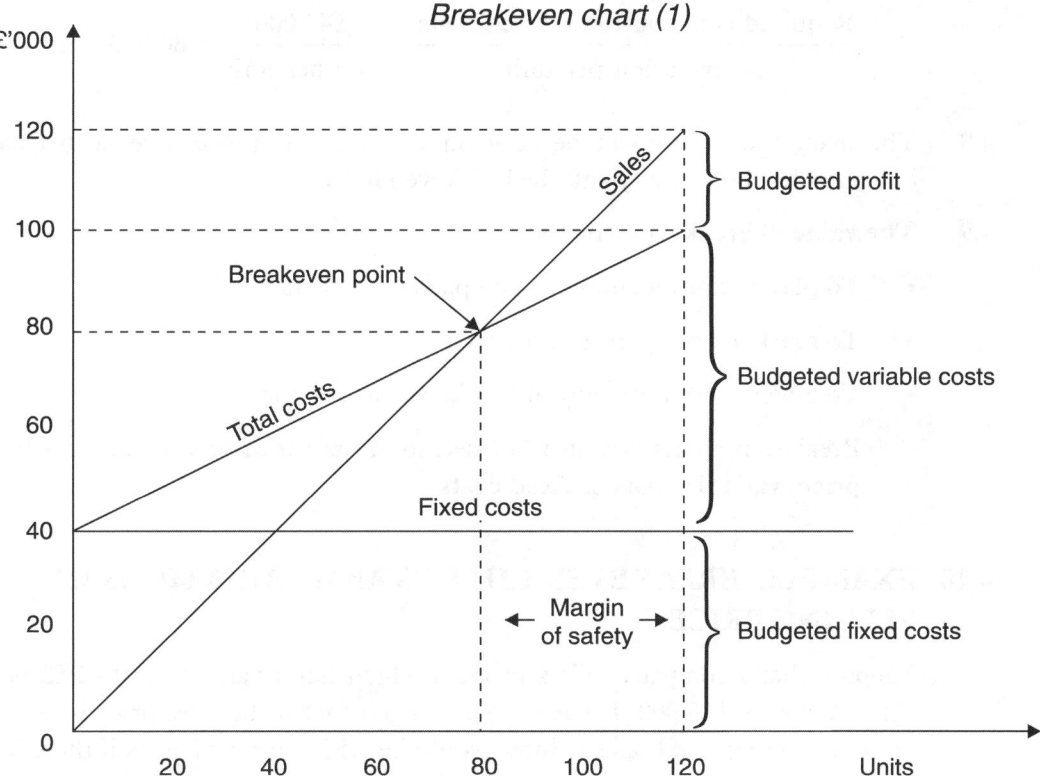

Breakeven chart (1)

The chart is drawn as follows.

(a) The vertical axis represents money (costs and revenue) and the horizontal axis represents the level of activity (production and sales).

(b) The fixed costs are represented by a straight line parallel to the horizontal axis (in our example, at £40,000).

(c) The variable costs are added 'on top of' fixed costs, to give total costs. It is assumed that fixed costs are the same in total and variable costs are the same per unit at all levels of output.

The line of costs is therefore a straight line and only two points need to be plotted and joined up. Perhaps the two most convenient points to plot are total costs at zero output, and total costs at the budgeted output and sales.

(i) At zero output, costs are equal to the amount of fixed costs only, £40,000, since there are no variable costs.

(ii) At the budgeted output of 120,000 units, costs are £100,000.

	£
Fixed costs	40,000
Variable costs 120,000 × 50p	60,000
Total costs	100,000

(d) The sales line is also drawn by plotting two points and joining them up.

(i) At zero sales, revenue is nil.
(ii) At the budgeted output and sales of 120,000 units, revenue is £120,000.

4.7 The breakeven point is where total costs are matched exactly by total revenue. From the chart, this can be seen to occur at output and sales of 80,000 units, when revenue and costs are both £80,000. This breakeven point can be proved mathematically as:

$$\frac{\text{Required contribution = fixed costs}}{\text{Contribution per unit}} = \frac{£40,000}{50\text{p per unit}} = 80,000 \text{ units}$$

4.8   The margin of safety can be seen on the chart as the difference between the budgeted level of activity and the breakeven level.

4.9   **The value of breakeven charts**

- To **plan** the production of a company's products

- To **market** a company's products

- To given a **visual display** of breakeven arithmetic

- Breakeven charts can also be used to **show variations** in the possible **sales price**, **variable costs** or **fixed costs**.

4.10 EXAMPLE: BREAKEVEN CHARTS AND VARIATIONS IN SELLING PRICE

Suppose that a company sells a product which has a variable cost of £2 per unit. Fixed costs are £15,000. It has been estimated that if the sales price is set at £4.40 per unit, the expected sales volume would be 7,500 units; whereas if the sales price is lower, at £4 per unit, the expected sales volume would be 10,000 units.

Task

Draw a breakeven chart to show the budgeted profit, the breakeven point and the margin of safety at each of the possible sales prices.

4.11 SOLUTION

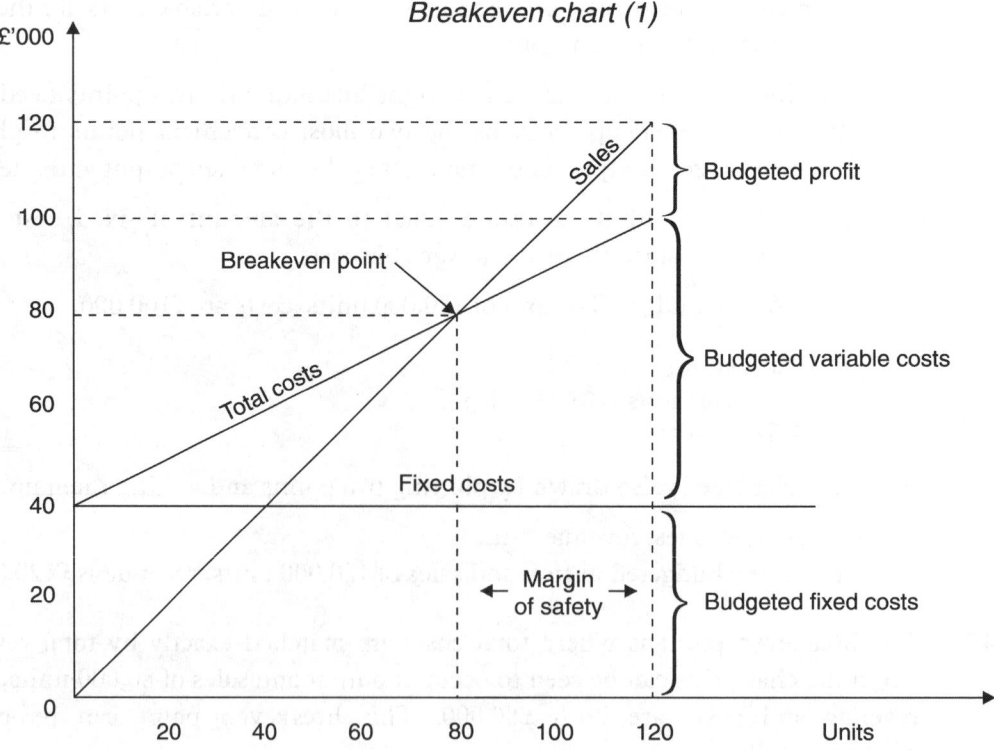

Workings	Sales price £4.40 per unit		Sales price £4 per unit
	£		£
Fixed costs	15,000		15,000
Variable costs (7,500 × £2.00)	15,000	(10,000 × £2.00)	20,000
Total costs	30,000		35,000
Budgeted revenue (7,500 × £4.40)	33,000	(10,000 × £4.00)	40,000

(a) Breakeven point A is the breakeven point at a sales price of £4.40 per unit, which is 6,250 units or £27,500 in costs and revenues.

(check:
$$\frac{\text{Required contribution to break even}}{\text{Contribution per unit}} = \frac{£15,000}{£2.40 \text{ per unit}} = 6,250 \text{ units})$$

The margin of safety (A) is 7,500 units – 6,250 units = 1,250 units or 16.7% of expected sales.

(b) Breakeven point B is the breakeven point at a sales price of £4 per unit which is 7,500 units or £30,000 in costs and revenues.

(check:
$$\frac{\text{Required contribution to break even}}{\text{Contribution per unit}} = \frac{£15,000}{£2 \text{ per unit}} = 7,500 \text{ units})$$

The margin of safety (B) = 10,000 units – 7,500 units = 2,500 units or 25% of expected sales.

4.12 Since a price of £4 per unit gives a higher expected profit and a wider margin of safety, this price will probably be preferred even though the breakeven point is higher than at a sales price of £4.40 per unit.

5 PROFIT/VOLUME CHARTS

KEY TERM

The **profit/volume (P/V) chart** is a variation of the breakeven chart which provides a simple illustration of the relationship of costs and profit to sales.

5.1 A P/V chart is constructed as follows. (Look at the chart in the example that follows as you read the explanation.)

(a) '**P**' is on the **y axis** and actually comprises not only 'profit' but **contribution to profit** (in monetary value), extending above and below the x axis with a zero point at the intersection of the two axes, and the **negative section below the x axis representing fixed costs**. This means that at **zero production**, the firm is incurring a **loss equal to the fixed cost**s.

(b) '**V**' is on the **x axis** and comprises either **volume of sales or value of sales** (revenue).

(c) The **profit-volume line** is a straight line drawn with its **starting point** (at zero production) at the **intercept on the y axis representing the level of fixed costs**, and with a **gradient of contribution/unit (or the C/S ratio if sales value is used rather than units)**. The P/V line will **cut the x axis at the breakeven point of sales volume**. Any point on the P/V line above the x axis

BPP PUBLISHING

represents the profit to the firm (as measured on the vertical axis) for that particular level of sales.

5.2 EXAMPLE: P/V CHART

Here, we draw a P/V chart for the example in Paragraph 4.5. At sales of 120,000 units, total contribution will be $120,000 \times £(1 - 0.5) = £60,000$ and total profit will be £20,000.

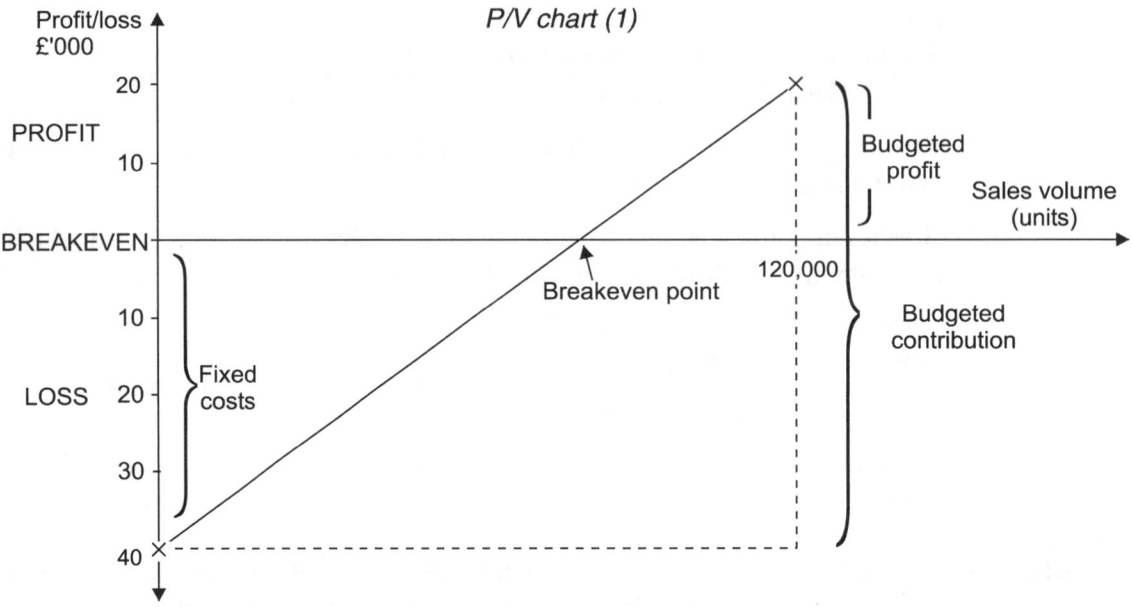

The value of P/V charts

5.3 Just as breakeven charts can be used to **show how variations in sales price, variable costs and fixed costs affect the breakeven point and the margin of safety,** so too can P/V charts. Two circumstances can be considered.

(a) Fixed cost changes do not alter the slope of the P/V line but change the point of intersection and therefore the breakeven point. Such a diagram shows how the breakeven point and the level of profit or loss at different levels of revenue will change depending on the level of fixed costs.

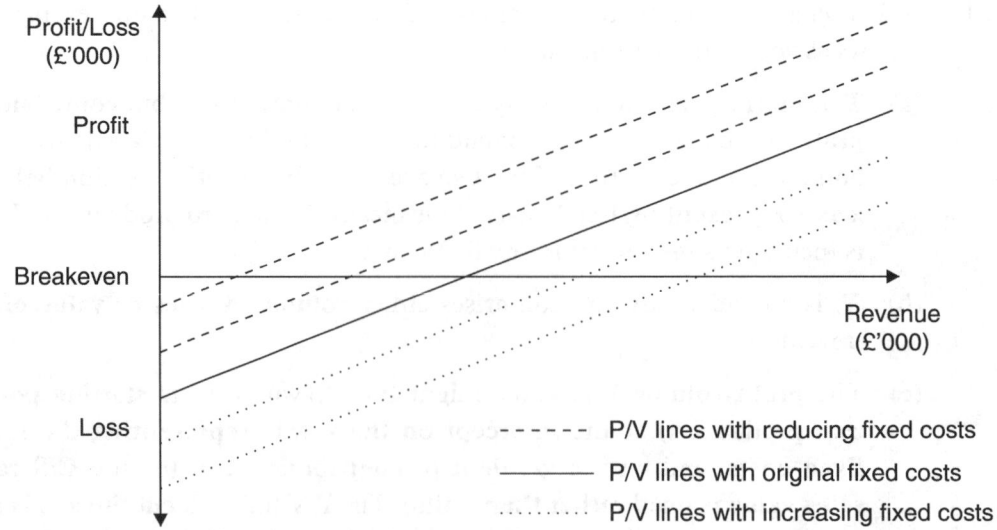

(b) **Variable cost and sales price changes alter the slope of the line and hence the breakeven point and the profit or loss.** Such a diagram shows how the breakeven point and the level of profit or loss at different levels of revenue will change depending on the contribution ratio.

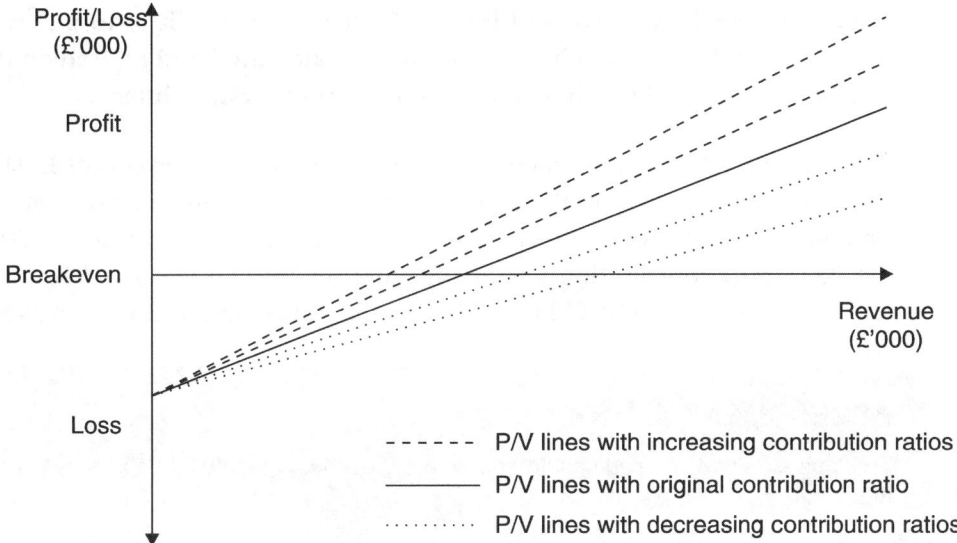

5.4 Suppose the budgeted selling price of the product in our example in Paragraphs 4.5 and 5.2 is increased to £1.20, with the result that demand drops to 105,000 units despite additional fixed costs of £10,000 being spent on advertising. We could add a line representing this situation to P/V chart (1). At a sales level of 105,000 units, contribution will be 105,000 × £(1.20 − 0.50) = £73,500 and total profit will be £23,500 (fixed costs being £50,000).

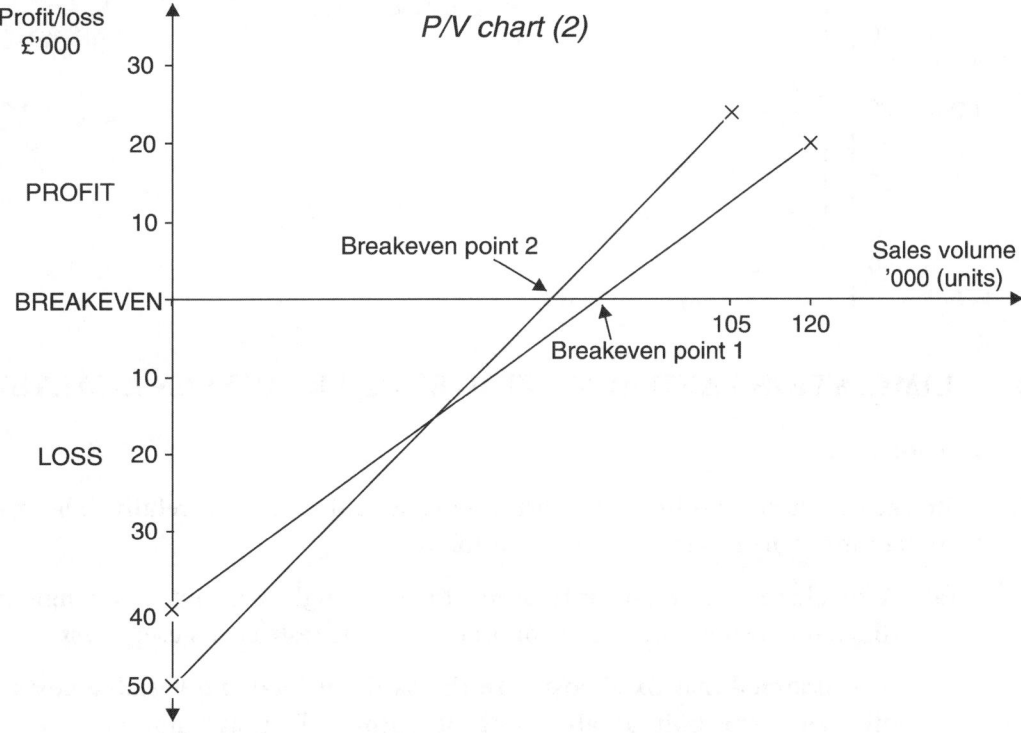

5.5 The diagram shows that if the selling price is increased, the breakeven point occurs at a lower level of sales revenue (71,429 units instead of 80,000 units), although this is not a particularly large increase when viewed in the context of the

127

projected sales volume. It is also possible to see that for sales above 50,000 units, the profit achieved will be higher (and the loss achieved lower) if the price is £1.20. For sales volumes below 50,000 units the first option will yield lower losses.

5.6 **Changes in the variable cost per unit or in fixed costs at certain activity levels** can also be **easily incorporated** into a P/V chart. The **profit or loss** at each point **where the cost structure changes should be calculated and plotted** on the graph so that the **profit/volume line becomes a series of straight lines**.

5.7 For example, suppose that in our example, at sales levels in excess of 120,000 units the variable cost per unit increases to £0.60 (perhaps because of overtime premiums that are incurred when production exceeds a certain level). At sales of 130,000 units, contribution would therefore be 130,000 × £(1 – 0.60) = £52,000 and total profit would be £12,000. This can be shown on the P/V chart as follows.

ASSESSMENT ALERT

Try to be sure that you can construct *both* breakeven charts and P/V charts *and* interpret them.

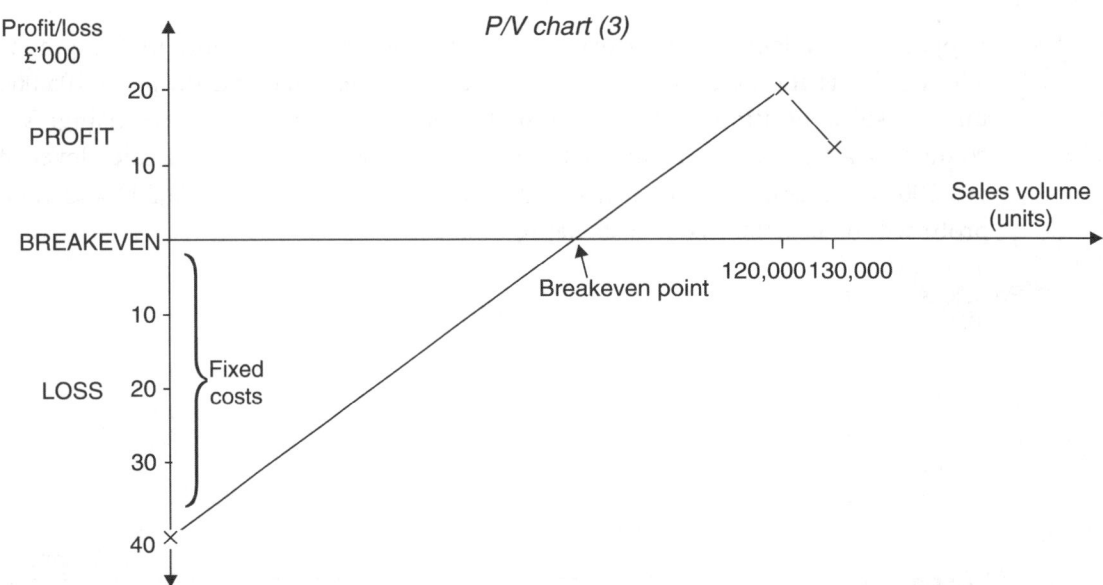

P/V chart (3)

6 LIMITATIONS AND ADVANTAGES OF BREAKEVEN ANALYSIS

Limitations

6.1 Breakeven charts and breakeven arithmetic should be used carefully. The major limitations of breakeven analysis are as follows.

(a) A breakeven chart can **only apply to one single product** or a single mix (fixed proportions) of a group of products. This restricts its usefulness.

(b) It is **assumed** that **fixed costs are the same in total and variable costs are the same per unit at all levels of output**. This assumption is a great simplification, for the following reasons.

(i) Fixed costs will change if output falls or increases substantially. (Most fixed costs are step costs).

(ii) The variable cost per unit will decrease where economies of scale are made at higher output volumes, and the variable cost per unit will also eventually rise where diseconomies of scale begin to appear at higher volumes of output (for example, the extra cost of labour in overtime working).

It is important to remember that although a breakeven chart is drawn on the assumption that fixed costs and the variable cost per unit are constant, this is **only correct within a normal range or relevant range of output**. It is generally assumed that both the budgeted output and also the breakeven point of sales lie within this relevant range.

(c) It is **assumed that sales prices will be constant at all levels of activity**. This may not be true, especially at higher volumes of output, where the price may have to be reduced to win the extra sales.

(d) **Production and sales are assumed to be the same**, therefore the consequences of any increase in stock levels (when production volumes exceed sales) or 'de-stocking' (when sales volumes exceed production levels) are ignored.

(e) **Uncertainty** in the estimates of fixed costs and unit variable costs is often **ignored** in breakeven analysis, and some costs (for example mixed costs and step costs) are not always easily categorised or divided into fixed and variable.

Advantages

6.2 In spite of limitations, however, breakeven analysis is a **useful technique** for managers in planning sales prices, the desired sales mix, and profitability. (Breakeven charts are 'decorative' in the sense that they merely provide a graphical representation of breakeven arithmetic.)

6.3 Breakeven arithmetic should be used with a full awareness of its limitations, but can usefully be applied to **provide simple and quick estimates of breakeven volumes or profitability given variations** in sales price, variable and fixed costs within a 'relevant range' of output/sales volumes.

Key learning points

- **CVP or breakeven analysis** has a number of purposes: to provide information to management about cost behaviour for routine **planning** and 'one-off' **decision making**; to determine what volume of sales is needed at any given budgeted sales price in order to **break even**; to identify the 'risk' in the budget by measuring the **margin of safety**; to calculate the effects on profit of changes in variable costs, sales prices, fixed costs, and so on.

- Make sure that you understand how to calculate the **breakeven point,** the **C/S ratio,** the **margin of safety** and **target profits,** and can apply the principles of CVP analysis to decisions about whether to change sales prices or costs. You should also be able to construct **breakeven charts** and **profit/volume charts**.

- Do not forget that CVP analysis does have **limitations**: it is only valid within a 'relevant range' of output volumes; it measures profitability, but does not consider the volume of capital employed to achieve such profits; and it is subject to the other limitations described in this chapter.

Quick quiz

1   What is the formula for calculating the breakeven point in terms of the number of units required to break even?

2   Give the formula which uses the C/S ratio to calculate the breakeven point.

3   What is the margin of safety?

4   What do the axes of a breakeven chart represent?

5   Give three uses of breakeven charts.

6   What is a profit/volume chart?

7   What does the horizontal axis of the P/V chart represent?

8   What are the limitations of breakeven charts and CVP analysis?

Answers to quick quiz

1   $$\text{Breakeven point (units)} = \frac{\text{Total fixed costs}}{\text{Contribution per unit}}$$

2   $$\text{Sales value at breakeven point} = \frac{\text{Fixed costs}}{\text{C / S ratio}} = \frac{\text{Required contribution}}{\text{C / S ratio}}$$

3   The margin of safety is the difference in units between the budgeted sales volume and the breakeven sales volume.

4   The vertical axis represents money (costs and revenue) and the horizontal axis represents the level of activity (production and sales).

5   Breakeven charts are used as follows.

   •   To plan the production of a company's products
   •   To market a company's products
   •   To given a visual display of breakeven arithmetic

6   The profit/volume chart is a variation of the breakeven chart which provides a simple illustration of the relationship of costs and profit to sales.

7   'V' on the horizontal axis is volume or value of sales.

8   •   A breakeven chart can only apply to a single product or a single mix of a group of products.

   •   A breakeven chart may be time-consuming to prepare.

   •   It assumes fixed costs are constant at all levels of output.

   •   It assumes that variable costs are the same per unit at all levels of output.

   •   It assumes that sales prices are constant at all levels of output.

   •   It assumes production and sales are the same (stock levels are ignored).

   •   It ignores the uncertainty in the estimates of fixed costs and variable cost per unit.

Answers to activities

Answer 6.1

$$\frac{\text{Required contribution}}{\text{C / S ratio}} = \frac{£50,000}{20\%} = £250,000$$

∴ Number of units = £250,000 ÷ £10 = 25,000.

Answer 6.2

(a) In 20X0, fixed costs are as follows.

		£
Production	20,000 × £5	100,000
Selling	20,000 × £1	20,000
		120,000

Contribution per medal is £15

Breakeven point is $\dfrac{£120,000}{£15}$ = 8,000 medals

(b)

	£
Fixed costs per (a)	120,000
Additional premises costs	210,000
Total fixed costs	330,000

Breakeven point = $\dfrac{£330,000}{£15}$ = 22,000 medals

George will be manufacturing and selling 40,000 medals. The margin of safety will therefore be (40,000 – 22,000) medals = 18,000 medals, or 45% of the target output of 40,000 medals.

Answer 6.3

Let S be budgeted level of sales
Margin of safety = 200 = S – 400
∴S = 600

Answer 6.4

(a) *Assumption.* Wages and standing costs are fixed costs and will not vary with the level of activity.

∴ Total fixed costs = £(10,000 + 6,000) = £16,000.

	£
Revenue	30,000
Variable costs	12,000
Contribution for next year	18,000

∴ Contribution per kilometre = $\dfrac{£18,000}{30,000}$ = £0.60

Breakeven point = $\dfrac{\text{fixed costs}}{\text{contribution per km}}$ = $\dfrac{£16,000}{£0.60}$ = 26,667 km.

Margin of safety = forecast activity – breakeven point
= 30,000 km – 26,667 km
= 3,333 km, or 11% of estimated activity

(b) Table of profit or loss at various levels of activity:

Level of activity (kilometres)	20,000	30,000	40,000
	£	£	£
Contribution (× £0.60)	12,000	18,000	24,000
Less fixed costs	16,000	16,000	16,000
Profit/(loss)	(4,000)	2,000	8,000

(c) The forecast of 28,500 kilometres is irrelevant to the calculation of the breakeven point.

Fixed costs are reduced to £14,000.

Breakeven point = $\dfrac{\text{fixed costs}}{\text{contribution per km}}$ = $\dfrac{£14,000}{£0.60}$ = 23,333 km

Answer 6.5

Required contribution	=	fixed costs plus profit	
	=	£47,000 + £23,000	
	=	£70,000	
Required sales	=	14,000 units	

	£
Required contribution per unit sold	5
Variable cost per unit	15
Required sales price per unit	20

Answer 6.6

(a)   Contribution per pair of shoes = £(40 − 25) = £15

$$\text{Breakeven point} = \frac{\text{fixed costs}}{\text{contribution, per pair}} = \frac{£240,000}{£15}$$

= 16,000 pairs

Margin of safety = 25,000 − 16,000 pairs = 9,000 pairs

(b)

		£
Contribution = 20,000 × £15	=	300,000
Fixed costs	=	240,000
Net income		60,000

(c)   Revised contribution per pair = £40 − £27 = £13

Required contribution   =   £240,000 fixed costs + £10,000 net income = £250,000

$$\text{Number of pairs} = \frac{£250,000}{£13} = 19,231 \text{ pairs}$$

(d)   Revised contribution per pair =   £(40 × 1.12) − £25 = £19.80

Revised fixed costs   =   £260,000

$$\text{Breakeven point} = \frac{£260,000}{£19.80} = 13,132 \text{ pairs}$$

Answer 6.7

At breakeven point, contribution = fixed costs.

Contribution = sales revenue − variable costs.

∴ At breakeven point, sale revenue − variable costs = fixed costs.

∴ At breakeven point, sales revenue = variable costs + fixed costs.
ie sales revenue = total costs.

7 Pricing

Chapter topic list

1   The importance of pricing

2   Factors affecting pricing policy

3   Price and the price elasticity of demand

4   The demand-based approach to pricing

5   Full cost plus pricing

6   Marginal cost plus pricing

7   Opportunity cost approach to pricing

8   Fixed price tenders

9   Practical considerations

Learning objectives

On completion of this chapter you will be able to:

	Performance criteria	Range statement
• Describe factors which may influence an organisation's pricing policy	16.2	16.2.2
• Explain the importance of the price elasticity of demand to an organisation setting or changing prices	16.2	16.2.2
• Explain and illustrate the demand-based approach to setting prices	16.2	16.2.2
• Understand approaches to pricing using absorption costing, marginal costing and opportunity costing	16.2	16.2.2
• Describe the procedure for preparing cost estimates for fixed price quotations and tenders	16.2	16.2.2
• Explain the procedure for monitoring costs against fixed prices	16.2	16.2.2

BPP PUBLISHING

1   THE IMPORTANCE OF PRICING

1.1   **Price** can go by many names: fares, tuitions, rent, assessments and so on. All profit organisations and many non-profit-making organisations face the task of setting a price for their products or services.

1.2   In the past, setting a price was typically the single most important decision made by the sales department, but in modern marketing philosophy, price, whilst important, is not necessarily the predominant factor. **Modern businesses** seek to interpret and **satisfy customer wants and needs by modifying existing products or introducing new products** to the range.

1.3   Nevertheless, **proper pricing** of an organisation's products or services is **essential to its profitability** and hence its **survival**. Also, price can be used to differentiate a product and an organisation from competitors.

2   FACTORS AFFECTING PRICING POLICY

2.1   In practice, there are many more influences on pricing policy than the **cost** of a product or service.

Influence	Explanation/example
Price sensitivity	Sensitivity to price levels will vary amongst purchasers. **Those that can pass on the cost of purchases will be the least sensitive** and will therefore respond more to other elements of perceived value.
	For example, the business traveller will probably be more concerned about the level of service and quality of food in looking for an hotel than price, since his or her employer will be paying the bill. In contrast, a family on holiday are likely to be very price sensitive when choosing an overnight stay.
Price perception	Price perception is **the way customers react to prices**. For example, customers may react to a price increase by buying more. This could be because they expect further price increases to follow (they are '**stocking up**').
Quality	This is an aspect of price perception. In the absence of other information, customers tend to **judge quality by price**. Thus a price change may send signals to customers concerning the quality of the product. A price rise may indicate improvements in quality, a price reduction may signal reduced quality, for example through the use of inferior components.
Intermediaries	If an organisation distributes products or services to the market through independent intermediaries, the **objectives of these intermediaries complicate the pricing decision**. Such intermediaries are likely to deal with a range of suppliers and their aims concern their own profits rather than those of suppliers.
Competitors	In setting prices, an organisation sends out signals to rivals. **Competitors are likely to react to these signals in some way**. In some industries (such as petrol retailing) **pricing** moves **in unison**; in others, price changes by one supplier may initiate a **price war**, with each supplier undercutting the others. Competition is discussed in more detail below.

Influence	Explanation/example
Suppliers	If an organisation's suppliers **notice a price rise** for the organisation's products, they **may seek a rise** in the price for their supplies to the organisation on the **grounds** that it is now able to pay a higher price.
Inflation	In periods of inflation the organisation may need to change prices to reflect increases in the prices of supplies, labour, rent and so on. Such changes may be needed to keep relative (real) prices unchanged.
Newness	When a **new product** is introduced for the first time there are no existing reference points such as customer or competitor behaviour; **pricing decisions are most difficult to make** in such circumstances. It may be possible to seek alternative reference points, such as the price in another market where the new product has already been launched, or the price set by a competitor.
Incomes	In times of **rising incomes**, **price** may become **less important than product quality** or convenience of access (distribution). When income levels are **falling** and/or unemployment levels rising, **price** will become much **more important.**
Product range	Products are often interrelated, being complements to each other or substitutes for one another. **Pricing** is then likely **to focus** on the profit from the **whole range** rather than the profit on each single product. Take, for example, the use of **loss leaders**: a very low price for one product is intended to make consumers buy additional products in the range which carry higher profit margins. A good example is selling razors at low prices whilst selling the blades for them at a higher profit margin.
Ethics	Ethical considerations may be a further factor, for example whether or not to **exploit** short-term shortages through higher prices.
Substitute products	These are **products which could be transformed for the same use**. For example if the price of train travel rises it comes under competition from cheaper coach travel and more expensive air travel.

Product life cycle

2.2 A typical product has a life cycle of four stages.

(a) **Introduction**. The product is introduced to the market. Heavy **capital expenditure** will be incurred on product development and perhaps also on the purchase of new fixed assets and building up stocks for sale.

On its introduction to the market, the product will begin to earn some revenue, but initially demand is likely to be small. Potential customers will be unaware of the product or service, and the organisation may have to spend further on **advertising** to bring the product or service to the attention of the market.

(b) **Growth**. The product gains a bigger market as demand builds up. Sales revenues increase and the product begins to make a profit. The initial costs of the **investment** in the new product are gradually **recovered**.

(c) **Maturity**. Eventually, the growth in demand for the product will slow down and it will enter a period of relative maturity. It will continue to be profitable. The product may be **modified or improved, as a means of sustaining its demand**.

(d) **Saturation and decline**. The market will, at some stage, have bought enough of a product and it will therefore reach 'saturation point'. Demand will start to fall. For a while, the product will still be profitable in spite of declining sales, but eventually it could become a **loss-maker** and this is the time when the organisation should decide to stop selling the product or service, and so the product's life cycle should reach its end.

Markets and competition

2.3 The price that an organisation can charge for its products will be determined to a greater or lesser degree by the type of market in which it operates.

> **KEY TERMS**
>
> **Perfect competition**: many buyers and many sellers all dealing in an identical product. Neither producer nor user has any market power and both must accept the prevailing market price.
>
> **Monopoly**: one seller who dominates many buyers. The monopolist can use his market power to set a profit-maximising price.
>
> **Oligopoly**: relatively few competitive companies dominate the market. Whilst each large firm has the ability to influence market prices, the unpredictable reaction from the other giants makes the final industry price indeterminate.

2.4 In **established industries** dominated by a few major firms, it is generally accepted that a price initiative by one firm will be countered by a price reaction by competitors. In these circumstances, **prices tend to be fairly stable**, unless pushed upwards by inflation or strong growth in demand.

2.5 If a **rival cuts its prices** in the expectation of increasing its market share, a **firm has several options**.

(a) It will **maintain its existing prices** if the expectation is that only a small market share would be lost, so that it is more profitable to keep prices at their existing level. Eventually, the rival firm may drop out of the market or be forced to raise its prices.

(b) It may maintain its prices but respond with a **non-price counter-attack**. This is a more positive response, because the firm will be securing or justifying its current prices with a product change, advertising, or better back-up services.

(c) It may **reduce its prices**. This should protect the firm's market share so that the main beneficiary from the price reduction will be the consumer.

(d) It may **raise its prices** and respond with a **non-price counter-attack**. The extra revenue from the higher prices might be used to finance an advertising campaign or product design changes. A price increase would be based on a campaign to emphasise the quality difference between the firm's own product and the rival's product.

Price leadership

2.6 It is not unusual to find that large corporations emerge as **price leaders**. The price leader **indicates to the other firms in the market what the price will be**, and **competitors then set their prices with reference to the leader's price**.

2.7 A price leader will have the dominant influence over price levels for a class of products and may actually lead without other firms moving its prices at all. For example, if other firms tried to raise prices and the leader did not follow, the upward move in prices would be halted.

2.8 The price leader generally has a large, if not necessarily the largest, market share. The greater the number of firms in an industry, the weaker will be the role of a price leader.

Market penetration pricing

2.9 Market penetration pricing is a policy of **low prices** when the product is **first launched** in order to obtain sufficient penetration into the market. A penetration pricing policy may be appropriate in the following circumstances.

   (a) If the firm wishes to **discourage new entrants** into the market.

   (b) If the firm wishes to **shorten the initial period of the product's life cycle** in order to enter the growth and maturity stages as quickly as possible.

   (c) If there are significant **economies of scale** to be achieved from a high volume of output, so that quick penetration into the market is desirable in order to gain unit cost reductions.

   (d) If **demand is likely to increase as prices fall**.

Market skimming pricing

2.10 In contrast, **market skimming** involves charging **high prices** when a product is **first launched** and **spending heavily on advertising** and sales promotion to obtain sales. As the product moves into the **later stages** of its life cycle (growth, maturity and decline) **progressively lower prices** will be charged. The profitable 'cream' is thus skimmed off in stages until sales can only be sustained at lower prices.

2.11 The aim of market skimming is to gain **high unit profits early** in the product's life. High unit prices make it more likely that **competitors** will enter the market than if lower prices were to be charged.

Differential pricing

2.12 In certain circumstances the **same product** can be sold at **different prices** to **different customers**. There are a number of bases on which such prices can be set.

Basis	Example
By **market segment**	A cross-channel ferry company would market its services at different prices in England, Belgium and France, for example. Services such as cinemas and hairdressers are often available at lower prices to old age pensioners and/or juveniles.
By **product version**	Many car models have 'add on' extras which enable one brand to appeal to a wider cross-section of customers. The final price need not reflect the cost price of the add on extras directly: usually the top of the range model would carry a price much in excess of the cost of provision of the extras, as a prestige appeal.
By **place**	Theatre seats are usually sold according to their location so that patrons pay different prices for the same performance according to the seat type they occupy.
By **time**	This is perhaps the most popular type of price discrimination. Rail operating companies, for example, are successful price discriminators, charging more to rush hour rail commuters whose demand remains the same whatever the price charged at certain times of the day.

Activity 7.1

Can you think of any more examples of products or services which are sold to different customers at different prices on the basis of time?

3   PRICE AND THE PRICE ELASTICITY OF DEMAND

3.1   Economists argue that the higher the price of a good, the lower will be the quantity demanded. We have already seen that in practice it is by no means as straightforward as this (some goods are bought *because* they are expensive, for example), but you know from your personal experience as a consumer that the theory is essentially true. An important concept in this context is **price elasticity of demand (PED).**

KEY TERM

The **price elasticity of demand** measures the extent of change in demand for a good following a change to its price.

3.2   Price elasticity of demand (η) is measured as:

$$\frac{\% \text{ change in sales demand}}{\% \text{ change in sales price}}$$

3.3   Demand is said to be **elastic** when a **small change in the price** produces a **large change in the quantity demanded**. The PED is then greater than 1. *Example:* A good with readily available substitutes, such as a Vauxhall Astra car, would be expected to have relatively high demand elasticity.

3.4 Demand is said to be **inelastic** when a **small change in the price** produces only a **small change in the quantity demanded**. The PED is then less than 1. *Example:* Mains electricity for domestic use cannot easily be replaced by alternative energy sources, and so demand will be relatively inelastic.

3.5 Strictly speaking, demand is elastic (PED > 1) when a cut in price results in a bigger **percentage** expansion in demand. Thus, in Figure 1 (a), a cut in price from £12 to £6 (50% reduction) leads to an expansion in demand from 100 to 300 (200% expansion).

$$\text{PED} = \frac{200\%}{50\%} = 4.0$$

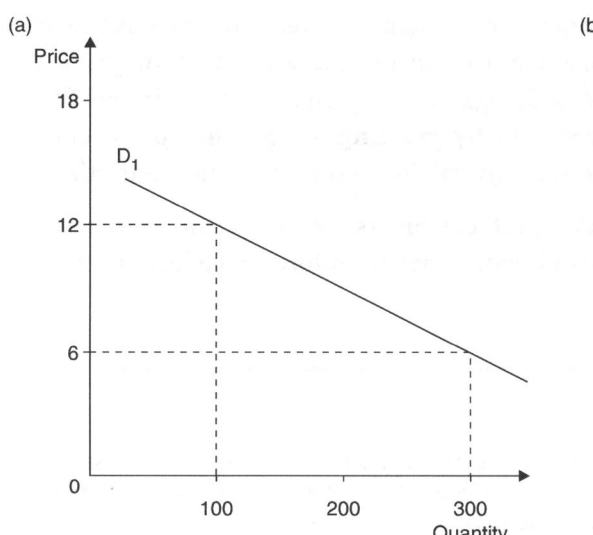 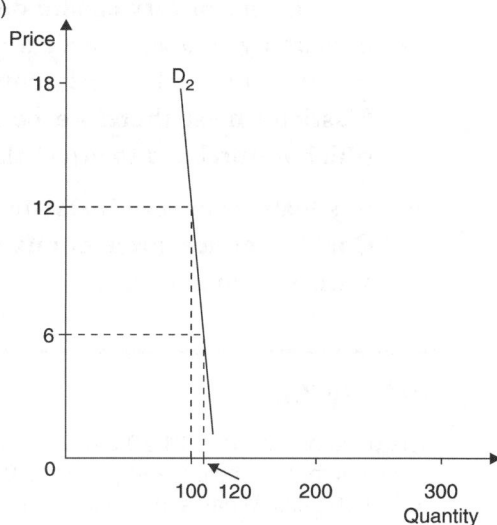

Figure 1

3.6 Demand is inelastic (PED < 1) when a cut in price results in a smaller **percentage** expansion in demand. Thus, in Figure 1(b), a cut in price from £12 to £6 (50% reduction) leads to an expansion in demand from 100 to 120 units (20% expansion).

$$\text{PED} = \frac{20\%}{50\%} = 0.4$$

(PED will be negative for all 'normal' demand curves. Hence it is usual to omit the use of + and − signs.)

3.7 Price elasticity can, of course, apply also to price rises. What has been stated so far merely operates in reverse. Therefore, if price is increased and revenue falls, demand is elastic. The following table summarises the situation.

Price	Revenue	Demand
Decrease	Rises	Elastic
Increase	Falls	Elastic
Decrease	Falls	Inelastic
Increase	Rises	Inelastic

BPP PUBLISHING

Elasticity and the pricing decision

3.8 An awareness of the concept of elasticity can help management with pricing decisions.

(a) In circumstances of **inelastic demand, prices should be increased** because revenues will increase and total costs will reduce (because quantities sold will reduce).

(b) In circumstances of **elastic demand**, increases in prices will bring decreases in revenue and decreases in price will bring increases in revenue. Management therefore have to **decide whether the increase/decrease in costs will be less than/greater than the increases/decreases in revenue.**

(c) In situations of **very elastic demand**, overpricing can lead to a massive drop in quantity sold and hence a massive drop in profits, whereas underpricing can lead to costly stock outs and, again, a significant drop in profits. **Elasticity must therefore be reduced by creating a customer preference which is unrelated to price** (through advertising and promotional activities).

(d) In situations of **very inelastic demand**, customers are not sensitive to price. **Quality, service, product mix and location are therefore more important** to a firm's pricing strategy.

Activity 7.2

The price of a good is £1.20 per unit and annual demand is 800,000 units. Market research indicates that an increase in price of 10 pence per unit will result in a fall in annual demand of 75,000 units. What is the price elasticity of demand?

4 THE DEMAND-BASED APPROACH TO PRICING

4.1 A difficulty with a demand-based approach to pricing is to find a balance between theory and practice.

(a) **Price theory** or **demand** theory is based on the idea that a connection can be made between price, quantity demanded and sold, and total revenue. Demand varies with price, and so if an estimate can be made of demand at different price levels, it should be **possible to derive either a profit-maximising price** or a revenue-maximising price.

The theory of demand cannot be applied in practice, however, unless realistic estimates of demand at different price levels can be made.

(b) In practice, businesses might not make estimates of demand at different price levels, but they might still make pricing decisions on the basis of demand conditions and competition in the market.

4.2 Some larger organisations go to considerable effort to estimate the demand for their products or services at differing price levels by producing estimated demand curves. A knowledge of demand curves can be very useful.

4.3 **For example,** a large transport authority might be considering an increase in fares. The effect on total revenues and profit of the increase in fares could be estimated from a knowledge of the demand for transport services at different price levels. If an increase in the price per ticket caused a large fall in demand, because

demand was price elastic, total revenues and profits would fall whereas a fares increase when demand is price inelastic would boost total revenue, and since a transport authority's costs are largely fixed, this would probably boost total profits too.

4.4 Many businesses enjoy something close to a monopoly position, even in a competitive market. This is because they develop a unique marketing mix, for example a unique combination of price and quality, or a monopoly in a localised area. The significance of a monopoly situation is as follows.

(a) The business does not have to 'follow the market' on price, in other words it is not a 'price-taker', but has more choice and flexibility in the prices it sets. **At higher prices**, demand for its products or services will be less. **At lower prices**, demand for its products or services will be higher.

(b) There will be a selling price at which the business can maximise its profits.

Activity 7.3

Skillmade Ltd sells a product which has a variable cost of £8 per unit. The sales demand at the current sales price of £14 is 3,000 units. It has been estimated by the marketing department that the sales volume would fall by 100 units for each addition of 25 pence to the sales price. Establish whether the current price of £14 is the optimal price which maximises contribution.

5 FULL COST PLUS PRICING

5.1 A traditional approach to pricing products is full cost plus pricing, whereby the sales price is determined by **calculating the full cost of the product and adding a percentage mark-up for profit.** The term **target pricing** is sometimes used, which means setting a price so as to achieve a target profit or return on capital employed.

5.2 In **full cost plus pricing**, the full cost may be a fully absorbed **production** cost only, or it may include some absorbed administration, selling and distribution overhead. The full cost might also include some opportunity costs as well, such as the opportunity cost of a production resource that is in short supply, so that '**full cost' need not be the cost as it might be established in the accounts**.

5.3 A business might have an idea of the percentage profit margin it would like to earn and so might decide on an average profit mark-up as a general guideline for pricing decisions. This would be particularly **useful for** businesses that carry out a large amount of **contract work** or **jobbing work**, for which individual job or contract prices must be quoted regularly to prospective customers. The **percentage profit mark-up** does not have to be fixed, but can be **varied to suit** demand conditions in the market.

5.4 The full cost plus approach to pricing is commonly used in practice, but varying the size of the profit mark-up gives the pricing decisions much-needed flexibility so as to adapt to demand conditions.

Problems with full cost plus pricing

5.5 There are serious problems with relying on a full cost approach as a basis for pricing decisions.

(a) Perhaps the most significant problem with cost plus pricing is that it **fails to recognise** that since demand may be determined by price, **there will be a profit-maximising combination of price and demand.** A cost plus based approach to pricing will be **most unlikely to arrive at the profit-maximising price**.

(b) Prices must be adjusted to market and demand conditions: the decision cannot simply be made on a cost basis only.

(c) Output volume, a key factor in the fixed overhead absorption rate, must be budgeted. **A full cost plus pricing decision cannot be made without a knowledge of demand and demand cannot be estimated without a knowledge of price:** a vicious circle.

   (i) One solution is to estimate likely demand (from past experience in the case of established products) and calculate an absorption rate on this assumed volume of output. Provided that actual volume equals or exceeds the estimated volume of sales, the company will achieve (or exceed) its target profit.

   (ii) Another solution is to set a price on the basis of a budgeted production volume and allow stocks to build up for a time if demand is below production volume at this price. A **price review** can be made when demand conditions are known better, and either of the following decisions could be taken. A **price reduction** could be made to stimulate demand if this seems appropriate. Production volumes could be reduced and **prices raised** if necessary in recognition of the lack of demand at the original budgeted volumes.

(d) Further objections to full cost plus pricing as the basis for pricing decisions can be listed as follows.

   (i) It **fails to allow for competition**. A company may need to match the prices of rival firms when these take a price-cutting initiative.

   (ii) A full cost plus basis for a pricing decision is a means of ensuring that, in the long run, a company succeeds in covering all its fixed costs and making a profit out of revenue earned. However, in the short term it is **inflexible**. A firm may tender a cost plus price that results in a contract going elsewhere, although a lower price would have been sufficient to cover incremental costs and opportunity costs. In the **short term**, rapidly-changing environmental factors might dictate the need for lower (or higher) prices than long-term considerations would indicate.

   (iii) Full cost plus prices tend to ignore opportunity costs.

   (iv) Where **more than one product is sold** by a company, the **price** decided by a cost plus formula **depends on the method of apportioning fixed costs** between the products.

5.6 EXAMPLE: FULL COST PLUS PRICING WITH MORE THAN ONE PRODUCT

Giraffe Ltd is attempting to decide sales prices for two products, Lyons and Tygers. The products are both made by the same workforce and in the same department. 30,000 direct labour hours are budgeted for the year.

The budgeted fixed costs are £30,000 and it is expected that the department will operate at full capacity. Variable costs per unit are as follows.

		Lyons		*Tygers*
		£		£
Materials		4		4
Labour	(2 hours)	6	(3 hours)	9
Expenses	(1 machine hour)	2	(1 machine hour)	2
		12		15

Expected demand is 7,500 Lyons and 5,000 Tygers. You are required to calculate the unit prices which give a profit of 20% on full cost if overheads are absorbed:

(a) On a direct labour hour basis

(b) On a machine hour basis

5.7 SOLUTION

(a) *A direct labour hour basis*

$$\frac{\text{Budgeted fixed costs}}{\text{Budgeted labour costs}} = \frac{£30,000}{(15,000 + 15,000)} = £1$$

Absorption rate: £1 per direct labour hour

	Lyons	*Tygers*
	£	£
Variable costs	12.00	15.00
Overhead absorbed	2.00	3.00
	14.00	18.00
Profit (20%)	2.80	3.60
Price	16.80	21.60

The total budgeted profit would be £(21,000 + 18,000) = £39,000.

(b) *A machine hour basis*

$$\frac{\text{Budgeted fixed costs}}{\text{Budgeted machine hours}} = \frac{£30,000}{(7,500 + 5,000)} = \frac{£30,000}{12,500} = £2.40$$

Absorption rate : £2.40 per machine hour

	Lyons	*Tygers*
	£	£
Variable costs	12.00	15.00
Overhead absorbed	2.40	2.40
Full cost	14.40	17.40
Profit (20%)	2.88	3.48
Price	17.28	20.88

The total budgeted profit would be £(21,600 + 17,400) = £39,000.

(c) The different bases for charging overheads result in different prices for both Lyons (difference of 48p per unit) and Tygers (difference of 72p per unit).

5.8 It is unlikely that the expected sales demand for the products would be the same at both sales prices. It is questionable whether one (or either) product might achieve expected sales demand at the higher price. In other words, although the budgeted profit is £39,000 whichever overhead absorption method is used, this assumes that budgeted sales would be achieved regardless of the unit price of each product. This is an unrealistic basis on which to make a decision.

5.9 **Advantages of full cost plus pricing**

(a) Since the size of the profit margin can be varied at management's discretion, a decision based on a price in excess of full cost should ensure that a company working at normal capacity will cover all its fixed costs and make a profit. Companies may benefit from cost plus pricing in the following circumstances.

(i) When they carry out large contracts which must make a sufficient profit margin to cover a fair share of fixed costs

(ii) If they must justify their prices to potential customers (for example for government contracts)

(iii) If they find it difficult to estimate expected demand at different sales prices

(b) It is a **simple, quick and cheap** method of pricing which can be delegated to junior managers. This may be particularly important with jobbing work where many prices must be decided and quoted each day.

Activity 7.4

A product's full cost is £4.75 and it is sold at full cost plus 70%. A competitor has just launched a similar product selling for £7.99. How will this affect the first product's mark up?

6 MARGINAL COST PLUS PRICING

6.1 Instead of pricing products or services by adding a profit margin on to full cost, a business might **add a profit margin on to marginal cost (either the marginal cost of production or else the marginal cost of sales)**. This is sometimes called **mark-up pricing**.

6.2 For example, if a company budgets to make 10,000 units of a product for which the variable cost of production is £3 a unit and the fixed production cost £60,000 a year, it might decide to fix a price by adding, say, $33^1/_3$% to full production cost to give a price of £9 × $1^1/_3$ = £12 a unit. Alternatively, it might decide to add a profit margin of, say, 250% on to the variable production cost, to give a price of £3 × 350% = £10.50.

6.3 **Advantages of a marginal cost plus approach to pricing**

(a) It is a **simple and easy** method to use.

(b) The **mark-up can be varied** and so, provided that a rigid mark-up is not used, mark-up pricing can be adjusted to reflect demand conditions.

(c) It draws management attention to contribution and the effects of higher or lower sales volumes on profit.

(d) Mark-up pricing is **convenient where there is a readily identifiable basic variable cost. Retail industries** are the most obvious example, and it is quite common for the prices of goods in shops to be fixed by adding a mark-up (20% or 33^1/$_3$%, say) to the purchase cost. A retailer might buy in items of pottery, for example at £3 each, add a mark-up of one third and resell the items at £4.

6.4 Disadvantages of marginal cost plus pricing

(a) Although the size of the mark-up can be varied in accordance with demand conditions, it **does not ensure that sufficient attention is paid to competitors' prices and profit maximisation.**

(b) It ignores fixed overheads in the pricing decision, but the price must be high enough to ensure that a profit is made after covering fixed costs. Pricing decisions **cannot ignore fixed costs altogether.**

Activity 7.5

A product has the following costs.

	£
Direct materials	5
Direct labour	3
Variable overhead	7

Fixed overheads are £10,000 per month. Budgeted sales for the month are 400 units. What profit margin needs to be added to marginal cost to break even?

7 OPPORTUNITY COST APPROACH TO PRICING

7.1 The opportunity cost approach to pricing can be used to **set a full cost plus price or marginal cost plus price which includes the opportunity costs of the resources consumed in making and selling the item.**

7.2 EXAMPLE: FULL COST-PLUS PRICING AND OPPORTUNITY COSTS

Oppo Ltd has begun to produce a new product, Product Tunity, for which the following cost estimates have been made.

	£
Direct materials	27
Direct labour: 4 hrs at £5 per hour	20
Variable production overheads: machining, ½ hr at £6 per hour	3
	50

Production fixed overheads are budgeted at £300,000 per month and because of the shortage of available machining capacity, the company will be restricted to 10,000 hours of machine time per month. The absorption rate will be a direct labour rate, however, and budgeted direct labour hours are 25,000 per month.

It is estimated that the company could obtain a minimum contribution of £10 per machine hour on producing items other than product Tunity. The company wishes to make a profit of 20% on full production cost from product Tunity.

Your task is to calculate the full cost plus price.

7.3 SOLUTION

Let us begin by calculating a price based on *not* including opportunity costs.

	£
Direct materials	27.00
Direct labour (4 hours)	20.00
Variable production overheads	3.00
Fixed production overheads	
(at $\dfrac{£300,000}{25,000}$ = £12 per direct labour hour)	48.00
Full production cost	98.00
Profit mark-up (20%)	19.60
Selling price per unit of product Tunity	117.60

The price if we include machine time opportunity costs is as follows.

	£
Full production cost as above	98.00
Opportunity cost of machine time:	
contribution forgone (½ hr × £10)	5.00
Adjusted full cost	103.00
Profit mark-up (20%)	20.60
Selling price per unit of product Tunity	123.60

The inclusion of opportunity costs therefore raises the price by £6.

Activity 7.6

Lanvollon Ltd and its rival Gatto Ltd both produce individually packaged biscuits and cakes which are sold through confectionery retailers and newsagents' shops throughout the country. It is estimated that Lanvollon currently has a 50% share of this market, while Gatto has approximately a 40% share. Discuss the options which are open to Lanvollon if Gatto cuts the prices of its products.

8 FIXED PRICE TENDERS

Special orders

8.1 A special order is a **one-off revenue earning opportunity**. These may arise in the following situations.

(a) When a business has a regular source of income but also has some **spare capacity** allowing it to take on extra work if demanded. For example a brewery might have a capacity of 500,000 barrels per month but only be producing and selling 300,000 barrels per month. It could therefore consider special orders to use up some of its spare capacity.

(b) When a business has no regular source of income and **relies exclusively** on its **ability to respond to demand**. A building firm is a typical example as are many types of sub-contractors. In the service sector consultants often work on this basis.

8.2 In the case of (a), a firm would normally attempt to cover its longer-term running costs in its prices for its regular product. Pricing for special orders need therefore take no account of unavoidable fixed costs. This is clearly not the case for a firm in (b)'s position, where special orders are the only source of income for the foreseeable future.

8.3   Questions featuring pricing for special orders typically present a scenario in which a firm has to decide whether to submit a fixed price tender for a contract. The basic approach in both situations is to determine the price at which the firm would break even if it undertook the work, that is, the minimum price that it could afford to charge.

Minimum pricing

8.4   A minimum price is the price that would have to be charged so that the **following costs are just covered**.

(a)   The **incremental costs** of producing and selling the item
(b)   The **opportunity costs** of the resources consumed in making and selling the item

A minimum price would leave the business no better or worse off in financial terms than if it did not sell the item.

8.5   Two essential points about a minimum price are as follows.

(a)   It is **based on relevant costs**.

(b)   It is **unlikely that a minimum price would actually be charged** because if it were, it would not provide the business with any incremental profit. However, the minimum price for a job shows the following.

(i)   An absolute minimum below which the price should not be set

(ii)   The incremental profit that would be obtained from any price that is actually charged in excess of the minimum (For example, if the minimum price is £20,000 and the actual price charged is £24,000, the incremental profit on the sale would be £4,000.)

8.6   If there are no scarce resources and a company has spare capacity, the minimum price of a job is the incremental cost of carrying it out. Any price in excess of this minimum would provide an incremental contribution towards profit.

8.7   If there are scarce resources, minimum prices must include an allowance for the opportunity cost of using the scarce resources on the job (instead of using the resources on the next most profitable product).

8.8   EXAMPLE: OPPORTUNITY COSTS AND MINIMUM PRICE

Minimax Ltd has just completed production of an item of special equipment for a customer, only to be notified that this customer has now gone into liquidation. After much effort, the sales manager has been able to interest a potential buyer who might buy the machine if certain conversion work could first be carried out.

(a)   The sales price of the machine to the original buyer had been fixed at £138,600 and had included an estimated normal profit mark-up of 10% on total costs. The costs incurred in the manufacture of the machine were as follows.

BPP PUBLISHING

	£
Direct materials	49,000
Direct labour	36,000
Variable overhead	9,000
Fixed production overhead	24,000
Fixed sales and distribution overhead	8,000
	126,000

(b) If the machine is converted, the production manager estimates that the cost of the extra work required would be as follows.

Direct materials (at cost) £9,600
Direct labour
 Department X: 6 workers for 4 weeks at £210 per worker per week
 Department Y: 2 workers for 4 weeks at £160 per worker per week

(c) Variable overhead would be 20% of direct labour cost, and fixed production overhead would be absorbed as follows.

Department X: 83.33% of direct labour cost
Department Y: 25% of direct labour cost

(d) Additional information is available as follows.

(i) In the original machine, there are three types of material.

(1) Type A could be sold for scrap for £8,000.

(2) Type B could be sold for scrap for £2,400 but it would take 120 hours of casual labour paid at £3.50 per hour to put it into a condition in which it would be suitable for sale.

(3) Type C would need to be scrapped, at a cost to Minimax Ltd of £1,100.

(ii) The direct materials required for the conversion are already in stock. If not needed for the conversion they would be used in the production of another machine in place of materials that would otherwise need to be purchased, and that would currently cost £8,800.

(iii) The conversion work would be carried out in two departments, X and Y. Department X is currently extremely busy and working at full capacity; it is estimated that its contribution to fixed overhead and profits is £2.50 per £1 of labour.

Department Y, on the other hand, is short of work but for organisational reasons its labour force, which at the moment has a workload of only 40% of its standard capacity, cannot be reduced below its current level of eight employees, all of whom are paid a wage of £160 per week.

(iv) The designs and specifications of the original machine could be sold to an overseas customer for £4,500 if the machine is scrapped.

(v) If conversion work is undertaken, a temporary supervisor would need to be employed for four weeks at a total cost of £1,500. It is normal company practice to charge supervision costs to fixed overhead.

(vi) The original customer has already paid a non-returnable deposit to Minimax Ltd of 12.5% of the selling price.

Task

Calculate the minimum price that Minimax Ltd should quote for the converted machine. Explain clearly how you have reached this figure.

8.9 SOLUTION

The minimum price is the price which reflects the opportunity costs of the work. These are established as follows.

(a) Past costs are not relevant, and the £126,000 of cost incurred should be excluded from the minimum price calculation. It is necessary, however, to consider the alternative use of the direct materials which would be forgone if the conversion work is carried out.

	£
Type A	
Revenue from sales as scrap (note (i))	8,000
Type B	
Revenue from sales as scrap,	
minus the additional cash costs necessary to	
prepare it for sale (£2,400 − (120 × £3.50)) (note (i))	1,980
Type C	
Cost of disposal if the machine is not converted	
(a negative opportunity cost) (note (ii))	(1,100)
Total opportunity cost of materials types A, B and C	8,880

By agreeing to the conversion of the machine, Minimax Ltd would therefore lose a net revenue of £8,880 from the alternative use of these materials.

Notes

(i) Scrap sales would be lost if the conversion work goes ahead.

(ii) These costs would be incurred unless the work goes ahead.

(b) The cost of additional direct materials for conversion is £9,600, but this is an historical cost. The relevant cost of these materials is the £8,800 which would be spent on new purchases if the conversion is carried out. If the conversion work goes ahead, the materials in stock would be unavailable for production of the other machine mentioned in item (d)(ii) of the question and so the extra purchases of £8,800 would then be needed.

(c) Direct labour in departments X and Y is a fixed cost and the labour force will be paid regardless of the work they do or do not do. The cost of labour for conversion in department Y is not a relevant cost because the work could be done without any extra cost to the company.

In department X, however, acceptance of the conversion work would oblige the company to divert production from other profitable jobs. The minimum contribution required from using department X labour must be sufficient to cover the cost of the labour and variable overheads and then make an additional £2.50 in contribution per direct labour hour.

Department X: costs for direct labour hours spent on conversion

6 workers × 4 weeks × £210 =	£5,040
Variable overhead cost	
£5,040 × 20% =	£1,008
Contribution forgone by diverting labour from other work	
£2.50 per £1 of labour cost = £5,040 × 250% =	£12,600

(d) Variable overheads in department Y are relevant costs because they will only be incurred if production work is carried out. (It is assumed that if the workforce is idle, no variable overheads would be incurred.)

Department Y   20% of (2 workers × 4 weeks × £160) = £256

(e) If the machine is converted, the company cannot sell the designs and specifications to the overseas company. £4,500 is a relevant (opportunity) cost of accepting the conversion order.

(f) Fixed overheads, being mainly unchanged regardless of what the company decides to do, should be ignored because they are not relevant (incremental) costs. The additional cost of supervision should, however, be included as a relevant cost of the order because the £1,500 will not be spent unless the conversion work is done.

(g) The non-refundable deposit received should be ignored and should not be deducted in the calculation of the minimum price. Just as costs incurred in the past are not relevant to a current decision about what to do in the future, revenues collected in the past are also irrelevant.

8.10   **Estimate of minimum price for the converted machine**

	£	£
Opportunity cost of using the direct materials types A, B and C		8,880
Opportunity cost of additional materials for conversion		8,800
Opportunity cost of work in department X		
Labour	5,040	
Variable overhead	1,008	
Contribution forgone	12,600	
		18,648
Opportunity cost: sale of designs and specifications		4,500
Incremental costs:		
Variable production overheads in department Y		256
Fixed production overheads (additional supervision)		1,500
Minimum price		42,584

Activity 7.7

Ship Ltd has recently shut down its London factory which used to make cushions, although all the stocks of raw materials and machinery are still there awaiting disposal. A former customer has just asked whether he could be supplied with one last delivery of 500 cushions. You ascertain the following facts.

(a) There is sufficient covering material in stock. This originally cost £400 but has a disposal value of £190.

(b) There is sufficient stuffing in stock. This originally cost £350. It was to have been shipped to the Bristol factory at a cost of £80. The Bristol factory would currently expect to pay £500 for this quantity.

(c) Labour costs would be £450.

(d) A supervisor could be spared from the Bristol factory for the week needed to produce the cushions. His normal wage is £160 and his rail fare and hotel bill in London would amount to £135.

(e) Before the factory was closed, fixed overheads were absorbed at 200% of direct labour cost.

Task

Calculate the minimum price that could be quoted.

Activity 7.8

DDD Ltd has decided to price its jobs as follows.

(a) It calculates the minimum price for the job using relevant costs.
(b) It adds £5,000 to cover fixed costs.
(c) It adds a 10% profit margin to the total cost.

A customer who has work to be performed in May says he will award the contract to DDD Ltd if its bid is reduced by £5,000. Assess whether the contract should be accepted.

9 PRACTICAL CONSIDERATIONS

9.1 In setting the price, management must decide **how much profit** it would consider reasonable on the job. A simple cost-plus approach can be used (for example, add 10% to the minimum price) but the company management should **consider the effect that the additional jobs will have** on the activities engaged in by the company and whether these activities will create additional unforeseen costs.

9.2 Sometimes an organisation may depart from its typical price-setting routine and 'low-ball' bid jobs. The rationale behind **low-ball bids** is to obtain the job so as to have the opportunity to introduce products or services to a particular market segment. During the recession of the early 1990s, there were many reports of accountancy firms 'low balling' - submitting tenders for audit and other work at very low prices. As well as the shortage of work resulting from the recession, one of the reasons behind this was probably often the desire to gain a competitive edge. By gaining new clients with low priced audit work, the firms helped to 'cross-sell' other more lucrative services, such as consultancy, to the same clients.

9.3 'Low ball' pricing may provide work for a period of time, but cannot be continued in the long term. To remain in business, an organisation must set selling prices which cover total variable costs and an appropriate amount of fixed costs, and provide a reasonable profit margin.

Qualitative factors

9.4 When setting prices, management must consider qualitative as well as quantitative issues.

(a) Will setting a low bid price cause the customer (or others) to feel that a **precedent** has been established for future prices?

(b) Will the contribution margin on a bid set low enough to acquire the job, **earn a sufficient amount to justify the additional burdens** placed on management or employees by the activity?

(c) How, if at all, will fixed price tenders **affect the organisation's normal sales**?

(d) If the job is taking place during a period of low business activity (off-season or during a recession), is management willing to take the business at a **lower contribution or profit margin simply to keep a valued workforce employed?**

Monitoring costs against fixed prices

9.5 Once a tender has been submitted and accepted, management must ensure that actual costs do not exceed the estimated costs, since for every cost overrun, profit is eroded. **Actual costs must therefore monitored in detail** on a regular basis. **Variances** between actual and estimated costs must be **investigated**. If the estimates are found to be incorrect then profit forecasts must be revised; if actual costs are too high they must be brought under control and back in line with estimates.

ASSESSMENT ALERT

In an assessment you could be asked to prepare a report in which you set out concerns you may have about a fixed price quotation you have drawn up.

Key learning points

- In practice in the modern world there are many more influences on pricing policy than the cost of a product or service.

- A typical product has a **life cycle** of four stages.

- **Competition** affects pricing policy. A **price leader** indicates to the other firms in the market what the price will be.

- **Market penetration pricing** and **market skimming pricing** are pricing policies for new products.

- **Differential pricing** involves selling the same product at different prices to different customers.

- The **price of elasticity of demand** measures the extent of change in demand for a good following a change in price. Demand can be **elastic** or **inelastic.**

- The **demand-based approach to pricing** involves determining a profit-maximising price.

- Using **full cost plus pricing,** the sales price is determined by calculating the full cost of the product and adding a percentage mark-up for profit. The approach is unlikely to arrive at a profit-maximising price.

- **Marginal cost plus pricing (mark-up pricing)** involves adding a profit margin to the marginal cost of production or the marginal cost of sales.

- The **opportunity cost approach to pricing** involves including the opportunity costs of resources consumed in making and selling the item in the cost of the product and then adding a profit margin.

- **Fixed price tenders** involve an analysis of relevant costs. A margin is often added to the **minimum price.**

Quick quiz

1 Name ten influences (apart from cost) on pricing policy.

2 What are the four stages of the product life cycle?

3 What price is first charged for a product under a policy of market penetration pricing?

4   What are the four bases on which the same product can be sold at different prices to different customers?

5   Demand is elastic when a small price change produces a large change in quantity demanded. True or false?

6   What form of pricing is useful for businesses that carry out a large amount of jobbing or contract work?

7   Describe two drawbacks to marginal cost plus pricing?

8   What costs does a minimum price cover?

9   What qualitative issues should management consider when submitting a fixed price quotation.

Answers to quick quiz

1   Price sensitivity, price perception, quality, intermediaries, competitors, suppliers, newness, incomes, product range, ethics, substitute products

2   Introduction, growth, maturity, decline

3   Low prices

4   By maker segment, by product version, by place, by time

5   True

6   Full cost plus pricing

7   Although the size of the mark-up can be varied in accordance with demand conditions, it does not ensure that sufficient attention is paid to demand conditions, competitors' prices and profit maximisation.

     It ignores fixed overheads in the pricing decision, but the price must be high enough to ensure that a profit is made after covering fixed costs. Pricing decisions cannot ignore fixed costs altogether.

8   • The incremental costs of producing and selling the item
     • The opportunity costs of the resources consumed in making and selling the item

9   Will setting a low bid price cause the customer (or others) to feel that a precedent has been established for future prices?

     Will the contribution margin on a bid set low enough to acquire the job, earn a sufficient amount to justify the additional burdens placed on management or employees by the activity?

     How, if at all, will fixed price tenders affect the organisation's normal sales?

     If the job is taking place during a period of low business activity (off-season or during a recession), is management willing to take the business at a lower contribution or profit margin simply to keep a valued workforce employed?

Answers to activities

Answer 7.1

Off-peak travel bargains, hotel prices, telephone and electricity charges are examples.

Answer 7.2

Annual demand at £1.20 per unit is 800,000 units.
Annual demand at £1.30 per unit is 725,000 units.

$$\% \text{ change in demand} = \frac{75,000}{800,000} \times 100\% = 9.375\%$$

% change in price $\qquad = \dfrac{10p}{120p} \times 100\% = 8.333\%$

Price elasticity of demand $\quad = \dfrac{-9.375}{8.333} = -1.125$

Ignoring the minus sign, price elasticity is 1.125.

The demand for this good, at a price of £1.20 per unit, would be referred to as *elastic* because the price elasticity of demand is greater than 1.

Answer 7.3

Sales price	Unit contribution	Sales volume	Total contribution
£	£	Units	£
13.00	5.00	3,400	17,000
13.25	5.25	3,300	17,325
13.50	5.50	3,200	17,600
13.75	5.75	3,100	17,825
14.00	6.00	3,000	18,000
14.25	6.25	2,900	18,125
14.50	6.50	2,800	18,200
14.75	6.75	2,700	18,225*
15.00	7.00	2,600	18,200

* Contribution would be maximised at a price of £14.75, and sales of 2,700 units.

The current price is not optimal.

Answer 7.4

Price needs to be reduced to £7.99

Mark-up therefore needs to be $\left(\dfrac{7.99 - 4.75}{4.75} \right) \times 100\% = 68\%$

The mark-up therefore needs to be reduced by 2%.

Answer 7.5

To breakeven, total contribution = fixed costs

Let selling price = p

Unit contribution = p – 15

Total monthly contribution $\qquad = 400\,(p - 15)$
At breakeven point, $\qquad 400(p - 15) = 10,000$
$$p - 15 = 25$$
$$p = 40$$

Profit margin $= \dfrac{40 - 15}{15} \times 100\% = 166^2/_3\%$

Answer 7.6

If a rival cuts its prices in the expectation of increasing its market share, a firm has several options.

(a) Lanvollon could *maintain its existing prices* if the expectation is that only a small market share would be lost, so that it is more profitable to keep prices at their existing level. Eventually Gatto may drop out of the market or be forced to raise its prices.

(b) Lanvollon may *maintain its prices but respond with non-price measures*. This is a more positive response, because the firm will be securing or justifying its current prices with a product change or advertising.

(c)   It may *reduce its prices.* This should protect the firm's market share so that the main beneficiary from the price reduction will be the consumer.

(d)   It may *raise its prices and respond with non-price measures.* The extra revenue from the higher prices might be used to finance an advertising campaign or packaging design changes. A price increase would be based on a campaign to emphasise the quality difference between the firm's own product and the rival's product.

Answer 7.7 _____

The minimum price is estimated from the relevant costs of producing the cushions.

	£
Covering material (The opportunity cost of this material is its scrap value of £190. The original cost is irrelevant because it is a historical cost, not a future cash flow)	190
Stuffing (The opportunity cost of the stuffing is the savings forgone by not sending it to Bristol, net of the transport costs of getting it to Bristol: £(500 – 80).)	420
Labour: incremental cost	450
Supervisor's expenses: incremental expense item	135
Minimum price	1,195

The supervisor's basic wage and the overheads are irrelevant to the decision because these are costs that would be incurred anyway, even if the cushions were not produced.

Answer 7.8 _____

Yes or no.

Yes, if there is no other work available, because DDD will at least earn a contribution towards fixed costs of 10% of the minimum cost.

No, if by accepting this reduced price it would send a signal to other prospective customers that they too could negotiate such a large reduction.

8 Contracts: cost estimating and price fixing

Chapter topic list

1   Project planning

2   Cost estimating

3   Price fixing

4   Contract terminology

Learning objectives

On completion of this chapter you will be able to:

	Performance criteria	Range statement
• Prepare estimates for price fixing and the submission of tenders or quotations		16.1.1
• Prepare estimates in an approved form to the appropriate people within an agreed timescale	16.1.5	
• Gather the views of appropriate specialists to inform analysis and any conclusions drawn	162.3	
• Agree the extent of the information within estimates with those who commission them	16.1.1	
• Clearly state assumptions made in conclusions	16.2.4	
• Base recommendations on clearly stated conclusions drawn from an accurate analysis of all relevant information	16.2.6	
• Present recommendations to the appropriate people in a clear and concise way, supported with a clear rationale	16.2.7	

1 PROJECT PLANNING

What is a project?

KEY TERM

A **project** can be defined as a scheme to be implemented over a definite timespan in order to achieve established goals within objective relating to cost, schedule and quality.

Activity 8.1

A research project undertaken on behalf of a client has already incurred costs of £200,000. It is estimated that a further £280,000 would be charged to the project before its completion in one year's time.

The further costs have been calculated as follows.

	£
Materials	100,000
Staff costs	60,000
Overheads	120,000

The overheads comprise depreciation of plant and equipment (£40,000), and an allocation of general overheads incurred by the business based on 80% of material costs.

You have been asked to review the project because the project's total estimated costs of £480,000 exceed the contracted value of £350,000 for the completed research.

If the project is abandoned the client will receive £150,000 as compensation. You obtain the following information about the estimated cost to completion of the project.

Materials: Contracts have already been exchanged for the purchase of £100,000 of materials. The material is highly specialised and has no alternative use on other projects. If not used on this project the material would have to be disposed of, incurring costs of £15,000.

Staffing: two highly skilled researchers each receive a salary of £25,000 pa. The other £10,000 is an allocation of part of the salary of a supervisor who is in overall charge of several projects. If the project is abandoned, the research workers would be declared redundant, each receiving £10,000 in compensation.

Overheads: plant and equipment costing £80,000 was bought at the commencement of the project, and a second year's depreciation charge (£40,000) is included in the estimated costs. The plant and equipment is highly specialised and has no other use.

Estimated scrap values:	Now	£10,000
	In one year	£4,000

Task

Give your recommendation whether on financial grounds the project should be continued or abandoned. Your calculations must be supported by clear statements of the reasons why a particular figure is included or excluded, and of any assumptions you make.

Guidance note

Pay particular attention to which costs are *relevant costs* of continuing with the research project. (We covered relevant costs earlier in this Text.)

ASSESSMENT ALERT

Non-financial factors will often need to be weighed against financial factors in evaluating a project, and you should be aware of this when doing assessed work. The following activity should get you thinking on the types of non-financial factor which could matter.

Activity 8.2

See if you can briefly explain any non-financial factors which need to be considered before finally deciding to abandon a research project, such as that in Activity 8.1.

The project life cycle

1.1 It is possible to identify all the stages of a typical project, whether it is a construction project or system design project. For example, the **project life cycle** has the following stages.

- Conceiving and defining the project
- Planning the project
- Carrying out the plan (project implementation)
- Completing and evaluating the project

1.2 Remember that, in all stages of the project, the most important guiding factors are **quality** (of design and conformance), **cost** and **time**.

1.3 The broad objectives of project management arise out of these factors.

(a) **Quality**. The end result should conform to the proper specification. In other words, the result should achieve what the project was supposed to do.

(b) **Budget**. The project should be completed without exceeding authorised expenditure.

(c) **Timescale**. The progress of the project must follow the planned process, so that the 'result' is ready for use at the agreed date. As time is money, proper time management can help contain costs.

Customers' and contractors' specifications

The customer's specification

1.4 The **specification** which may be provided by a potential customer relating to contract work may take a variety of forms. There will probably be some written matter on the objective of the project, and plans or drawings may also be provided. Some requests may be communicated verbally, at least initially.

1.5 Subsequent communication, verbally or in writing between the customer and the contractor, may lead to changes to the original specification. The contractor must do his best to make sure that the customer's specification is met in every possible respect if the quotation is to be successful in winning a firm order. All communications between customer and contractor on the project can be considered part of the customer's specification for these purposes.

The contractor's specification. The tender

1.6 If the contracting firm is interested in gaining the work set out in the customer's specification and feels able to do the work, it will prepare a **tender** which consists of proposals for undertaking the work. The contractor's own provisional design specification is likely to have been based on these proposals.

1.7 Obviously, the technical aspects of the proposal need to be worked out before cost estimations can be made, since the use of different techniques may involve incurring widely differing costs. The techniques decided upon should be included in the provisional design specification to ensure that other more costly techniques are not used later on because of original design concept has been forgotten.

1.8 A project plan aims to ensure that the project objective is achieved within the objectives of the quality, cost and time. This involves three stages, once the basic project objective and the underlying activities have been agreed.

(a) Break the project down into manageable units. As a simple example, if your objective is to cook a dinner party for your friends, you will break down this task into preparing the entrée, the main course, and then the dessert. If you were a stickler for planning, you could break these down further into detailed tasks (chop onions, peel potatoes). This is sometimes called establishing a **work breakdown structure**, which we discuss further below.

(b) For each unit, the resources needed must be estimated (in materials, money and time).

(c) The varying times and resource requirements of each sub-unit are then estimated, and co-ordinated into a planning framework to schedule and group the activities in the most appropriate way. One way in which this can be done (**Gantt charts**) is illustrated a little later.

Cost estimating, which we look at later in this chapter, is part of the project planning stage.

Implementation

1.9 The project implementation stage is when the plans are put into action. Frequently a project is directed by a project manager whose role is as follows.

1.10 **Control over work in progress**

(a) The project manager will review progress to see that standards, outlined in the project specifications, are maintained.

(i) **Control point** identification charts indicate the sort of things that might go wrong, and the action taken to rectify them.

(ii) **Project control** charts use budget and schedule plans to give a status report on progress (eg cumulative time and cost) so that variances can be calculated.

(b) Performance is also monitored, by:

(i) Inspection
(ii) Progress reviews (at regular stages)
(iii) Quality testing
(iv) Financial audit

(c) Corrective action can be taken, if deficiencies are not self-correcting. Falling behind schedule, because of some circumstance unforeseen at the planning stage, might require the rescheduling of the project or a change in resource configuration. If the project is over budget, cost savings can be found, or alternatively more funds might be available from the client.

1.11 Finally, the project must be delivered to the customer, of course after final testing and review. Note that 'delivery' might include preparation of subsidiary matters such as instruction manuals. (Instruction manuals and aids to use are vital in successful implementation of information systems.)

2 COST ESTIMATING

2.1 Projects are carried out within objectives relating to cost, schedule and quality. Our main concern in AAT Unit 16 is with **cost**. We have mentioned the task of estimating costs in our discussion of the management of projects above, and we now look at cost estimating in more detail. The Activity below gives you a chance to practise some cost calculations.

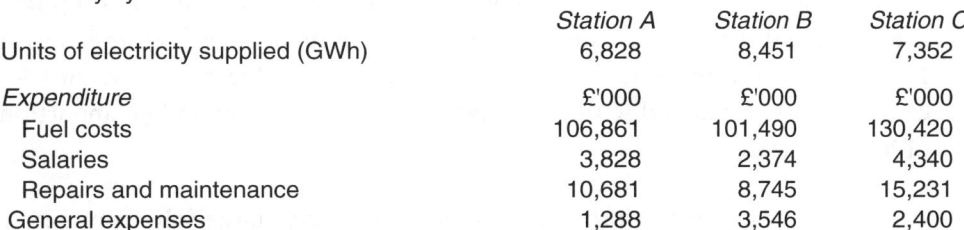

Activity 8.3

The following data relates to three power stations which supply electricity to the national electricity system.

	Station A	Station B	Station C
Units of electricity supplied (GWh)	6,828	8,451	7,352
Expenditure	£'000	£'000	£'000
Fuel costs	106,861	101,490	130,420
Salaries	3,828	2,374	4,340
Repairs and maintenance	10,681	8,745	15,231
General expenses	1,288	3,546	2,400

(*Note.* GWh = 1 gigawatt hour = 1 million kilowatt hours.)

Task

Prepare a table showing the expenditure of each power station in pence per kilowatt hour of electricity supplied, to three decimal places.

2.2 One of the main reasons why project costs need to be estimated is so that a price can be fixed for the project. But that is not the only reason.

Activity 8.4

See if you can think for yourself some other reasons why project costs need to be estimated as accurately as possible, before looking at the next paragraph.

2.3 Apart from the reason of fixing of the price, accurate cost estimation for contracts is needed for the following reasons.

(a) **Budgeting.** So that business can forecast costs and revenues in future periods, it is important to know the estimated costs of projects to be undertaken.

(b) **Allocation of project resources.** Cost estimates will help to indicate the stages at which various resources (including finance) need to be allocated to the project.

(c) **Cost control.** Estimates of expected costs provide a yardstick against which actual costs can be compared. Is too much being spent on particular aspects or stages of the project?

(d) **Comparison of achievement against expected performance.** Cost estimates, especially for labour, help to indicate whether at a particular stage achievement on the project matches what was expected originally at that stage.

Labour burden and materials burden

2.4 The term **labour burden** is sometimes used for the amount which is added to the basic hourly or weekly rate for labour to make allowance for the incidence of holidays, illness and other absence, plus employer's national insurance contributions which must be paid on top of employees' wages or salaries. The labour burden will normally be stated as a percentage.

2.5 The **materials burden** is a mark-up imposed by contractors on the cost of direct materials in order to compensate for administration and handling costs. 15% is a commonly used rate for the materials burden.

Problems in accounting for contract costs

2.6 Many projects are carried out on construction sites away from the supplier's own premises, and it is not unusual for a site to have its own cashier and timekeeper. For cost accounting purposes, each contract is regarded as a cost unit, or cost centre, which is charged with the direct costs of production and an apportionment of head office overheads.

2.7 An important feature of project work is its duration; large jobs may take a long time to complete, perhaps two or three years. Even when a contract is completed within less than twelve months, it is quite possible that the work may have begun during one financial year ended during the supplier's next financial year; therefore the profit on the contract will relate to more than one accounting period.

2.8 The following issues may arise in costing for projects.

(a) **Identifying direct costs.** Because of the large size of the job, many cost items which are usually thought of as production overhead are charged as direct cost of the contract (for example supervision, hire of plant, depreciation or loss in value of plant which is owned, sub-contractors' fees or charges and so on).

(b) **Adding overheads.** Because many costs normally classed as overheads are charged as direct cost of contract, the absorption rate for overheads should only apply a share of the cost of those items which are not already direct costs. In the case of large capital projects, customers may be critical of the overhead rates charged on their projects, and may ask for detailed explanations of the overhead costs to be included. The overhead rate for the project might need to be negotiated so that the order can be won.

(c) **Subcontractors.** On large contracts, much work may be done by subcontractors. The invoices of subcontractors will be treated as a direct expense to the contract, although the invoiced amounts are small, it may be more convenient to account for them as 'direct materials' rather than as direct expenses.

(d) **The cost of plant.** Plant used on a project may be owned by the company, or hired from a plant hire firm. If the plant is hired, the cost will be a direct expense of the contract. If the plant is owned by the company, a variety of accounting methods may be employed.

  (i) The project may be charged with depreciation on the plant.

  (ii) More commonly, the project is charged with the current book value of the plant, and credited with the written down value at the end of the accounting period.

  (iii) Thirdly, a separate plant account may be set up, and a notional hire charge made to the project.

Standard costs in estimating

2.9 Although different individuals doing the same job may be earning different salaries, for example if one is paid more in recognition of longer service with the company, the cost estimator cannot practically take this into account in preparing estimates. Estimates may be made for work which is to be carried out years from the date of the estimate, and it may therefore not be known who will do the job.

2.10 The cost estimator will usually make use of a number of categories or grades in estimating labour costs, to cover the various functions involved in the project, such as engineering, purchasing and construction management.

2.11 The average salary cost for all those within a specific standard grade can then be used as the standard cost for estimating purposes. As pointed out by Dennis Lock (*Project Management*), this method has an advantage of confidentiality: if the standard rate is calculated by accounting staff, then cost estimators and project administrators only need to know the standard rate, and not individuals' salaries.

2.12 Standard cost rates for use in estimating can also be worked out for materials and purchased components.

Recovery of overheads

2.13 The most common method of recovering or absorbing overheads is to charge direct labour costs, including the **labour burden**, as:

Time recorded on job × standard hourly cost for labour grade

The indirect overhead costs of the business are then recovered by adding a percentage to the labour costs.

2.14 EXAMPLE: COST ESTIMATE

The cost and price structure for a simple manufacturing project might be as follows.

Direct materials			£	£
Steel tubing			44.00	
Laminated board			69.00	
Other			27.00	
Total direct material cost				140.00
Direct labour, at standard rates				
Design				
Engineer	8 hours	@ £28.00	224.00	
Draughtsman	10 hours	@ £18.00	180.00	
Manufacture				
Metal worker	15 hours	@ £14.00	210.00	
Turner	6 hours	@ £12.50	75.00	
Assembly	3 hours	@ £12.50	37.50	
Inspection	1 hour	@ £14.00	14.00	
Total direct labour cost				740.50
Prime cost				880.00
Overheads @ 80% of direct labour cost				592.40
Factory cost				1,472.90
Mark-up at 40%				589.16
Selling price				2,062.06

The overhead recovery rate

2.15 Usually, the same overhead rate (80% in the above example) will be applied by the company for all similar projects which it is involved in. The overhead rate will vary between industries and will need to take account of distribution and administration costs.

In an industry with high research and development costs, the recovery rate might be 200% or even higher. In a labour intensive industry with little or no research and development to fund and with low premises costs, the overhead rate might be 50% or lower. Clearly, a company which keeps its indirect costs and therefore its overhead rate lower than its competitors will have a competitive pricing advantage: with the same direct materials and labour and mark-up, it would be able to quote a lower price.

2.16 Setting the correct overhead recovery rate depends on making accurate forecasts of workload and overhead costs, and on controlling costs to within planned levels.

(a) Overhead under-recovery will occur if there is not as much work as was anticipated: there is then less direct labour charged to projects and consequently less recovery of overhead.

(b) Overhead over-recovery will occur if the workload and the direct labour charged exceed expectations. This can raise profitability: more money is being charged to cover the overheads than is being spent on the overheads. The disadvantage is that the over-recovery may be reflected in high prices relative to competitors and the company's future order prospects may be damaged as a result.

Accuracy of estimates

2.17 Any estimate must be accompanied by a proviso detailing its expected accuracy. However, project estimation inevitably involves fallible guess work. It is unreasonable to expect exact accuracy, but the project manager should be able to

keep within estimates, particularly for projects where there is no 'margin of safety', or which have *tight* profit margins.

2.18 Some industries use different classifications to denote the accuracy of estimates.

(a) **Ball-park estimates** are made before a project starts. These are very rough indeed and might be accurate to within 25%.

(b) **Comparative estimates** are made if the project under consideration has some similarities with previous ones. Accuracy will depend, of course, on how similar the project is to the projects it is compared with. Lock suggests that it is possible to be accurate to within 15%.

(c) **Feasibility estimates** (probably accurate to within 10%) arise from preliminary aspects of the design. Building companies use feasibility estimates.

(d) **Definitive estimates** (accurate to within 5%) are only made when *all* the design work has been done.

Activity 8.5

Springfield Builders has agreed to do some building work at Gowley House, a stately home in Hertfordshire. Springfield Builders are charging the owners of Gowley House the sum of £10,000. They estimate that the job will cost them £8,000, plus an estimated profit of £2,000. What would be the effect on profit of cost estimating errors of:

(a) +/- 5%
(b) +/- 10%
(c) +/- 20%

2.19 Estimates can be improved:

(a) By a company learning from its mistakes over time
(b) By ensuring sufficient design information
(c) By ensuring as detailed a specification as possible from the customer
(d) By properly analysing the job into its constituent units, especially labour costs

Collecting information for estimates

2.20 Costs should be analysed into **component parts**.

(a) Direct costs of a project include labour, raw materials and sub-components

(b) Project overhead costs include heating, lighting and so on, and can be fixed and/or variable

2.21 In some projects, a large element of the work might be fixed costs. For example, a building company is unlikely to buy a brand new crane for every house it builds. For systems design work, a company may have developed a set of unique design tools for modelling work. The cost of such items might be spread over individual projects according to some measure. For example, an element of crane's depreciation charge might be charged to a project.

2.22 The various costs identified need to be collated, in such a way as:

(a) To provide a useful cost analysis for various business functions
(b) To be a mechanism for controlling costs

(c)   To provide evidence, in any dispute, that the costs are reasonable

On this last point, technical cost investigations might occur in some contracts. This means that the client will send technical cost officers to examine the books. The right to do so might be incorporated in the original contract. (As more and more public services are contracted out, such investigations are likely to be increasingly frequent.)

2.23   Estimating forms could be designed to be based on the work breakdown structure, so that by each work unit number, there are columns for labour, materials and so on.

2.24   Collecting estimates can be a difficult task especially if large numbers of people need to be involved in providing them. The project manager might be best advised to canvass for opinion. Again, if there is only a short time scale to put in a tender, these estimates will inevitably be rough and ready. The following considerations are to be expected if **labour time** is the issue.

(a)   A project manager often relies on the personal opinions of the individuals in each department as to the time it would take to do a job. Lock holds that 'estimates for any work will more frequently be understated than overstated'.

(i)   Many people are eager to please the project manager.

(ii)   According to Lock, people do not learn to estimate better. In some companies, a rule of thumb is to add 50% on to the estimated time given by production or design staff.

(b)   On occasions when people's estimates are over-pessimistic, a cause might be a desire to inflate departmental budgets.

(c)   Finally, some estimators are inconsistent. The project manager can probably cope with the person who **consistently** underestimates **or** overestimates, but someone who is inconsistent could be a major problem.

2.25   Materials require an estimate of **lead times for receipt,** as well as **costs.** Failure to receive materials on time can result in unexpected delay.

2.26   Estimates should always be reviewed by a competent person who is independent of the person who compiled it. Once a project has begun, actual costs incurred should be monitored against the cost estimates and any significant discrepancies should be investigated.

Estimating forms

2.27   **Estimating forms** vary between industries and between companies. An example of an estimating form for general purposes is shown **below.**

			Direct labour costs by grade											1	2	3	4	
Code	Description	Qty	A		B		C		D		E		Total direct labour cost	Over-head %	Materials		Total cost 1+2+3+4
															Std/net cost	Burden %	
			Hrs	£	Hrs	£	Hrs	£	Hrs	£	Hrs	£					

COST ESTIMATE FORM

Project code: ☐☐ / ☐☐☐   Estimate for: Date of estimate ☐☐/☐☐/☐☐

Estimate No: ☐☐ / ☐☐☐   Compiled by: Reviewed by: Sheet   of   sheets

Activity 8.6

The production manager of your organisation has approached you for some costing advice on project X, a one-off order from overseas that he intends to tender for. The costs associated with the project are as follows.

	£
Material A	4,000
Material B	8,000
Direct labour	6,000
Supervision	2,000
Overheads	12,000
	32,000

You ascertain the following.

(a)   Material A is in stock and the above was the cost. There is now no other use for Material A, other than the above project, within the factory and it would cost £1,750 to dispose of. Material B would have to be ordered at the cost shown above.

(b)   Direct labour costs of £6,000 relate to workers that will be transferred to this project from another project. Extra labour will need to be recruited to the other project at a cost of £7,000.

(c)   Supervision costs have been charged to the project on the basis of $33\frac{1}{3}$% of labour costs and will be carried out by existing staff within their normal duties.

(d)   Overheads have been charged to the project at the rate of 200% on direct labour.

(e)   The company is currently operating at a point above breakeven.

(f)   The project will need the utilisation of machinery that will have no other use to the company after the project has finished. The machinery will have to be purchased at a cost of £10,000 and then disposed of for £5,250 at the end of the project.

The production manager tells you that the overseas customer is prepared to pay up to a maximum of £30,000 for the project and a competitor is prepared to accept the order at that price. He also informs you the minimum that he can charge is £40,000 as the above costs show £32,000 and this does not take into consideration the cost of the machine and profit to be taken on the project.

BPP
PUBLISHING

Tasks

(a) Cost the project for the production manager clearly stating how you have arrived at your figures and giving reasons for the exclusion of other figures.

(b) Write a report to the production manager stating whether the organisation should go ahead with the tender for the project, the reasons why and the price, bearing in mind that the competitor is prepared to undertake the project for £30,000. (*Note.* The project should only be undertaken if it shows a profit.)

Guidance notes

1   In a task of this sort you might find it useful to set up a 'do/don't do' table. The costs of doing something less the cost of not doing it are the incremental costs for the project.

2   In the case of materials, ensure that you distinguish costs *saved* from costs *incurred*.

Activity 8.7

This Activity is based on the scenario given in the previous Activity 8.6.

(a) State four non-monetary factors that should be taken into account before tendering for this project.

(b) Describe the advice you would give if you were told that the organisation was operating below breakeven point. Give reasons for your advice.

3   PRICE FIXING

3.1   We looked at the general principles of how prices can be set in Chapter 7. How in general terms is a price for a project to be fixed? Given that the objective of a business is to make profits, this might be seen as a relatively simple matter of adding a specified level of **'mark-up'** to the estimated costs to arrive at a fixed price for the project as in the example at Paragraph 2.14. In reality, fixing a price is rarely as straightforward as this.

3.2   As noted earlier, a firm may submit a tender with a **'low-ball' bid** or accept an order at a price which is too low for there to be a prospect of making a reasonable profit. It might even be virtually certain that the firm will make a **loss** from the project. A firm may adopt such tactics if it is temporarily short of work or if it wishes to gain a **short-term competitive advantage,** perhaps in the hope that competitors will give up its operations in the market in which the firm and its competitors operate.

3.3   A temporary **shortage of work** may arise in a recession. While management of a business may see good prospects in the future once an economic recessing has ended, it may wish to ensure that there is a steady flow of work in the meantime even if this work is loss-making. **Keeping work teams idle** may be poor for morale and may prevent employees from acquiring on-the-job skills from work experience. **Laying off workteams** may prove to be excessively costly when both redundancy costs and the costs of building up new teams when activity levels may rise again are considered. In the case of highly skilled employees, it may be virtually impossible to rebuild a workteam once it has been disbanded.

3.4   **Payment terms** can be another important factor in determining how much is earned from a project and may be influenced by the desire of the customer to set performance incentives for the contractor. **Penalty payments** may be imposed

which are calculated according to the length of time by which successful completion of the project is delayed beyond a stated period.

3.5 Projects can be delayed because of design errors, production mistakes, material and component failures. An allowance is sometimes built in (50% might be a typical figure). An appropriate **contingency allowance** can usually be estimated by reviewing problems in previous projects.

Cost escalation

3.6 Over the short term, **inflation in costs** can often be predicted fairly accurately for projects of short duration, and allowed for in cost estimates calculated to fixed prices.

3.7 The effects of inflation on project costs become less predictable if there is a significant delay between when a cost estimate is prepared and the project actually begins, or the project is of longer duration.

3.8 The enterprise can protect itself against these risks by:

(a) **Placing a time limit** on the applicability of rates or prices included in the tender, or

(b) **Negotiating a cost escalation clause** in the contract, so that cost rises can be passed on to the customer by getting him to agree to pay more if costs rise.

Estimating and pricing form

3.9 A form which could be used for general purpose estimating and pricing for manufacturing projects is reproduced on the **next page**.

3.10 The items included on a **cost estimation form** will, of course, vary from one enterprise or organisation to another and from one industry to another. In a service industry such as accountancy, there is likely to be a detailed breakdown of estimated staff time of different grades and of the different tasks on which it is to be spent. In providing services such as accountancy, there will be no direct materials. Overheads and a margin for profit may be absorbed into a charge-out rate per hour for each grade of staff; to the total of time charged will be added expenses such as travelling which will be billed directly to the client, and a contingency allowance, if any.

PROJECT COST AND PRICE SUMMARY

Project name: **Sales ref:** ☐☐☐☐☐☐

Customer: **Date:** ☐☐ / ☐☐ / ☐☐

Summary prepared by: **Reviewed by:**

Item		£	£
	Direct labour		
1			
2			
3			
4			
5			
6	*Total direct labour*		
	Materials, equipment and bought-in services		
7			
8			
9			
10			
11			
12	*Total materials etc*		
	Other expenses		
13			
14			
15			
16	*Total other expenses*		
17	PRIME COST (6 + 12 + 16)		

Overheads

Item	Item numbers charged	%	£	£
18				
19				
20				
21	*Total overheads*			
22	BASIC ESTIMATED PROJECT COST (17 +21)			

Allowances

Item		%	£	£
23	Contingencies allowance			
24	Escalation allowance			
25				
26	*Total allowances*			
27	TOTAL ESTIMATED PROJECT COST (22 + 26)			

Mark-up

Item	Item numbers	%	£	£
28				
29				
30	*Total mark-up*			
31	INDICATED SELLING PRICE (27 +30)			

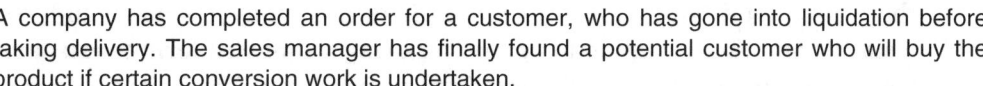

Activity 8.8

A company has completed an order for a customer, who has gone into liquidation before taking delivery. The sales manager has finally found a potential customer who will buy the product if certain conversion work is undertaken.

The company has already spent £20,000 on manufacturing the product, and the following information relating to the proposed conversion work is collected.

	£
Materials required at cost	2,000
Direct wages: four workers	2,000
Variable overhead	400
Depreciation	1,000
Foreman	150
Fixed production overhead	800
	6,350

It is company policy to price its products at 25% mark up on cost, and accordingly a price of £32,937.50 (20,000 + 6,350 + 6,587.50) would be quoted.

Notes

(a) The materials which are to be used on the conversion are in stock. The material could be used in the production of another good in place of material that the company would otherwise have to buy at a cost of £4,000.

(b) Four workers would be required to complete the conversion. They would be taken from a department which is currently working well below full capacity.

(c) The conversion work will require the use of machinery which cost £120,000 eight years ago. It has an estimated life of ten years. Depreciation is charged on a straight line basis.

(d) The conversion work will be supervised by a foreman who is currently employed by the company. The foreman receives a salary which is equivalent to £1,500 per month. It is estimated that the conversion will occupy 10% of the foreman's time.

(e) The conversion will take one month.

(f) The original customer had paid a non-returnable deposit of £3,000.

(g) It is company policy to charge production with a proportion of general fixed overheads at an absorption rate of 40% of material costs.

(h) In its existing condition the product could be sold for scrap, earning a revenue of £1,000.

Task

Prepare calculations to show the minimum price which you would recommend the company to quote to the new customer. Assume that no other customer will be found. Give reasons for the inclusion or exclusion of items in your computations.

4   CONTRACT TERMINOLOGY

4.1   The process of agreeing plans and specifications and drawing up contracts governing contracts for projects is complex, technical and specialised. Some of the **terminology** in general use is set out in the following paragraphs.

4.2   **The articles of agreement.** This is the formal agreement between the contracting parties and will contain the names of the parties, say the contractor and a public authority, a description of the work to be performed, the contract price and details of the plans and documents which are to be included and construed as part of the contract. It is signed and sealed by the contracting parties.

4.3 **The standard conditions.** These set out the rights, duties an obligations of the contracting parties during the progress of the contract. The parties could draw up their own conditions of contract but there are many common and recurring elements and there is much to be said for using a standard form that is familiar to contractors and on which interpretations are available. The standard forms can be with or without quantities. A contract with quantities will have a bill of quantities attached to it; a contract without quantities will be based upon a plan and specification only and is suitable for small and simple capital projects.

4.4 **The bills of quantities.** This is detailed analysis of the different quantities of labour and materials which will be required to carry out the work to be undertaken. The bills are prepared by the quantity surveyor from the specification, plans and drawings supplied by the architect or engineer appointed to supervise the works. There will be separate bills for each trade, and each bill has a space for a description of the items, the unit rates and results of the calculations.

4.5 **Variation orders.** These are orders to alter details of the work originally agreed, issued by the architect or engineer. Variation becomes necessary when unforeseen conditions arise or because of changes after the contract has been agreed, say to roof a building with higher quality tiles.

4.6 **Progress payments.** A customer is likely to be required under the terms of the contract to make progress payments to the contractor throughout the course of the work. The amount of the payments will be based on the value of work done, as assessed by the architect or surveyor (for a building contract) or qualified engineer.

4.7 **Interim certificates.** These are issued periodically, usually monthly, as the contract progresses. They are calculated by first valuing the work completed up to a point in time and then deducting the payments already made to the contractor. A percentage will be deducted from all interim payments in respect of retention money, for example:

		Retention	
	Gross	*10%*	*Net*
	£	£	£
Valuation of work completed to 31 October	430,000	43,000	387,000
Paid to 30 September - Certificates 1-4	340,000	34,000	306,000
Payable 31 October - Certificate 5	90,000	9,000	81,000

4.8 **Retention money.** This is an agreed percentage of the contract price and is retained, during the contract, by deduction from interim payments. After the work is completed the retention money will be held for the retention period. This arrangement encourages the contractor to work well and maintain progress throughout the contract's duration and to put right any faults discovered before the retention money is finally released.

4.9 **Final accounts.** These must be considered in detail and fully audited before the final payment is made. Agreement of the final account on a major contract will take some time because adjustments will probably be necessary for provisional sums, variation orders, fluctuating prices and so on.

4.10 **Liquidated damages and penalties.** These terms refer to clauses in the contract which enable the authority to penalise the contractor if work is not done within the agreed time period. There may be genuine reasons for late work where both

parties agree to extending the time, for instance outside painting incomplete due to long periods of heavy rain, or concreting put off due to frost.

4.11 **Contracts register.** This is a key record and shows for each contract the original approval details and tender price, variation orders, interim payments made, retention percentage and period and running totals. The register must be kept up to date in order that the current financial position on each contract can be quickly established.

Activity 8.9

You are presented with the following information for the coming year about a coach company that operates in your area.

	30-seat coaches	50-seat coaches
Number of coaches	5	10
Number of drivers	5	10
Weekly wage costs per driver	£220	£250
Cost of each coach	£20,000	£32,000
Fuel consumption - miles per gallon	12.5	8.0
Licence fee per coach	£350	£500
Insurance per coach	£340	£400

Repairs and maintenance for the year are budgeted at £65,000 and are to be apportioned between the coaches in the ratio of their total mileage. Administration expenses are budgeted at £93,600 and are to be apportioned to each coach in the ratio of drivers' wage costs.

You are told that each 30-seat coach is kept for six years, at which time it will have a resale value of £2,000 and that every 50-seat coach will be replaced after seven years and have a resale value of £4,000. It is the policy of the company to depreciate the coaches on a straight line basis.

It is envisaged that each 30-seat coach will travel 500 miles per week and each 50-seat coach will travel 400 miles per week. The cost of fuel is budgeted at £2.20 per gallon. It is budgeted that each coach will be in operation 50 weeks per year and the drivers will be paid for 52 weeks.

Tasks

(a) Prepare costings to determine the operating cost per passenger mile on an absorption basis for the following.

  (i) Each 30-seat coach
  (ii) Each 50-seat coach

(b) The company has been asked to tender for a contract to provide transport for an education authority for 40 weeks in the coming year. The contract would involve three of the coaches carrying 25 students 10 miles a day, 5 days a week and two coaches carrying 40 students 15 miles a day, 5 days a week.

   Provide a total tender price on the basis of the costings you have prepared in (a) above, given that the company requires a profit of 40% on contract price.

Key learning points

- **Cost estimating** forms an important part of project planning. Cost estimates are likely to be required for all projects carried out in a commercial enterprise, for pricing and other reasons.

- **Projects documentation** is likely to include the customer's or contractor's specification, on which the tender is based.

- Once a project has begun, the **costs** need to be recorded as accurately as possible so that they can be correctly identified with the project.

Quick quiz

1   What are the stages of the typical project life cycle?

2   What is meant by 'labour burden' and 'materials burden' in cost estimating?

3   How can a business protect itself against the unpredictable effects of inflation in projects it carries out for customers?

4   What is a 'variation order'?

5   What is 'retention money'?

Answers to quick quiz

1   Conceiving and defining the project; planning the project; carrying out the plan (project implementation); completing and evaluating the project.

2   The term labour burden refers to an amount or percentage added to a basic hourly or weekly labour rate to allow for holidays, illness and other absence, plus employer's national insurance contributions.

The materials burden is a mark-up (commonly 15%) imposed by contractors on the cost of direct materials to compensate for administration and handling costs.

3   The enterprise can protect itself against inflation by:

(a)   Placing a time limit on the applicability of rates or prices included in the tender

(b)   Negotiating a cost escalation clause in the contract, so that cost rises can be passed on to the customer by getting him to agree to pay more if costs rise

4   A variation orders is an order to alter details of the work originally agreed, issued by the architect or engineer. Variation becomes necessary when unforeseen conditions arise or following changes after the contract has been agreed.

5   Retention money is an agreed percentage of the contract price and is retained during the contract by deduction from interim payments. After the work is completed the retention money will be held for the retention period.

Answers to activities

Answer 8.1

Relevant cost of continuing with the research project

	Note	£	
Costs already incurred	1	0	
Materials	2	(15,000)	saving
Staff costs	3	30,000	
Overheads: plant and equipment	4	6,000	
general overhead	5	0	
		21,000	
Contracted value		350,000	
Relevant future contribution from project		329,000	
Saving in compensation		150,000	
Total gain from continuing with project		479,000	

Therefore, on financial grounds the project should be continued.

Notes

1   Costs already incurred are sunk and are not relevant to any future decision.

2   Contracts have already been exchanged and so the material must be paid for and the £100,000 cost is sunk. Using the material on this project would save the disposal costs.

3   The £10,000 allocated salary of the supervisor would not be affected by this project and so is not relevant. To continue to employ the skilled researchers would cost £15,000 each more than declaring them redundant.

4   The original cost of the equipment is a sunk cost. Depreciation is not a cash flow and is irrelevant. The relevant cost of using the equipment for this project is the £6,000 reduction in scrap value which would occur.

5   General overheads are allocations of business overheads which are unaffected by this decision.

Activity 8.2

Non-financial factors which would need to be considered are as follows.

(a)   The effect on the company's reputation for completing projects once commenced.

(b)   The likelihood of further projects being received from the same customer.

(c)   The effect on the morale of the research staff.

(d)   Other opportunities for research projects which could use the facilities currently being employed on the project under consideration.

(e)   The ease with which the skilled researchers could be replaced for future projects.

Answer 8.3

	Station A	Station B	Station C
Units of electricity (GWh)	6,828	8,451	7,352
Expenditure (pence per kilowatt hour)			
Fuel costs	1.565	1.201	1.774
Salaries	0.056	0.028	0.059
Repairs and maintenance	0.156	0.103	0.207
General expenses	0.019	0.042	0.033
	1.796	1.374	2.073

Answer 8.4

See paragraph 2.3 of the chapter.

Answer 8.5

(a)   An error of +/- 5% would mean that the profit would be increased or reduced by £400 (ie 5% × £8,000), in other words 20%.

(b)   A 10% error would increase or reduce profits by £800 which is 40% of the profit.

(c)   A 20% error would increase or decrease profits by £1,600 or 80% of profit.

Answer 8.6

(a)

	Note	Tender (a) £	Do not tender (b) £	Incremental costs (a - b) £
Material A	1	-	1,750	(1,750)
Material B	2	8,000	-	8,000
Direct labour	3	7,000	-	7,000
Supervision	4	-	-	-
Overheads	5	-	-	-
Machinery (net cost)		4,750	-	4,750
		19,750	1,750	18,000
Competitor's price				30,000
Contribution				12,000

BPP PUBLISHING

Notes

1   If the project does not go ahead, material A will have to be disposed of. The original cost is a sunk cost and not relevant.

2   Material B will be purchased specially, so the actual cost is relevant.

3   The workers in question will be paid £6,000 whatever the case, but if they are transferred to this project an additional £7,000 will also be paid so that the other project can proceed.

4   Supervision will be carried out by staff who will receive their salaries whatever decision is taken and who will not receive any extra amount for supervising this project. This cost can therefore be ignored.

5   Overheads are currently being fully recovered by existing operations (the company is breaking even) and there is therefore no need to charge an amount to this project.

(b)   REPORT

To: Production Manager
From: Management Accountant
Date: 30 April 20X5
Subject: Project X

On the basis of the detailed figures and explanations at (a) the company will make a profit of £12,000 if it matches the price tendered by the competition.

In brief this is because a number of the costs associated with the project cannot be avoided whatever decision is taken. They are therefore not relevant to this decision and they will be met by the revenue from existing operations in any case.

For this reason, the tender should go ahead. The price to be quoted should be between £18,000 and £30,000. A price of a little less than £30,000 is recommended in order to beat the competition.

Answer 8.7

(a)   Non-monetary factors to be taken into account are as follows.

(i)   The organisation may lack experience in this sort of work. Labour may need to be trained and this may put undue pressure upon supervisors. There may be unforeseen technical difficulties.

(ii)   The project may disrupt existing operations depending upon its duration and the extent to which it uses shared resources.

(iii)   The overseas aspects should be considered. The order may be cancelled without notice for political reasons. There may be legal requirements (such as safety standards) that have to be met. The customer may not be creditworthy.

(iv)   The project may provide an opportunity to break into a new market: it may be worth quoting a price significantly below that of the competition in order to attract further orders.

(*Note.* The above includes more than four factors. You should only give four.)

(b)   If the organisation were operating below breakeven point, this would mean that existing operations were not generating sufficient contribution to cover fixed costs. Some or all of the costs of supervision and of overheads would need to be charged to the project giving a tender price of £18,000 + £2,000 + £12,000 = £32,000. The organisation would be unable to match the price tendered by the competitor and should therefore only tender for the contract if it felt that the customer could be swayed into paying a higher price by non-monetary factors such as quality of product or speed of delivery.

Answer 8.8 _____

> *Tutorial note.* Since there are many possible interpretations of the data, it is important to state any assumptions which you make.

As the company requires the absolute minimum price for this contract, the only relevant costs are those which will be incurred in the future as a direct result of the sale to the new customer.

The original manufacturing cost and the deposit already paid are not relevant to future cash flows as they occurred in the past. Since a special price is required, the company pricing policy is also not relevant.

	Note	Relevant cost £
Materials required	1	4,000
Direct wages	2	-
Variable overhead	3	400
Depreciation	4	-
Foreman	5	-
General fixed overhead	6	-
Opportunity cost of sale forgone	7	1,000
Minimum price		5,400

Notes and assumptions

1. The original historical cost of the material in stock is a sunk cost and not relevant. The relevant cost is the opportunity cost of the saving forgone on the other materials which now have to be purchased for £4,000. The material could have been used elsewhere.

2. The workers would be paid even if the contract was not undertaken. There is thus no opportunity cost as the department is already working below capacity.

3. The variable overhead is assumed to be an incremental cost. They are included in the minimum price, as it is assumed they are specifically incurred in conversion work.

4. Depreciation is not a cash flow and is therefore not relevant. Depreciation apportions the original cost of the machine, a cost which was sunk eight years ago. There is no indication of the current resale value of the machine and so it is assumed that there is no intention of selling it. It is also assumed that there is no opportunity cost involved in its use for this contract, as it would not be needed elsewhere.

5. The foreman is already being paid. Therefore his salary is not an incremental cost. It is assumed that there is no opportunity cost associated with the use of his time for this contract.

6. It is assumed that general fixed overheads will not increase as a result of this contract, therefore absorbed overhead is not relevant.

7. Scrap revenue forgone will be an opportunity cost, if the product is converted rather than sold as scrap.

BPP PUBLISHING

Answer 8.9

(a)

	30-seat coaches		50-seat coaches
Miles per annum (5 × 500 × 50)	125,000	(10 × 400 × 50)	200,000
Fuel (125,000 ÷ 12.5)	10,000	(200,000 ÷ 8)	25,000
	£'000		£'000
Wages (5 × 52 × £220)	57.20	(10 × 52 × £250)	130.00
Fuel (10,000 × £2.20)	22.00	(25,000 × £2.20)	55.00
Licences (5 × £350)	1.75	(10 × £500)	5.00
Insurance (5 × £340)	1.70	(10 × £400)	4.00
Repairs and maintenance (£65,000 in ratio 125:200)	25.00		40.00
Administrative expenses (£93,600 in ratio 57.2:130.0)	28.60		65.00
Depreciation			
[(5 × 20,000) − (5 × 2,000)] ÷ 6	15.00		
[(10 × 32,000) − (10 × 4,000)] ÷ 7			40.00
	151.25		339.00
Cost per mile (151.25 ÷ 125)	£1.21	(339 ÷ 200)	£1.695

(b)   Three 30-seat and two 50-seat coaches will be required.

	£
3 coaches × 5 days × 40 weeks × 10 miles × £1.21	7,260
2 coaches × 5 days × 40 weeks × 15 miles × £1.695	10,170
	17,430
Profit (40/60)	11,620
Tender price	29,050

(*Note*. Whatever profit is 'on' is 100%. The question says 'profit on contract price' so the contract price is 100% and profit is 40% of that price.)

9 Index numbers

Chapter topic list

1   Indexation

2   Multi-item price indices

3   Chain based index numbers

4   Limitations of index numbers

5   Using index numbers in comparing performance

Learning objectives

On completion of this chapter you will be able to:

	Performance criteria	Range statement
• Understand the nature of an index number	16.1	
• Calculate simple price and quantity indices	16.1	
• Use price indices for adjusting for changing price levels	16.1	
• Use indices for comparing performance between cost units and cost/profit centres	16.1	

BPP PUBLISHING

1   INDEXATION

The need for index numbers

1.1   If we are making comparisons of costs and revenues over time to see how well an organisational unit is performing, we need to take account of the fact that general shifts in costs (ie prices) take place.

If a business achieves an increase in sales of 10% in monetary (cash) terms over a year, this result becomes less impressive if we are told that there was general price inflation of 15% over the year. If the business has raised its prices in line with this inflation rate of 15%, then a 10% increase in sales in cash terms indicates a fall in the physical volume of sales. The business is now selling less at the new higher prices.

1.2   In financial accounting, there has been much debate over whether the financial results declared in the annual report of companies should be adjusted to reflect inflation. Understandably, the amount of discussion on this subject has tended to be greater in periods of high inflation. When results of a business are being compared over a period of time for internal management purposes, it is up to managers of the business to agree and use an appropriate method of allowing for changing price levels. The usual method is to use a series of **index numbers**.

> **KEY TERM**
>
> An **index** is a measure, over a period of time, of the average changes in the values (prices or quantities) of a group of items.

1.3   An example of an index is the **'cost of living'** index. This is made up of a large variety of items including bread, butter, meat, rent, insurance etc. The raw data giving the prices of each commodity for successive years would be confusing and useless to most people; but a **simple index** stating that the cost of living index is 145 for the year 2002 compared with 100 for 1996 is easily understood.

Price indices and quantity indices

1.4   An index may be a **price index** or a **quantity index**.

> **KEY TERM**
>
> A **price index** measures the change in the money value of a group of items over a period of time.

(a)   The best known UK price index is the Retail Prices Index (RPI) which measures changes in the costs of items of expenditure of the average household, and which used to be called the 'cost of living' index. Another example which you may have heard reported in the news is the FT-SE (or 'footsie') 100 share index, which measures how the top 100 share prices in general have performed from one day to the next.

> **KEY TERM**
>
> A **quantity index** measures the change in the non-monetary values of a group of items over a period of time.

(b) A well-known example is a productivity index, which measures changes in the productivity of various departments or groups of workers.

Index points

1.5 The term '**points**' is used to measure the difference in the index value in one year with the value in another year. In the example given in Paragraph 1.3 above, the cost of living index rose 45 points between 1994 and 2000 (ie rose from an index of 100 to 145). Points are used for measuring changes in an index because they provide an easy method of arithmetic. The alternative is to use percentages, because indices are based on percent-ages, as we shall see.

The base period, or base year

1.6 Index numbers are normally expressed as **percentages**, taking the value for a **base date** as 100. The choice of a base date or base year is not significant, except that it should normally be 'representative'. In the construction of a **price index**, the base year preferably should not be one in which there were abnormally high or low prices for any items in the 'basket of goods' making up the index.

Calculation of an index

1.7 Suppose sales for a company over the last five years were as follows.

Year	Sales
	£'000
20X5	35
20X6	42
20X7	40
20X8	45
20X9	50

The managing director decided that he wanted to set up a sales index (ie an index which measures how sales have done from year to year), using 20X5 as the base year. The £35,000 of sales in 20X5 is given the index 100%. What are the indices for the other years?

1.8 If £35,000 = 100%, then:

(a) £42,000 $= \dfrac{42,000}{35,000} \times 100\% = 120\%$

(b) £40,000 $= \dfrac{40,000}{35,000} \times 100\% = 114\%$

(c) £45,000 $= \dfrac{45,000}{35,000} \times 100\% = 129\%$

(d) £50,000 $= \dfrac{50,000}{35,000} \times 100\% = 143\%$

BPP
PUBLISHING

1.9   Now the table showing sales for the last five years can be completed, taking 20X5 as the base year.

Year	Sales	Index
	£'000	
20X5	35	100
20X6	42	120
20X7	40	114
20X8	45	129
20X9	50	143

1.10 EXAMPLE: PRICE INDEX

If the price of a cup of coffee in the Café Frederick was 40p in 20X0, 50p in 20X1 and 76p in 20X2, using 20X0 as a base point the price index numbers for 20X1 and 20X2 would be:

$$20\text{X1 price index} = \frac{50}{40} \times 100 = 125$$

$$20\text{X2 price index} = \frac{76}{40} \times 100 = 190$$

1.11 EXAMPLE: QUANTITY INDEX

Similarly, if the Café Frederick sold 500,000 cups of coffee in 20X0, 700,000 cups in 20X1, and 600,000 in 20X2, then quantity index numbers for 20X1 and 20X2, using 20X0 as a base year, would be:

$$20\text{X1 quantity index} = \frac{700,000}{500,000} \times 100 = 140$$

$$20\text{X2 quantity index} = \frac{600,000}{500,000} \times 100 = 120$$

Activity 9.1

A price index measuring the price of a litre of milk over the period 20X0-20X3 is as follows.

Year	Index
20X0	96
20X1	98
20X2	100
20X3	113

(a)   What year is the base year of this index, as far as you can tell from the table above?
(b)   By how many points has the index risen between 20X0 and 20X2?
(c)   By what percentage has the index risen between 20X0 and 20X2?
(d)   If a litre of milk cost £0.54 in 20X1, how much did it cost in 20X3?

2   MULTI-ITEM PRICE INDICES

2.1   In the examples we have seen so far in this chapter, it is not really necessary to calculate an index, because only one product or item has been under consideration. Knowing that sales have risen by 20% from £35,000 to £42,000, for instance, is just as informative as knowing that the index has risen 20 points (from 100 to 120). There was no real need to calculate the index.

2.2 Most practical indices are made up of more than one item. For example, suppose that the cost of living index is calculated from only three commodities: potatoes, coffee and beef and that the prices for 20X1 and 20X5 were as follows.

	20X1	*20X5*
Potatoes	20p a bag	40p a bag
Coffee	25p a jar	30p a jar
Beef	450p a kilo	405p a kilo

2.3 Note that the prices above are given in different units, and there is no indication of the relative importance of each item. In formulating index numbers, these aspects can be overcome by **weighting**. To decide the weighting, we need information about the **relative importance** of each item. In our example of a simple cost of living (or retail price) index, it would be necessary to find out how much the average person or household spends per week (or month) on each item in the 'basket' of goods.

2.4 Research may suggest that the average spending by each household in a week was as follows in 20X1 (rounding to the nearest penny).

	Quantity	*Price per unit*	*Total spending* £	*% of total spending* *= weighting factor*
Potatoes	6 pounds	20p	1.20	60
Coffee	2 jars	25p	0.50	25
Beef	0.067 kilos	450p	0.30	15
			2.00	100 %

The weighting factor of each item in the index will depend on the proportion of total weekly spending taken up by the item. In our example, the weighting factors of potatoes, coffee and beef would be 60%, 25% and 15% respectively.

2.5 If 20X1 is a base year, the index for 20X5 is obtained as follows.

(a) Calculate the price of each item in 20X5 as a percentage of the price in 20X1. This percentage figure is called a **price relative**, because it shows the new price level of each item relative to the base year price.

(b) Multiply the price relative by the weighting factor for each item in the 'basket of goods' to give a weighted average for each item. The result for all items is added together to give a weighted average total for 20X5.

(c) Make a similar weighted average total for the base year (the price relative for each item will be 100 as it is the base year).

(d) As the base year index = 100, the 20X5 index is:

$$\frac{\text{Weighted average total in 20X5}}{\text{Weighted average total in 20X1}} \times 100$$

2.6 In our example:

(a) 20X5 price relatives (ie 20X5 prices as a percentage of 20X1 prices):

(i) Potatoes $\dfrac{40p}{20p} \times 100 = \quad 200$

(ii) Coffee $\dfrac{30p}{25p} \times 100 =$ 120

(iii) Beef $\dfrac{405p}{450p} \times 100 =$ 90

(b) Multiply the 20X5 price relative of each item by the weighting factor of the item to give a weighted average for each item.

Item	Weighting factor	Price relative	Weighted average
Potatoes	60%	200	120
Coffee	25%	120	30
Beef	15%	90	13.5
	100%		163.5

(c) Calculate the weighted averages for the base year 20X1 (total is always 100).

Item	Weighting factor	Price relative	Product
Potatoes	60%	100	60
Coffee	25%	100	25
Beef	15%	100	15
	100%		100

(d) The 20X5 index is:

$$\dfrac{163.5}{100} \times 100 = 163.5$$

2.7 The formula for a weighted price index of this type may be shown as follows.

> **KEY TERM**
>
> **Price index** $= \dfrac{\sum p_1 w}{\sum p_0 w} \times 100$
>
> where $\quad p_1$ represents prices in the 'new' year
> p_0 represents prices in the base year
> w is the weighting factor (same for both years).

2.8 A quantity index measures the change in the **non-monetary** values of a group of items. It is calculated in much the same way as a price index, but because it deals with non-monetary values, it ignores any changes in price: there is no need to work out price relatives when calculating a quantity index. We do not look at quantity indices further here.

3 CHAIN BASED INDEX NUMBERS

3.1 In all the previous examples in this chapter, we have used a **fixed base** method of indexing, whereby a base year is selected (index 100) and all subsequent changes are measured against this base. The **chain base** method of indexing is an alternative approach, whereby (in a price index), the changes in prices are taken as a percentage of the period immediately before. This method is suitable where weightings are changing rapidly, and new items are continually being brought into the index and old items taken out.

3.2 EXAMPLE: THE CHAIN BASE METHOD

The price of a particular model of car varied as follows over the years 20X5 to 20X8.

Year	20X5	20X6	20X7	20X8
Price	£10,000	£11,120	£12,200	£13,880

Tasks

(a) Construct a fixed base index for the years 20X5 to 20X8, using 20X6 as the base year.

(b) Construct a chain base index for the years 20X5 to 20X8.

Round all answers to the nearest index point.

3.3 SOLUTION

(a) Constructing a fixed base index is exactly the same sort of problem we have already met in this chapter.

Year			*Index*
20X5	$\dfrac{10,000}{11,120} \times 100$	=	90
20X6			100
20X7	$\dfrac{12,200}{11,120} \times 100$	=	110
20X8	$\dfrac{13,880}{11,120} \times 100$	=	125

(b) Constructing a chain base index is almost the same, except that the index is always calculated using the percentage increase (or decrease) on the previous year, rather than on a base year.

Year			*Index*
20X5			100
20X6	$\dfrac{11,120}{10,000} \times 100$	=	111
20X7	$\dfrac{12,200}{11,120} \times 100$	=	110
20X8	$\dfrac{13,800}{12,200} \times 100$	=	114

3.4 The chain base index shows the rate of change in prices from year to year, whereas the fixed base index shows the change more directly against prices in the base year.

ASSESSMENT ALERT

Remember that the index number of the base year is normally 100. The base year should not be a year in which prices were abnormally high or low, so if you are asked to select a base year in an assessment, make sure that your choice of year is 'representative' and that you can give reasons for your choice.

BPP PUBLISHING

Activity 9.2

Bone is a popular brand of dog food. It is produced by mixing the four ingredients B, O, N and E, in the proportions 6, 5, 4 and 3 respectively.

Indices of the cost prices of the four ingredients for the years 20X5 to 20X8, using 20X4 as the base year are as follows.

	20X5	20X6	20X7	20X8
B	103	107	115	120
O	104	111	118	123
N	107	113	117	121
E	102	106	110	118

Tasks

(a) For each of the years 20X5 to 20X8, calculate the material cost index of Bone.

(b) For 20X8, calculate the material cost index using 20X7 as the base year.

4   LIMITATIONS OF INDEX NUMBERS

4.1   Index numbers are easy to understand and fairly easy to calculate, so it is not surprising that they are frequently used. However, they are not perfect.

(a) **Index numbers are usually only approximations** of changes in price (or quantity) over time, and must be interpreted with care and reservation.

(b) **Weighting factors become out of date as time passes**. Unless a chain base index is used, the weightings will gradually cease to reflect the current 'reality'.

(c) **New products or items may appear, and old ones cease to be significant.** For example, spending has changed in recent years, to include new items such as mobile phones, PCs and video recorders, whereas the demand for large black and white televisions and spin dryers has declined. These changes would make the weightings of a retail price index for consumer goods out of date and the base of the index would need revision.

(d) **Sometimes, the data used to calculate index numbers might be incomplete, out of date, or inaccurate.** For example, the quantity indices of imports and exports are based on records supplied by traders which may be prone to error or even falsification.

(e) The base year of an index should be a 'normal' year, but there is probably no such thing as a perfectly normal year. **Some error in the index will be caused by untypical values in the base period.**

(f) **The 'basket of items' in an index is often selective.** For example, the Retail Prices Index (RPI) is constructed from a sample of households and, more importantly, from a basket of only about 600 items.

(g) **A national index cannot necessarily be applied to an individual town or region.** For example, if the national index of wages and salaries rises from 100 to 115, it does not follow that the wages and salaries of people in, say, Birmingham, have gone up from 100 to 115.

(h) **An index may exclude important items**, for example the RPI excludes payments of income tax out of gross wages.

Misinterpretation of index numbers

4.2 You must be careful not to misinterpret index numbers. Several possible mistakes will be explained using the following example of a retail price index.

	20X0		*20X1*		*20X2*
January	340.0	January	360.6	January	436.3
		February	362.5	February	437.1
		March	366.2	March	439.5
		April	370.0	April	442.1

(a) It would be wrong to say that prices rose by 2.6% between March and April 20X2. It is correct to say that prices rose 2.6 **points**, or:

$$\frac{2.6}{439.5} = 0.6\%$$

(b) It would be wrong to say that because prices are continually going up, then there must be rising inflation. If prices are going up, then there must be **inflation**. But is the rate of price increases going up, or is the rate slowing down? In our example, it so happens that although the trend of prices is still upwards, the rate of price increase (inflation) is slowing down. For example:

(i) Annual rate of inflation, March 20X1 to March 20X2

$$\frac{439.5 - 366.2}{366.2} \times 100 = 20\%$$

(ii) Annual rate of inflation, April 20X1 to April 20X2

$$\frac{442.1 - 370.0}{370.0} \times 100 = 19.5\%$$

The **rate of inflation** has dropped from 20% per annum to 19.5% per annum between March and April 20X2, even though prices went up in the month between March and April 20X2 by 0.6%.

(c) It is also wrong to state (except as an approximation) that the average annual rate of inflation between January 20X0 and January 20X2 is:

$$\frac{1}{2} \text{ of } \frac{436.3 - 340.0}{340.0} = 14.2\% \text{ per annum}$$

The reason for this is that the annual increase has been compounded, ie it has been multiplied by itself. To calculate the average annual increase over the two years we must use a square root.

$$\text{Average annual increase} = \left(\sqrt{\frac{436.3}{340.0}} - 1\right) \times 100 = 13.3\% \text{ per annum}$$

5 USING INDEX NUMBERS IN COMPARING PERFORMANCE

5.1 For the purpose of internal management reporting, results recorded over a number of periods can be adjusted using an appropriate price index to convert the figures from money terms to **'real' terms**.

5.2 As well as the Retail Prices Index (RPI) - also known as the General Index of Retail Prices - which measures the average level of prices of goods and services purchased by most households in the United Kingdom, the Office for National Statistics publishes a large number of producer price indices for different sectors of industry as well as index numbers of agricultural prices. These indices track changes in prices facing businesses in different industries. Annual average figures for these indices covering the previous five years are published in the *Annual Abstract of Statistics*.

(a) Someone needing to track the trend in prices of raw material inputs could use the Index of Producer Prices: Materials and Fuels, which measures prices of goods as they enter the factory.

(b) The price of finished manufactured goods is tracked by the Index of Producer Prices: Manufactured Products, which is sometimes called a measure of 'factory gate prices'.

5.3 The various price indices for specific industry sectors will usually provide a more useful way of comparing results in different periods than more general indices such as the RPI. The RPI measures price changes over a varied 'basket' of retail goods and services, including housing costs. The price trends facing a wholesaler or producer in any particular industry may be very different.

5.4 Let us now look at an example which considers the way in which index numbers may be used to compare the performance over several years of a single profit centre in a manufacturing company.

5.5 EXAMPLE: USING INDEX NUMBERS TO COMPARE PERFORMANCE

(a) Loving Lawns Ltd manufactures a range of lawnmowers. The results for one of its most popular models, the Baritone are collected in profit centre 12. The results for profit centre 12 for the periods 20X5 to 20Y0 were as follows.

	£'000
20X5	3,422
20X6	3,608
20X7	3,862
20X8	4,036
20X9	4,072
20Y0	4,114

(b) The trend in profits is to be expressed at 20Y0 prices, using the producer price index numbers for lawnmowers set out below (the base year is 20X5). The year-on-year 'real' change in profit is then to be calculated.

	Producer price index
20X5	100.0
20X6	106.3
20X7	110.4
20X8	115.4
20X9	120.1
20Y0	125.7

5.6 SOLUTION

(a)

	Rebased index (20Y0=100)	Profit £'000	Profit at 20Y0 prices £'000	Real year-on-year increase %
20X5	79.6	3,422	4,299	
20X6	84.6	3,608	4,265	– 0.8
20X7	87.8	3,862	4,399	+ 3.1
20X8	91.8	4,036	4,397	0.0
20X9	95.5	4,072	4,264	– 3.0
20Y0	100.0	4,114	4,114	– 3.5

(b) Each index number is rebased to 20Y0 by dividing it by the 20Y0 index number and multiplying by 100. For example:

$$20X9: \frac{120.1}{125.7} \times 100 = 95.5$$

(c) Profits at 20Y0 prices are calculated by dividing the profit figures in cash terms by the rebased index and multiplying by 100. The real year-on-year increase is the percentage change in profit at 20Y0 prices over the previous year.

(d) Different results in a business may be adjusted in a similar way, using an appropriate index. For example the unit cost of a product and the expenditure incurred in cost centres may be compared by following steps (a) - (c) above.

5.7 EXAMPLE: DEFLATION

Mick Payne works for Eastleigh Ltd. Over the last five years he has received an annual salary increase of £500. Despite his employer assuring him that £500 is a reasonable annual salary increase, Mick is unhappy because, although he agrees £500 is a lot of money, he finds it difficult to maintain the standard of living he had when he first joined the company. Consider the figures below.

Year	(a) Wages £	(b) RPI	(c) Real wages £	(d) Real wages index
1	12,000	250	12,000	100.0
2	12,500	260	12,019	100.2
3	13,000	275	11,818	98.5
4	13,500	295	11,441	95.3
5	14,000	315	11,111	92.6

(a) This column shows Mick's wages over the five-year period.

(b) This column shows the current RPI.

(c) This column shows what Mick's wages are worth taking prices, as represented by the RPI, into account. The wages have been deflated relative to the new base period (year 1). Economists call these deflated wage figures **real wages**. The real wages for years 2 and 4, for example, are calculated as follows.

Year 2: £12,500 × 250/260 = £12,019
Year 4: £13,500 × 250/295 = £11,441

(d) This column is calculated by dividing the entries in column (c) by £12,000, his starting salary.

$$\text{Real index} = \frac{\text{current value}}{\text{base value}} \times \frac{\text{base indicator}}{\text{current indicator}}$$

So, for example, the real wage index in year $4 = \dfrac{£13,500}{£12,000} \times \dfrac{250}{295} = 95.3$

The real wages index shows that the real value of Mick's wages has fallen by 7.4% over the five-year period. In real terms he is now earning £11,111 compared to £12,000 in year 1. He is probably justified, therefore, in being unhappy.

Key learning points

- **Index numbers** are used to make comparisons of costs and revenues over time, in order to see how well an organisational unit is performing.

- An index may be a **price index** or a **quantity index.**

- The index number for a **base year** is normally 100. The base year is chosen as a representative year.

- Index numbers are easy to calculate and understand. They do however have a number of limitations.

- **Weighting** is used to reflect the importance of each item in the index.

- Index numbers are used to **compare the performances** of cost units, cost centres and profit centres.

Quick quiz

1   What is an index?
2   Which value is the base year normally assigned when calculating index numbers?
3   What does a quantity index measure?
4   List four limitations of index numbers.

Answers to quick quiz

1   A measure over a period of time of the average changes of a group of items.

2   100.

3   The change in the non-monetary values of a group of items.

4   • Usually only approximations of changes in price or quantity.

 • Weighting factors often become out of date with time.

 • Spending on products may change. This would result in weightings of a retail price index for consumer goods to become out of date.

 • Data used to calculate index numbers may be incomplete, out-of-date or inaccurate.

 • See paragraph 4.1 for complete list.

Answers to activities

Answer 9.1

(a)   The base year appears to be 20X2, because the index is 100. We cannot be absolutely sure about this, because the base year *could* be before 20X0 or after 20X3, and the price of a litre of milk in 20X2 just happened to be the same as in the base year.

(b)   The index has moved from 96 points to 100 points, a rise of 4 points.

(c) $\dfrac{4}{96} \times 100\% = 4.17\%$

(d) $£0.54 \times \dfrac{113}{98} = £0.62$

Answer 9.2

Tutorial note. An index covering the prices of several items is an indication of the average of changes in the prices, with weights being used to allow for the relative importance of the different items.

Ingredient	Weight	20X5 Index	20X5 W ted	20X6 Index	20X6 W ted	20X7 Index	20X7 W ted	20X8 Index	20X8 W ted
B	6	103	618	107	642	115	690	120	720
O	5	104	520	111	555	118	590	123	615
N	4	107	428	113	452	117	468	121	484
E	3	102	306	106	318	110	330	118	354
	18		1,872		1,967		2,078		2,173

(a)   Material cost index

(20X4 = 100)   104   109   115   121

Each total is divided by 18 (the sum of the weights) to derive the index number.

(b)   Using 20X7 as the base year, the index for 20X8 is:

$\dfrac{2,173 \times 100}{2,078} = 105.$

192

10 Time series analysis

Chapter topic list

1 The components of time series

2 Finding the trend

3 Forecasting using time series analysis

Learning objectives

On completion of this chapter you will be able to:

	Performance criteria	Range statement
• Describe the components of a time series	16.1	
• Use moving averages to isolate the trend	16.1	
• Chart time series data	16.1	
• Comment on the use of time series analysis for forecasting	16.1	

BPP
PUBLISHING

1   THE COMPONENTS OF TIME SERIES

KEY TERM

A **time series** is a series of figures or values recorded over time.

1.1   *Examples of time series*

- Output at a factory each day for the last month
- Monthly sales over the last two years
- Total annual costs for the last ten years
- The Retail Prices Index each month for the last ten years
- The number of people employed by a company each year for the last 20 years

1.2   A graph of a time series is called a **historigram**. For example, consider the following time series.

Year	Sales
	£'000
20X0	20
20X1	21
20X2	24
20X3	23
20X4	27
20X5	30
20X6	28

The historigram is as follows.

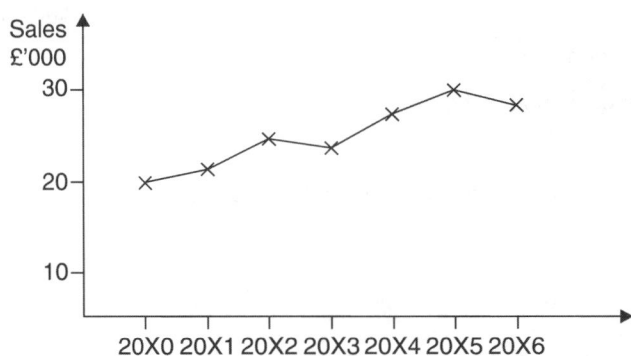

The horizontal axis is always chosen to represent time, and the vertical axis represents the values of the data recorded.

1.3   The main features of a time series which it may be necessary to identify include the following.

(a)   A **trend**

(b)   **Seasonal variations** or fluctuations

(c)   Cycles, or **cyclical variations**

(d)   Non-recurring **random variations**

The trend

1.4 In the following examples of time series, there are three types of trend.

	Output per labour hour Units	Cost per unit £	Number of employees
20X4	30	1.00	100
20X5	24	1.08	103
20X6	26	1.20	96
20X7	22	1.15	102
20X8	21	1.18	103
20X9	17	1.25	98
	(A)	(B)	(C)

(a) In time series (A) there is a **downward trend** in the output per labour hour. Output per labour hour did not fall every year, because it went up between 20X5 and 20X6, but the long-term movement is clearly a downward one.

(b) In time series (B) there is an **upward trend** in the cost per unit. Although unit costs went down in 20X7 from a higher level in 20X6, the basic movement over time is one of rising costs.

(c) In time series (C) there is no clear movement up or down, and the number of employees remained fairly constant around 100. The trend is therefore a **static**, or **level** one.

Seasonal variations

Activity 10.1

Can you think of some examples of seasonal variations?

1.5 'Seasonal' is a term which may appear to refer to the seasons of the year, but its meaning in time series analysis is somewhat broader, as the examples given in the key term above show.

1.6 EXAMPLE: A TREND AND SEASONAL VARIATIONS

The number of customers served by a company of travel agents over the past four years is shown in the following historigram.

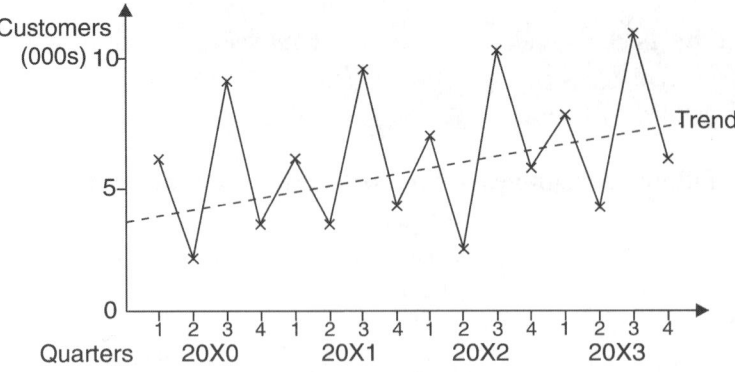

In this example, there would appear to be large seasonal fluctuations in demand, but there is also a basic upward trend.

Cyclical variations

> **KEY TERM**
>
> **Cyclical variations** are fluctuations which take place over a longer time period than seasonal variations.

1.7   It may take several years to complete the cycle, as in the case of the 'trade cycle'. Economists observed in the late 19th century that the level of economic activity or output, which may be measured as the Gross Domestic Product of a country, often fluctuated over a cycle of approximately nine years in length. The length of the cycle of economic boom and recession is not now generally of this length, although the cycle of economic activity nevertheless does affect the economy in general and individual businesses in particular.

2   FINDING THE TREND

2.1   Look at these monthly sales figures.

20X6	Sales £'000
August	0.02
September	0.04
October	0.04
November	3.20
December	14.60

2.2   It looks as though the business is expanding rapidly - and so it is, in a way. But when you know that the business is a Christmas pudding manufacturer, then you see immediately that the January sales will no doubt slump right back down again.

2.3   It is obvious that the business will do better in the Christmas season than at any other time. That is the **seasonal variation** with which the statistician has to contend. Using the monthly figures, how can he tell whether or not the business is doing well overall - whether there is a rising sales trend over time other than the short-term rise over Christmas?

2.4 One possibility is to compare figures with the equivalent figures of a year ago. However, many things can happen over a period of twelve months to make such a comparison misleading - for example, new products might now be manufactured and prices will probably have changed.

2.5 In fact, there are a number of ways of overcoming this problem of distinguishing trend from seasonal variations. One such method is called **moving averages**. This method attempts to remove seasonal (or cyclical) variations from a time series by a process of averaging so as to leave a set of figures representing the trend.

Finding the trend by moving averages

KEY TERM

A **moving average** is an average of the results of a fixed number of periods.

2.6 Since a moving average is an average of several time periods, it is related to the mid-point of the overall period.

2.7 EXAMPLE: MOVING AVERAGES

Year	Sales
	Units
20X0	390
20X1	380
20X2	460
20X3	450
20X4	470
20X5	440
20X6	500

Required

Take a moving average of the annual sales over a period of three years.

2.8 SOLUTION

(a) Average sales in the three year period 20X0 – 20X2 were:

$$\left(\frac{390+380+460}{3}\right) = \frac{1,230}{3} = 410$$

This average relates to the middle year of the period, 20X1.

(b) Similarly, average sales in the three year period 20X1 – 20X3 were:

$$\left(\frac{380+460+450}{3}\right) = \frac{1,290}{3} = 430$$

This average relates to the middle year of the period, 20X2.

(c) The average sales can also be found for the periods 20X2 - 20X4, 20X3 - 20X5 and 20X4 - 20X6, to give the following.

Year	Sales	Moving total of 3 years' sales	Moving average of 3 year's sales (÷ 3)
20X0	390		
20X1	380	1,230	410
20X2	460	1,290	430
20X3	450	1,380	460
20X4	470	1,360	453
20X5	440	1,410	470
20X6	500		

Note the following points.

(i) The moving average series has five figures relating to the years from 20X1 to 20X5. The original series had seven figures for the years from 20X0 to 20X6.

(ii) There is an upward trend in sales, which is more noticeable from the series of moving averages than from the original series of actual sales each year.

2.9 The above example averaged over a three-year period. Over what period should a moving average be taken? The answer to this question is that **the moving average which is most appropriate will depend on the circumstances and the nature of the time series.** Note the following points.

(a) A moving average which takes an average of the results in many time periods will represent results over a longer term than a moving average of two or three periods.

(b) On the other hand, with a moving average of results in many time periods, the last figure in the series will be out of date by several periods. In our example, the most recent average related to 20X5. With a moving average of five years' results, the final figure in the series would relate to 20X4.

(c) When there is a known cycle over which seasonal variations occur, such as all the days in the week or all the seasons in the year, the most suitable moving average would be one which covers one full cycle.

Moving averages of an even number of results

2.10 In the previous example, moving averages were taken of the results in an odd number of time periods, and the average was then related to the mid-point of the overall period.

2.11 If a moving average were taken of results in an even number of time periods, the basic technique would be the same, but the mid-point of the overall period would not relate to a single period. For example, suppose an average were taken of the following four results.

Spring	120	
Summer	90	average 115
Autumn	180	
Winter	70	

The average would relate to the mid-point of the period, between summer and autumn.

2.12 The trend line average figures need to relate to a particular time period; otherwise, seasonal variations cannot be calculated. To overcome this difficulty, we take a **moving average of the moving average**. An example will illustrate this technique.

2.13 EXAMPLE: MOVING AVERAGES OVER AN EVEN NUMBER OF PERIODS

Calculate a moving average trend line of the following results of Lileth Ltd.

Year	Quarter	Volume of sales '000 units
20X5	1	600
	2	840
	3	420
	4	720
20X6	1	640
	2	860
	3	420
	4	740
20X7	1	670
	2	900
	3	430
	4	760

2.14 SOLUTION

(a) A moving average of four will be used, since the volume of sales would appear to depend on the season of the year, and each year has four quarterly results. The moving average of four does not relate to any specific period of time; therefore a second moving average of two will be calculated on the first moving average trend line.

Year	Quarter	Actual volume of sales '000 units (A)	Moving total of 4 quarters' sales '000 units (B)	Moving average of 4 quarters' sales '000 units (B ÷ 4)	Mid-point of 2 moving averages Trend line '000 units (C)
20X5	1	600			
	2	840			
	3	420	2,580	645.0	650.00
	4	720	2,620	655.0	657.50
20X6	1	640	2,640	660.0	660.00
	2	860	2,640	660.0	662.50
	3	420	2,660	665.0	668.75
	4	740	2,690	672.5	677.50
20X7	1	670	2,730	682.5	683.75
	2	900	2,740	685.0	687.50
	3	430	2,760	690.0	
	4	760			

(b) By taking a mid point (a moving average of two) of the original moving averages, we can relate the results to specific quarters (from the third quarter of 20X5 to the second quarter of 20X7).

Activity 10.2

What can you say about the trend in sales of Lileth Ltd in Paragraph 2.14 above?

Moving averages on graphs

2.15 One way of displaying the trend clearly is to show it by plotting the moving average on a graph.

2.16 EXAMPLE: MOVING AVERAGES ON GRAPHS

Actual ice cream sales for Mr Frosty Ltd for 20X5 and 20X6 were as follows.

	Sales (£)	
	20X5	*20X6*
January	100	110
February	120	130
March	200	220
April	200	210
May	240	230
June	250	240
July	210	250
August	210	300
September	200	150
October	110	110
November	90	80
December	50	40
	1,980	2,070

Task

Calculate the trend in the ice cream sales and display it on a graph. (*Hint.* Calculate an annual moving total.)

2.17 SOLUTION

20X6	*Sales*	*Moving total*	*Moving average (trend)*
	£	£	£
January	110	1,990	165.83
February	130	2,000	166.67
March	220	2,020	168.33
April	210	2,030	169.17
May	230	2,020	168.33
June	240	2,010	167.50
July	250	2,050	170.83
August	300	2,140	178.33
September	150	2,090	174.17
October	110	2,090	174.17
November	80	2,080	173.33
December	40	2,070	172.50

2.18 There is one very important point not immediately obvious from the above table, and that is to do with the time periods covered by the moving total and moving average.

(a) The moving total, as we have seen, is the total for the previous twelve months. The figure of £1,990, for instance, represents total sales from February 20X5 to January 20X6.

(b) The moving average is the average monthly sales over the previous twelve months. The figure of £165.83, for instance, represents average monthly sales for each month during the period February 20X5 to January 20X6.

2.19 When plotting a moving average on a graph, it is therefore important to remember that the points should be located at the **mid-point** of the period to which they apply. For example, the figure of £165.83 (moving average at end of January 20X6) relates to the 12 months ending January 20X6 and so it must be plotted in the **middle** of that period (31 July 20X5).

2.20 The moving data on ice cream sales for Mr Frosty Ltd could be drawn on a graph as follows.

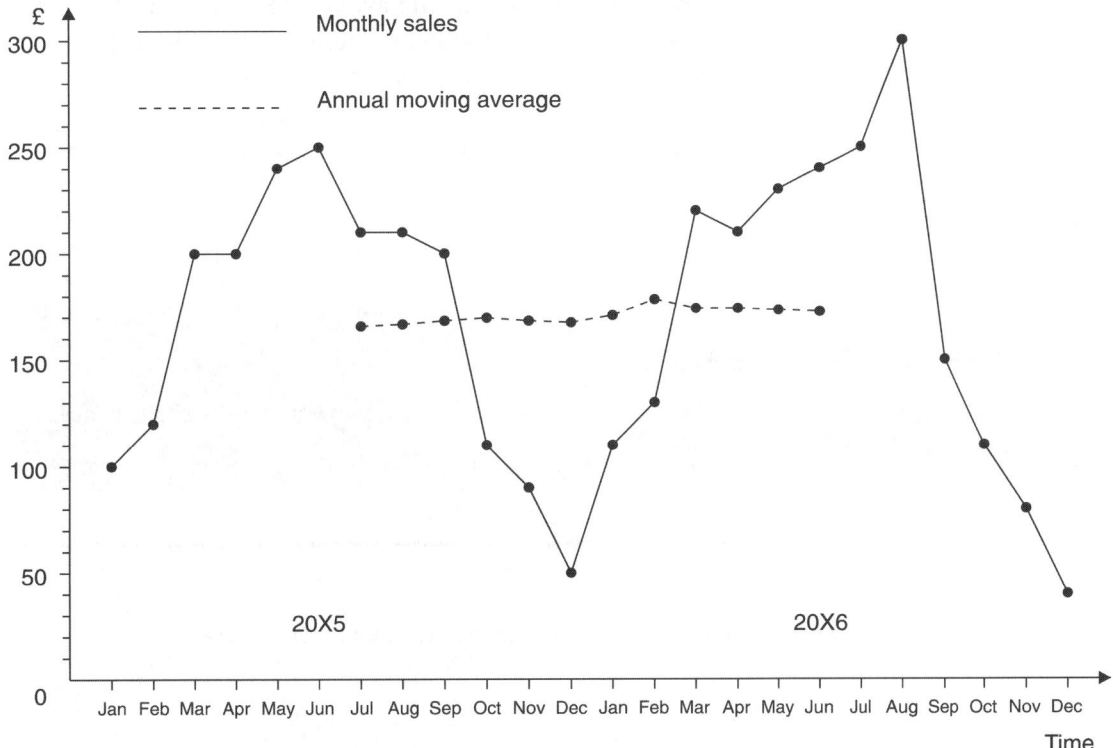

2.21 Points to note about this graph are as follows.

(a) The annual moving average can only be plotted from July 20X5 to May 20X6 as we have no data prior to January 20X5 or after December 20X6.

(b) The moving average has the effect of smoothing out the seasonal fluctuations in the ordinary sales graph (which is the reason why moving averages are used in the first place).

2.22 Once the trend has been established, we can find the **seasonal variations.**

2.23 The actual and trend sales for Lileth Ltd (as calculated in Paragraph 2.14) are set out below. The difference between the actual results for any one quarter and the trend figure for that quarter will be the seasonal variation for that quarter.

Year	Quarter	Actual (Y)	Trend (T)	Seasonal variation (Y – T)
20X5	1	600		
	2	840		
	3	420	650.00	–230.00
	4	720	657.50	62.50
20X6	1	640	660.00	–20.00
	2	860	662.50	197.50
	3	420	668.75	–248.75
	4	740	677.50	62.50
20X7	1	670	683.75	–13.75
	2	900	687.50	212.50
	3	430		
	4	760		

2.24 The variation between the actual result for any one particular quarter and the trend line average is not the same from year to year, but an average of these variations can be taken. This average is called the average seasonal variation, and is used in forecasting as we shall see in the following section of this chapter.

	Q_1	Q_2	Q_3	Q_4
20X5			–230.00	62.50
20X6	–20.00	197.50	–248.75	62.50
20X7	–13.75	212.50		
Total	–33.75	410.00	–478.75	125.00
Average (÷ 2)	–16.875	205.00	–239.375	62.50

ASSESSMENT ALERT

You may be asked to plot time series data, so make sure that you have a sharp pencil, rubber and ruler for drawing graphs.

Activity 10.3

The data below relates to the sales of Tudor Ltd for the years 20X1 to 20X8.

	Actual sales £'000
20X1	1,000
20X2	1,200
20X3	1,500
20X4	2,100
20X5	3,000
20X6	4,200
20X7	5,700
20X8	8,100

Task

Calculate the three-period moving average of Tudor Ltd's sales. Comment on your results.

3   FORECASTING USING TIME SERIES ANALYSIS

Using time series analysis in practice

3.1   The analysis of a time series allows historical aspects of data to be monitored. In other words, it is possible to observe how a variable has performed over the period of time being monitored. So, for example, the cost of raw materials, the price of a particular bought-in component or the rate per hour paid to labour can be monitored and analysed.

Equally, if not more important, is the potential to use the historical data once analysed to forecast future performance, which is a necessary part of business planning, budgeting and decision making.

Forecasting using time series analysis

3.2   Time series analysis data may be used to make forecasts as follows.

(a)   Find a trend line either by finding the line of best fit or by moving averages. If the moving averages method is used, the calculated trend values need to be plotted on a graph.

(b)   Extend the trend line so that readings for points outside the span of time covered by the original data can be taken. Forecasting the future from a trend line based on historical data is known as extrapolation.

(c)   Adjust the readings found by extrapolation by the average seasonal variation applicable to future periods in order to determine future forecasts for these periods.

The following example will demonstrate how time series analysis may be used for forecasting.

3.3   EXAMPLE: FORECASTING USING TIME SERIES ANALYSIS

The following data relate to output at a factory which appears to vary with the day of the week.

		Actual (Y)	Moving total of five days' output	Trend (T)	Seasonal variation (Y–T)
Week 1	Monday	80			
	Tuesday	104			
	Wednesday	94	460	92.0	+2.0
	Thursday	120	462	92.4	+27.6
	Friday	62	468	93.6	−31.6
Week 2	Monday	82	471	94.2	−12.2
	Tuesday	110	476	95.2	+14.8
	Wednesday	97	478	95.6	+1.4
	Thursday	125	480	96.0	+29.0
	Friday	64	486	97.2	−33.2
Week 3	Monday	84	489	97.8	−13.8
	Tuesday	116	494	98.8	+17.2
	Wednesday	100	496	99.2	+0.8
	Thursday	130			
	Friday	66			

The seasonal variations above (Y – T) have been used to calculate the average or estimated seasonal variations which are given below.

Monday	*Tuesday*	*Wednesday*	*Thursday*	*Friday*	*Total*
–13	+16	+1	+28	–32	0

Use the trend values and the estimates of seasonal variations to forecast sales in week 4.

(*Note.* You do not need to know how to calculate the average or estimated seasonal variations at this stage of your studies. You must, however, be able to comment on their use in forecasting methods.)

3.4 SOLUTION

We begin by plotting the trend values on a graph and extrapolating the trend line.

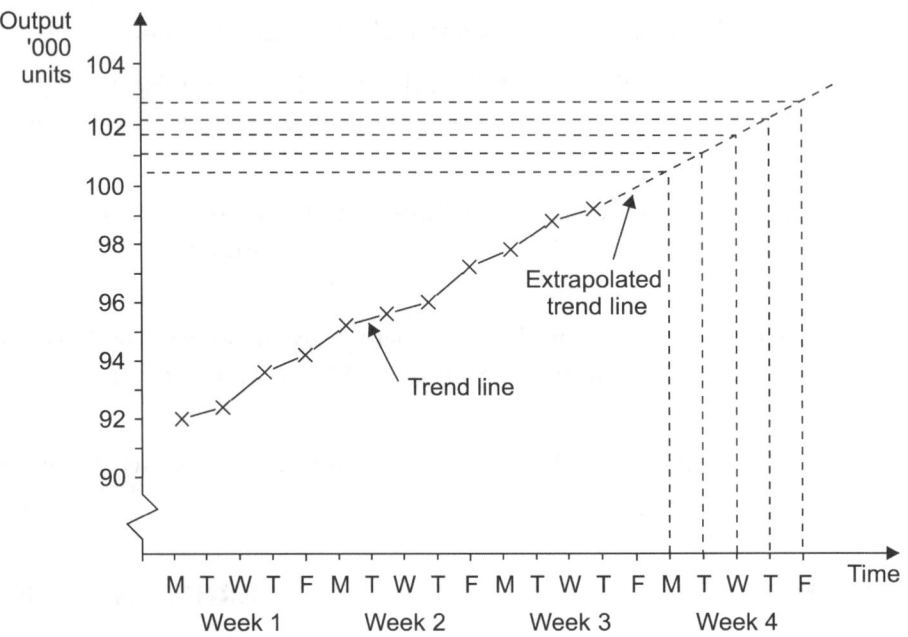

From the extrapolated trend line we can take the following readings and adjust them by the seasonal variations.

Week 4	*Trend line readings*	*Average seasonal variations*	*Forecast*
Monday	100.5	–13	87.5
Tuesday	101.5	+16	117.5
Wednesday	101.7	+1	102.7
Thursday	102.2	+28	130.2
Friday	102.8	–32	70.8

3.5 All forecasts are subject to error, but the likely errors vary from case to case.

(a) The further into the future the forecast is for, the more unreliable it is likely to be.

(b) The less data available on which to base the forecast, the less reliable the forecast.

(c) The pattern of trend cannot be guaranteed to continue in the future.

(d) There is always the danger of random variations upsetting the pattern of trend and seasonal variation.

(e) The extrapolation of the trend line is done by judgement and can introduce error.

Key learning points

- A **time series** is a series of figures or values recorded over time.

- A graph of a time series is called a **historigram**.

- There are four components of a time series: **trend, seasonal variations, cyclical variations** and **random variations**.

- The **trend** is the underlying long-term movement over time in the values of the data recorded. **Seasonal variations** are short-term fluctuations due to different circumstances which affect results at different points in time. **Cyclical variations** are medium-term changes in results caused by circumstances which repeat in cycles.

- One method of finding the trend is by the use of **moving averages**.

- When finding the moving average of an even number of results, a **second moving average** has to be calculated so that trend values can relate to specific actual values or periods.

- **Seasonal variations** are the differences between actual and trend figures.

- Time series analysis can be used both to **analyse** the **performance** of a variable over a period of time and in **forecasting**.

Quick quiz

1   What is the definition of a time series?
2   What are the three main features of a time series?
3   What is the trend?
4   When plotting a moving average on a graph, where should the plotted points be located?
5   Which are the two principal uses of time series analysis in practice?

Answers to quick quiz

1   A series of figures or values recorded over time.

2   • Trend
     • Seasonal variations or fluctuations
     • Cycles or cyclical variations
     • Non-recurring random variations

3   The underlying long-term movement over time in the values of data recorded.

4   At the mid-point of the period to which they apply.

5   • To analyse the performance of a variable over a period of time
     • Forecasting future performances

Answers to activities

Answer 10.1

Here are some suggestions.

(a)   Sales of ice cream will be higher in summer than in winter, and sales of overcoats will be higher in autumn than in spring.

(b)   Shops might expect higher sales shortly before Christmas, or in their winter and summer sales.

(c)   Sales might be higher on Friday and Saturday than on Monday.

(d)   The telephone network may be heavily used at certain times of the day (such as mid-morning and mid-afternoon) and much less used at other times (such as in the middle of the night).

Answer 10.2

The trend in sales is upward.

Answer 10.3

	Actual sales £'000	Three- year moving total £'000	Moving average £'000
20X1	1,000		
20X2	1,200	3,700	1,233
20X3	1,500	4,800	1,600
20X4	2,100	6,600	2,200
20X5	3,000	9,300	3,100
20X6	4,200	12,900	4,300
20X7	5,700	18,000	6,000
20X8	8,100		

Sales of Tudor Ltd are on a steeply rising trend.

11 Capital expenditure appraisal

Chapter topic list

1   Capital expenditure and appraisal methods

2   Accounting rate of return method

3   The payback period

4   The time value of money

5   Relevant costs and project appraisal

6   Discounting and compound interest

7   Discounted cash flow

8   Allowing for inflation

9   Taxation and project appraisal

10   Public sector capital budgeting decisions

Learning objectives

On completion of this chapter you will be able to:

	Performance criteria	Range statement
• Identify and use information relevant to estimating current and future costs and revenue	16.2.1	
• Explain and apply methods of project appraisal: payback and discounted cash flow methods		16.2.3
• Identify relevant cash flows	16.2	
• Understand the implications of taxation and inflation in discounted cash flow		16.2.3
• Present recommendations to the appropriate person in a clear and concise way, supported with a clear rationale	16.2.7	

1 CAPITAL EXPENDITURE AND APPRAISAL METHODS

Fixed assets

> **KEY TERM**
>
> A **fixed asset** is an asset which is acquired and retained in the business with a view to earning profits and not merely turning into cash. It is normally used over more than one accounting period.

1.1 **Examples of fixed assets**

(a) Motor vehicles (except for a motor trader)
(b) Plant and machinery
(c) Fixtures and fittings
(d) Land and buildings

1.2 Fixed assets are different from **stocks** which we buy or make in order to sell. Stocks are *current* assets and, as we have already seen, a part of the **working capital** of a business, along with cash and amounts owed to us by debtors.

Capital and revenue expenditure

> **KEY TERM**
>
> **Capital expenditure** is expenditure that results in the acquisition of fixed assets, or an improvement in their earning capacity.

1.3 How is capital expenditure accounted for in a company's financial statements?

(a) Capital expenditure is not charged as an expense in the profit and loss account of a business enterprise, although a **depreciation charge** will usually be made to write off the capital expenditure gradually over time. Depreciation charges are expenses in the profit and loss account of the business.

(b) Capital expenditure on fixed assets results in the appearance of a fixed asset in the **balance sheet** of a business.

1.4 Special methods of accounting for capital expenditure apply in local authorities and in some other public sector organisations. These are not explained further here.

> **KEY TERM**
>
> **Revenue expenditure** is expenditure incurred for either of the following reasons.
>
> (a) For the purpose of the trade of the business. This includes expenditure classified as selling and distribution expenses, administration expenses and finance charges.
>
> (b) To maintain the existing earning capacity of fixed assets.

1.5   Revenue expenditure is charged to the **profit and loss account** of a period, provided that it relates to the trading activity and sales of that particular period.

For example, if a business buys ten widgets for £200 (£20 each) and sells eight of them during an accounting period, it will have two widgets left in stock at the end of the period. The full £200 is revenue expenditure but only £160 is a cost of goods sold during the period. The remaining £40 (cost of two units) will be included in the balance sheet in the stock of goods held, ie as a current asset valued at £40.

1.6   Suppose that a business purchases a building for £30,000. It then adds an extension to the building at a cost of £10,000. The building needs to have a few broken windows mended, its floors polished and some missing roof tiles replaced. These cleaning and maintenance jobs cost £900.

In the example, the original purchase (£30,000) and the cost of the extension (£10,000) are capital expenditures, because they are incurred to acquire and then improve a fixed asset. The other costs of £900 are revenue expenditure, because these merely maintain the building and thus the 'earning capacity' of the building.

Capital income and revenue income

1.7   **Capital income** is the proceeds from the sale of non-trading assets (ie proceeds from the sale of fixed assets, including fixed asset investments). The profits (or losses) from the sale of fixed assets are included in the profit and loss account of a business, for the accounting period in which the sale takes place.

1.8   **Revenue income** is derived from the following sources.

   (a)   The sale of trading assets
   (b)   Interest and dividends received from investments held by the business

Other capital transactions

1.9   The categorisation of capital and revenue items given above does not mention raising additional capital from the owner(s) of the business, or raising and repaying loans. These are transactions which either:

   (a)   Add to the cash assets of the business, thereby creating a corresponding liability (capital or loan), or

   (b)   When a loan is repaid, reduce the liabilities (loan) and the assets (cash) of the business

Activity 11.1

Explain briefly the effect on the final accounts if:

(a)   Capital expenditure is treated as revenue expenditure
(b)   Revenue expenditure is treated as capital expenditure

Evaluating capital projects

1.10   If an enterprise is considering making an investment of capital expenditure, eg to buy a new computer system or to build a new production assembly line, it will want to establish whether the decision to invest is of benefit to the enterprise. It

will want to **evaluate** the project. There are three principal methods of evaluating whether a capital project is of value to an enterprise.

(a) **Accounting rate of return** (or **return on investment**)

This method calculates the profits that will be earned by a project and expresses this as a percentage of the capital invested in the project. The higher the rate of return, the higher a project is ranked. This method is based on **accounting results** rather than **cash flows**.

(b) **Payback period**

This method of investment appraisal calculates the length of time a project will take to recoup the initial investment, in other words how long a project will take to pay for itself. The method is based on **cash flows**.

(c) **Discounted cash flow (DCF)**, which may be sub-divided into two approaches.

(i) **Net present value (NPV)**

This method considers all relevant cash flows associated with a project over the whole of its life and adjusts those occurring in future years to their '**present value**' by discounting at a rate called the '**cost of capital**'.

(ii) **Internal rate of return (IRR)**

This method involves comparing the rate of return expected from the project calculated on a discounted cash flow basis with the rate used as the cost of capital. Projects with an IRR higher than the cost of capital are worth undertaking.

Cash flow forecasting

1.11 Before looking at each of these methods in turn it is worth emphasising one problem common to all of them, that of estimating future cash flows. Cash flow forecasting is never easy, but in capital budgeting the problems are particularly acute. This is because the period under consideration may not be merely a year or two, but five, ten, perhaps twenty years. It is therefore important that decision makers should consider that variations in the estimates might affect their decision.

2   ACCOUNTING RATE OF RETURN METHOD

2.1 A capital investment project may be assessed by calculating the **return on investment (ROI)** or **accounting rate of return (ARR)** and comparing it with a pre-determined target level.

KEY TERM

A formula for the **accounting rate of return** is:

$$\text{ARR} = \frac{\text{Estimated average profits}}{\text{Estimated average investment}} \times 100\%$$

ASSESSMENT ALERT

Other formulae you may come across use total profits for the numerator, or initial investment for the denominator. Various combinations are possible, but the important thing for an assessment is to be consistent once a method has been selected.

2.2 EXAMPLE: EVALUATING A PROJECT USING ARR

Bee Limited is contemplating the purchase of a new machine and has two alternatives.

	Machine X	Machine Y
Cost	£10,000	£10,000
Estimated scrap value	£2,000	£3,000
Estimated life	4 years	4 years
Estimated future cash flows		
Year 1	£5,000	£2,000
2	£5,000	£3,000
3	£3,000	£5,000
4	£1,000	£5,000

The only difference between annual cash flows and annual profits is depreciation. Based on the ARR method, which of the two machines would be purchased?

2.3 SOLUTION

Since ARR is based on accounting results rather than cash flows we must adjust the cashflows for depreciation.

We can think of the value of the investment as the amount of money tied up in it. The average of this value is the average of the initial investment and the residual value.

	X	Y
	£	£
Total cash flows	14,000	15,000
Total depreciation	8,000	7,000
Total profits after depreciation	6,000	8,000
Average profits (4 years)	£1,500	£2,000
Value of investment initially	10,000	10,000
Eventual residual value	2,000	3,000
	12,000	13,000
∴ Average value of investment (÷ 2)	6,000	6,500

The accounting rates of return are:

$$X = \frac{£1,500}{£6,000} = 25\%$$

$$Y = \frac{\text{£}2,000}{\text{£}6,500} = 31\%$$

Machine Y would therefore be chosen.

2.4　Note how, in the problem above as much weight was attached to cash inflows at year four as to those at year one, whereas the management of Bee Limited would favour high cash inflows in the early years. Early cash flows are less risky and they improve liquidity. For this reason, they might choose machine X despite its lower ARR. One of the disadvantages of the ARR method is that it does not take account of the timing of cash inflows and outflows.

Advantages of ARR	Disadvantages of ARR
A wisely understood measure of accounting profitability. Readily available from accounting data.	Based on accounting profits rather than cash flow, giving too much emphasis to costs as conventionally defined which are not relevant to project performance. Fails to take account of the timing of cash inflows and outflows.

3　THE PAYBACK PERIOD

3.1　The **payback period** method for evaluating capital expenditure is one which gives greater weight to cash flows generated in earlier years.

KEY TERM

The **payback period** is the length of time required before the total cash inflows received from the project is equal to the original cash outlay. In other words, it is the length of time the investment takes to pay itself back.

3.2　In the previous example (Paragraph 2.2), machine X pays for itself within two years and machine Y in three years. Using the payback method of investment appraisal, machine X is preferable to machine Y.

3.3　The payback method has obvious **disadvantages**. Consider the case of two machines for which the following information is available.

		Machine P	*Machine Q*
		£	£
Cost		10,000	10,000
Cash inflows year	1	1,000	5,000
	2	2,000	5,000
	3	6,000	1,000
	4	7,000	500
	5	8,000	500
		24,000	12,000

Machine Q pays back at the end of year two and machine P not until early in year four. Using the payback method machine Q is to be preferred, but this ignores the fact that the total profitability of P (£24,000) is double that of Q.

Advantages of payback method	Disadvantages of payback method
It is widely used in practice, even if often only as a supplement to more sophisticated methods. Its use will tend to minimise the effects of risk and help liquidity, because greater weight is given to earlier cash flows which can probably be predicted more accurately than distant cash flows.	Total profitability is ignored. It ignores any cash flows that occur after the project has paid for itself. A project that takes time to get off the ground but earns substantial profits once established might be rejected if the payback method is used.

3.4 A more scientific method of investment appraisal is the use of **discounted cash flow** (DCF) techniques. Before DCF can be understood it is necessary to know something about the **time value of money**.

4 THE TIME VALUE OF MONEY

4.1 Money is spent to earn a profit. For example, if an item of machinery costs £6,000 and would earn profits (ignoring depreciation) of £2,000 per year for three years, it would not be worth buying because its total profit (£6,000) would only just cover its cost.

4.2 Clearly, items of capital expenditure must earn profits or make savings to justify their costs. Also, the size of profits or return must be sufficiently large to justify the investment. In the example given in the previous paragraph, if the machinery costing £6,000 made total profits of £6,300 over three years, the return on the investment would be £300, or an average of £100 per year. This would be a very low return, because it would be much more profitable to invest the £6,000 somewhere else (for example on deposit at a bank).

4.3 If a capital investment is to be worthwhile, it must therefore earn at least a minimum profit or return so that the size of the return will compensate the investor (the business) for the **length** of time which the investor must wait before the profits are made. For example, if a company could invest £6,000 now to earn revenue of £6,300 in one week's time, a profit of £300 in seven days would be a very good return. If it takes three years to earn the revenue, however, the return would be very low.

4.4 When capital expenditure projects are evaluated, we should therefore decide whether the investment will make enough profits to allow for the 'time value' of capital tied up. The time value of money reflects people's **time preference** for £100 now over £100 at some time in the future. **DCF** (discounted cash flow), which we look at further below, is a technique which takes into account the time value of money.

5 RELEVANT COSTS AND PROJECT APPRAISAL

5.1 We looked at the distinction between **relevant costs** and **non-relevant costs** earlier in this Interactive Text. The fundamental principle is that **relevant costs should be used for decision making purposes.** This applies to capital project evaluation just as it does to other short-term business decisions.

ASSESSMENT ALERT

You will be expected to understand clearly the principles of relevant and non-relevant costs and of cash flows in the context of capital expenditure appraisal. Look back at Chapter 5 to revise these principles if you are in any doubt.

Relevant costs are cash flows

5.2 Following the principles set out in Chapter 5, it is important to see that **relevant costs are cash flows**. Thus, we do not look at the amounts of costs accruing to particular periods. We look at the actual flows of cash.

Depreciation is a non-cash item

5.3 **Depreciation** is a non-cash item: it is a way of **allocating costs for accounting purposes**. Given that in long-term projects we will normally be considering items of capital expenditure on which depreciation is charged for accounting purposes, you need to be alert to the point that depreciation is a non-cash item - **it is not a cash flow**.

5.4 Disregarding taxation for the moment, the **actual cash flows** involved in ownership of a capital asset are typically:

(a) The initial expenditure (a **cash outflow**), and

(b) The eventual disposal proceeds, if any, for example on scrapping the asset (a **cash inflow**)

Activity 11.2

(a) Explain why depreciation is generally considered not to be relevant to making project appraisal decisions.

(b) What method sometimes used for project appraisal (and covered earlier in this chapter) nevertheless does take into account depreciation? Explain your answer briefly.

Activity 11.3

A customer has asked whether your company would be willing to undertake a contract for him. The work would involve the use of certain equipment for five hours and its running costs would be £2 per hour. However, your company faces heavy demand for usage of the equipment which earns a contribution of £7 per hour from this other work. If the contract is undertaken, some of this work would have to be forgone.

Task

Explain briefly what is the opportunity cost of using the equipment and explain the relevance of this to the decision about whether to undertake the contract. How much should the contract under consideration be expected to earn?

6 DISCOUNTING AND COMPOUND INTEREST

6.1 If we were to invest £1,000 now in a bank account which pays interest of 10% per annum, with interest calculated once each year at the end of the year, we would expect the following returns.

(a) After one year, the investment would rise in value to:

£1,000 plus 10% = £1,000 (1 + 10%) = £1,000 × (1.10) = £1,100

Interest for the year would be £100. We can say that the rate of **simple interest** is 10%.

(b) If we keep all our money in the bank account, after two years the investment would now be worth:

£1,100 × 1.10 = £1,210.

Interest in year two would be £(1,210 − 1,100) = £110.

Another way of writing this would be to show how the original investment has earned interest over two years as follows.

£1,000 × (1.10) × (1.10) = £1,000 × (1.10)² = £1,210

(c) Similarly, if we keep the money invested for a further year, the investment would grow to £1,000 × (1.10) × (1.10) × (1.10) = £1,000 × (1.10)³ = £1,331 at the end of the third year. Interest in year three would be £(1,331 − 1,210) = £121.

6.2 This example shows, in a different way to that given earlier in this text, how **compound interest** works. The amount of interest earned each year gets larger because we earn interest on both the original capital and also on the interest now earned in earlier years.

6.3 A formula which can be used to show the value of an investment after several years which earns compound interest is:

$$S = P(1 + r)^n$$

where

S = future value of the investment after n years
P = the amount invested now
r = the rate of interest, as a proportion. For example, 10% = 0.10, 25% = 0.25, 8% = 0.08
n = the number of years of the investment

6.4 For example, suppose that we invest £2,000 now at 10%. What would the investment be worth after the following number of years?

(a) Five years
(b) Six years

The future value of £1 after n years at 10% interest is given in the following table.

n	$(1 + r)^n$ with $r = 0.10$
1	1.100
2	1.210
3	1.331
4	1.464
5	1.611
6	1.772
7	1.949

6.5 The solution is as follows.

(a) *After five years*:

$$S = £2,000 (1.611)$$
$$= £3,222$$

(b) *After six years*:

$$S = £2,000 (1.772)$$
$$= £3,544$$

6.6 The principles of compound interest are used in discounted cash flow, except that discounting is compounding in reverse.

Discounting

6.7 With **discounting**, we look at the size of an investment after a certain number of years, and we calculate how much we would need to invest now to build up the investment to that size, given a certain rate of interest. This may seem complicated at first, and an example might help to make the point clear. With discounting, we can calculate how much we would need to invest now at an interest rate, of say, 6% to build up the investment to (say) £5,000 after four years.

6.8 The compound interest formula shows how we calculate a future sum S from a known current investment P, so that if $S = P (1 + r)^n$, then:

$$P = \frac{S}{(1+r)^n} = S \times \frac{1}{(1+r)^n}$$

This is the basic formula for discounting, which is sometimes written as: $P = S(1 + r)^{-n}$

[$(1 + r)^{-n}$ and $\frac{1}{(1+r)^n}$ mean exactly the same thing.]

6.9 To build up an investment to £5,000 after four years at 6% interest, we would need to invest now:

$$P = £5,000 \times \frac{1}{(1 + 0.06)^4}$$

$$= £5,000 \times 0.792 = £3,960$$

Further examples of discounting

6.10 If you have not done any discounting before, the basic principle and mathematical techniques might take some time to get used to. The following examples might help to make them clearer.

(a) A businessman wants to have £13,310 in three years' time, and has decided to put some money aside now which will earn interest of 10% per annum. How much money must he put aside in order to build up the investment to £13,310 as required?

Answer $P = £13,310 \times \frac{1}{(1.10)^3} = £10,000$

Proof

After one year the investment would be worth £10,000 × 1.10 = £11,000; after two years it would be £11,000 × 1.10 = £12,100; and after three years it would be £12,100 × 1.10 = £13,310.

(b) Another businessman has two sons who are just 18 years and 17 years old. He wishes to give them £10,000 each on their 20th birthdays and he wants to know how much he must invest now at 8% interest to pay this amount.

The following table is relevant, giving values r = 8% or 0.08. Note that you can read the figures in the 'present value' column from the Present Value Table in the Appendix to this Study Text: look down the 8% column.

Year n	Future value of £1 $(1 + r)^n$	Present value of £1 $(1 + r)^{-n}$
1	1.080	0.926
2	1.166	0.857
3	1.260	0.794
4	1.360	0.735

The investment must provide £10,000 after two years for the elder son and £10,000 after three years for the younger son.

	After n years n =	Discount factor 8%		Amount provided £	Present value £
Elder son	2	0.857	×	10,000	8,570
Younger son	3	0.794	×	10,000	7,940
Total investment required					16,510

Proof

After two years the investment of £16,510 will be worth £16,510 × 1.166 = £19,251. After paying £10,000 to the elder son, £9,251 will be left after two years. This will earn interest of 8% in year three, to be worth £9,251 × 1.08 = £9,991 at the end of the year. This is almost enough to pay £10,000 to the younger son. The difference (£9) is caused by rounding errors in the table of discount (present value) factors and compound (future value) factors.

(c) A company is wondering whether to invest £15,000 in a project which will pay £20,000 after two years. It will not invest unless the return from the investment is at least 10% per annum. Is the investment worthwhile?

The present value of £1 in two years time at 10% interest is 0.826.

Answer

The return of £20,000 after two years is equivalent to an investment now at 10% of £20,000 × 0.826 = £16,520.

In other words, in order to obtain £20,000 after two years, the company would have to invest £16,520 now at an interest rate of 10%. The project offers the same payment at a cost of only £15,000, so that it must provide a return in excess of 10% and it is therefore worthwhile.

	£
Present value of future profits at 10%	16,520
Cost of investment	15,000
The investment in the project offers the same return, but at a cost lower by	1,520

7   DISCOUNTED CASH FLOW

> **KEY TERM**
>
> **Discounted cash flow** is a technique of evaluating capital investment projects, using discounting arithmetic to determine whether or not they will provide a satisfactory return.

7.1   A typical investment project involves a payment of capital for fixed assets at the start of the project and then there will be profits coming in from the investment over a number of years.

7.2   The word **'profits'** however, is not really appropriate in DCF, for the following reasons.

(a)   The cost of a fixed asset is charged against profits each year as depreciation in the normal financial accounts. In DCF, however, depreciation must be ignored because the full cost of the asset is treated as a capital investment at the start of the project. It would be wrong to charge depreciation against profits as well because this would be 'double-counting' the cost.

(b)   The return on an investment only occurs when the investor receives payments in cash. There is a difference between accounting profits and cash receipts less cash payments and in DCF it is the cash flows which are considered more relevant. For example, suppose that a company makes profits of £5,000 before depreciation during one year, but in that time increases its debtors by £1,000. The cash received in the year would not be £5,000, but only £4,000. In DCF, the return for the year would be taken as the cash flow of £4,000, not the profit of £5,000.

7.3   DCF can be used in either of two ways.

(a)   The **net present value method**

(b)   The **internal rate of return** (sometimes called DCF yield, DCF rate of return) method

We will now look at each method in turn.

The net present value (NPV) method of DCF

7.4   The **net present value (NPV) method** of evaluation is as follows.

(a)   Determine the present value of costs. In other words, decide how much capital must be set aside to pay for the project. Let this be £C.

(b)   Calculate the present value of future cash benefits from the project. To do this we take the cash benefit in each year and discount it to a present value. This shows how much we would have to invest now to earn the future benefits, if our rate of return were equal to the cost of capital. ('Cost of capital' is explained below.) By adding up the present value of benefits for each future year, we obtain the total present value of benefits from the project. Let this be £B.

(c)   Compare the present value of costs £C with the present value of benefits £B. The net present value is the difference between them: £(B − C).

(d) If the NPV is positive, the present value of benefits exceeds the present value of costs. This in turn means that the project will earn a return in excess of the cost of capital. Therefore, the project should be accepted.

(e) If the NPV is negative, this means that it would cost us more to invest in the project to obtain the future cash receipts than it would cost us to invest somewhere else, at a rate of interest equal to the cost of capital, to obtain an equal amount of future receipts. The project would earn a return lower than the cost of capital and would not be worth investing in.

7.5 EXAMPLE: THE NPV METHOD

Suppose that a company is wondering whether to invest £18,000 in a project which would make extra profits (before depreciation is deducted) of £10,000 in the first year, £8,000 in the second year and £6,000 in the third year. Its cost of capital is 10% (in other words, it would require a return of at least 10% on its investment).

Task

Evaluate the project.

7.6 SOLUTION

In DCF we make several assumptions. One such assumption is that discounted cash flows (payments or receipts) occur on the last day of each year. For example, although profits are £10,000 during the course of year 1, we assume that the £10,000 is not received until the last day of year 1. Similarly, the profits of £8,000 and £6,000 in years 2 and 3 are assumed to occur on the last day of years 2 and 3 respectively. The cash payment of £18,000 occurs 'now' at the start of year 1. To be consistent, we say that this payment occurs on the last day of the current year which is often referred to as year 0.

The NPV is now calculated with discounting arithmetic. Note that the Present Value Table in the Appendix to this Text gives us the following values.

Year	Present value of £1	
n	$(1 + r)^{-n}$	where r = 0.10
1	0.909	
2	0.826	
3	0.751	

Year	Cash flow £	Present value factor 10%	Present value £
0	(18,000)	1.000	(18,000)
1	10,000	0.909	9,090
2	8,000	0.826	6,608
3	6,000	0.751	4,506
		NPV	2,204

The NPV is positive, which means that the project will earn more than 10%. (£20,204 would have to be invested now at 10% to earn the future cash flows; since the project will earn these returns at a cost of only £18,000 it must earn a return in excess of 10%.)

Activity 11.4

A project would involve a capital outlay of £24,000. Profits (before depreciation) each year would be £5,000 for six years. The cost of capital is 12%. Is the project worthwhile? (Use the Present Value Table in the Appendix.)

Discounted payback method

7.7 While we are discussing the **NPV** method, it is worth looking briefly at the related **discounted payback method**. We have seen how discounting cash flows is a way of reflecting the time value of money in investment appraisal. The further into the future a cash flow is expected to be, the more uncertain it tends to be, and the returns or interest paid to the suppliers of capital (ie to investors) in part reflect this uncertainty.

7.8 The **discounted payback technique** is an adaptation of the payback technique, which we looked at earlier, taking some account of the time value of money. To calculate the discounted payback period, we establish the time at which the net present value of an investment becomes positive.

7.9 EXAMPLE: DISCOUNTED PAYBACK PERIOD

We can calculate the discounted payback period for the example above (Paragraphs 7.5 and 7.6). Having produced a net present value analysis as in the solution above, we calculate the discounted payback period as follows.

Year	Present value	Cumulative PV
	£	£
0	(18,000)	(18,000)
1	9,090	(8,910)
2	6,608	(2,302)
3	4,506	2,204
	2,204	

7.10 SOLUTION

If we assume now that cash flows in year 3 are even, instead of occurring on the last day of the year, the discounted payback period can be estimated as follows.

Discounted payback period = 2 yrs + 2,302/4,506 yrs
= 2.51 yrs, say 2 ½ years

7.11 Note that this compares with a non-discounted payback period of 2 years for the same project, since the initial outlay of £18,000 is recouped in money terms by year 2.

The discounted payback period of 2½ years suggests that if the project must be terminated within that period, it will not have added value to the company.

Comparison with the basic payback method

7.12 Like the basic payback method, the discounted payback method fails to take account of positive cash flows occurring after the end of the payback period.

The cost of capital

7.13 We have mentioned that the appropriate discount rate to use in investment appraisal is the company's **cost of capital**. In practice, this is a difficult figure to determine. It is often suggested that the discount rate which a company should use as its cost of capital is one that reflects the return expected by its investors in shares and loan stock. Investors will expect to receive a return at least as high as that which they could receive from alternative investments with the same level of risk, and this level of return can be termed the **opportunity cost of finance.**

7.14 Shareholders expect dividends and capital gains; loan stock investors expect interest payments. A company must make enough profits from its own operations (and this includes capital expenditure projects) to pay dividends and interest. The average return is the weighted average of the return required by shareholders and loan stock investors. The cost of capital is therefore the **weighted average cost** of all the sources of capital which a company uses.

Annuities

7.15 In DCF the term 'annuities' refers to an annual cash payment which is the same amount every year for a number of years, or else an annual receipt of cash which is the same amount every year for a number of years.

In Activity 12.4, the profits are an annuity of £5,000 per annum for six years. The present value of profits (£20,560 as shown in the answer at the end of the chapter) is the present value of an annuity of £5,000 per annum for six years at a discount rate of 12%.

7.16 When there is an annuity to be discounted, there is a shortcut method of calculation. You may already have seen what it is.

Instead of multiplying the cash flow each year by the present value factor for that year, and then adding up all the present values (as shown in the solution above) we can multiply the annuity by the sum of the present value factors.

Thus we could have multiplied £5,000 by the sum of (0.893 + 0.797 + 0.712 + 0.636 + 0.567 + 0.507) = 4.112. We then have £5,000 × 4.112 = £20,560.

7.17 This quick calculation is made even quicker by the use of 'annuity' tables. These show the sum of the present value factors each year from year one to year n.

The Annuity Table in the Appendix to this Text shows the following.

Years n	*Present value of £1 received per year* $\dfrac{[1-(1+r)^{-n}]}{r}$	Notes
1	0.893	PV factor for year 1 only
2	1.690	(0.893 + 0.797)
3	2.402	(add 0.712)
4	3.038	(add 0.636)
5	3.605	(add 0.567)
6	4.112	(add 0.507)

7.18 EXAMPLE: ANNUITIES

A project would involve a capital outlay of £50,000. Profits (before depreciation) would be £12,000 per year. The cost of capital is 10%. Would the project be worthwhile if it lasts the following numbers of years?

(a) Five years
(b) Seven years

7.19 SOLUTION

We can find the discount factors from the Annuity Table in the Appendix.

(a) *If the project lasts five years*

Years	Cash flow £	Discount factor 10%	Present value £
0	(50,000)	1.000	(50,000)
1 - 5	12,000 pa	3.791	45,492
		NPV	(4,508)

(b) *If the project lasts seven years*

Years	Cash flow £	Discount factor 10%	Present value £
0	(50,000)	1.000	(50,000)
1 - 7	12,000 pa	4.868	58,416
		NPV	8,416

The project is not worthwhile if it last only five years, but it would be worthwhile if it lasted for seven years. The decision to accept or to reject the project must depend on management's view about its duration.

Activity 11.5

(a) A project would cost £39,500. It would earn £10,000 per year for the first three years and then £8,000 per year for the next three years. The cost of capital is 10%. Is the project worth undertaking?

(b) Another project would cost £75,820. If its life is expected to be five years and the cost of capital is 10%, what are the minimum annual savings required to make the project worthwhile?

Use the Annuity Table in the Appendix to derive your answers.

Working capital

7.20 You might be given a problem in which you are told that in addition to capital expenditure on plant and machinery, a project would require some investment in **working capital** (ie stocks and debtors). To understand how this situation would be treated in DCF, it is necessary to remember the following.

(a) An increase in working capital leads to a reduction in expected total cash receipts and a decrease in working capital leads to an increase in cash receipts.

(b) If a project needs working capital, the amount of capital required should be treated as an **outflow** (payment of cash), usually at the start of the project life (ie year 0).

(c) Once the project ends, the working capital will no longer be needed and can be reduced to zero. This will cause an additional inflow of cash, usually in the last year of the project.

7.21 EXAMPLE: WORKING CAPITAL

A project would involve the purchase of some plant for £25,000 and an investment in working capital of £6,000. It would earn £10,000 per year for four years. The cost of capital is 9%. Is the project worthwhile?

7.22 SOLUTION

Year		Cash flow £	Discount factor 9%	Present value ££
0	Plant	(25,000)	1.000	(25,000)
0	Working capital increase	(6,000)	1.000	(6,000)
1-4		10,000pa	3.239	32,390
4	Working capital decrease	6,000	0.708	4,248
			NPV	5,638

The NPV is positive and the project is worthwhile. Note that the net cost of the working capital invested makes a difference of £(6,000 − 4,248) = £1,752 to the NPV.

Internal rate of return (IRR)

7.23 Using the NPV method of discounted cash flow, present values are calculated by discounting at a target rate of return, or cost of capital, and the difference between the PV of costs and the PV of benefits is the NPV. In contrast, the **internal rate of return (IRR)** method is to calculate the exact DCF rate of return which the project is expected to achieve, in other words the rate at which the NPV is zero.

7.24 The internal rate of return method involves two steps.

(a) Calculating the rate of return which is expected from a project

(b) Comparing the rate of return with the cost of capital

> **KEY TERM**
>
> The **internal rate of return** is the rate of return that a project is expected to achieve. This can be found as the discount rate at which the net present value of the project is zero.

7.25 (a) If a project earns a higher rate of return than the cost of capital, it will be worth undertaking (and its NPV would be positive).

(b) If it earns a lower rate of return, it is not worthwhile (and its NPV would be negative).

(c) If a project earns a return which is exactly equal to the cost of capital, its NPV will be 0 and it will only just be worthwhile.

BPP PUBLISHING

Calculating the internal rate of return: example

7.26 Suppose that a project would cost £20,000 and the annual net cash inflows are expected to be as follows. What is the internal rate of return of the project?

Year	Cash flow
	£
1	8,000
2	10,000
3	6,000
4	4,000

7.27 The IRR is a rate of interest at which the NPV is 0 and the discounted (present) values of benefits add up to £20,000.

7.28 We need to find out what interest rate or cost of capital would give an NPV of 0. The way we do this is to guess what it might be, and calculate the NPV at this cost of capital. It is most unlikely that the NPV will turn out to be 0, but we are hoping that it will be nearly 0.

7.29 We repeat this exercise until we find two rates of return.

(a) One at which the NPV is a small positive value (The actual IRR will be higher than this rate of return.)

(b) One at which the NPV is a small negative value (The actual IRR will be lower than this rate of return.)

The actual IRR will then be found (approximately) by using the two rates in (a) and (b).

7.30 In our example (above), we might begin by trying discount rates of 10%, 15% and 20%.

Year	Cash flow	Discount factor at 10%	Present value at 10%	Discount factor at 15%	Present value at 15%	Discount factor at 20%	Present value at 20%
	£		£		£		£
0	(20,000)	1.000	(20,000)	1.000	(20,000)	1.000	(20,000)
1	8,000	0.909	7,272	0.870	6,960	0.833	6,664
2	10,000	0.826	8,260	0.756	7,560	0.694	6,940
3	6,000	0.751	4,506	0.658	3,948	0.579	3,474
4	4,000	0.683	2,732	0.572	2,288	0.482	1,928
Net present value			2,770		756		(994)

The IRR is more than 15% but less than 20%. We could try to be more accurate by trying a discount rate of 16%, 17%, 18% or 19%, but in this solution we will use the values for 15% and 20% to estimate the IRR.

7.31 To estimate the IRR, we now assume that the NPV falls steadily and at a constant rate between £756 at 15% and £(994) at 20%. This represents a fall of £(756 + 994) = £1,750 in NPV between 15% and 20%. This is an average fall of:

$$\frac{£1,750}{(20-15)\%} = £350 \text{ in NPV for each 1\% increase in the discount rate.}$$

Since the IRR is where the NPV is 0, it must be $\frac{£756}{£350} \times 1\%$ above 15%, ie about 2.2% above 15% = 17.2%.

A formula for the IRR

7.32 A formula for making this calculation (which is known as **interpolation**) is as follows.

$$IRR = A + \left[\frac{a}{a + b} \times (B - A) \right]$$

where   A   is the discount rate which provides the positive NPV
           a   is the amount of the positive NPV
           B   is the discount rate which provides the negative NPV
           b   is the amount of the negative NPV but the minus sign is ignored

7.33 In our example, using this formula, the IRR would be calculated as follows.

$$15\% + \left[\frac{756}{756 + 994} \times (20 - 15) \right]\%$$

$$= \quad 15\% + [\, 0.432 \times 5\,]\%$$
$$= \quad 15\% + 2.16\%$$
$$= \quad 17.16\%, \text{ say } 17.2\%$$

NPV is preferable to IRR

7.34 An **advantage** of the IRR method is that it is fairly easily understood since it is expressed in percentage terms. However, a major **disadvantage** is that IRR ignores the relative size of investments. A larger project may be preferable to a much smaller one because it generates more revenue or saves more costs, even though the IRR of the much smaller project may be higher. The IRR method can also be ambiguous where the direction of cash flows varies during the course of a project. The **NPV method** is to be preferred to the **IRR method**, as it gives clear and ambiguous results.

8   ALLOWING FOR INFLATION

8.1 We now consider briefly the effect of **inflation** on the appraisal of capital investment proposals. As we saw earlier, inflation refers to a sustained increase in the level of prices over a period of time. As the inflation rate increases so will the minimum return required by an investor. For example, you might be happy with a return of 5% in an inflation-free world, but if inflation was running at 15% you would expect a considerably greater yield.

ASSESSMENT ALERT

You won't be expected to carry out detailed calculations of a net present value involving inflation - but looking at some examples involving calculations will help you understand the points involved.

BPP
PUBLISHING

8.2 EXAMPLE: INFLATION (1)

A company is considering investing in a project with the following cash flows.

Time	Actual cash flows
	£
0	(15,000)
1	9,000
2	8,000
3	7,000

The company requires a minimum return of 20% under the present and anticipated conditions. Inflation is currently running at 10% a year, and this rate of inflation is expected to continue indefinitely. Should the company go ahead with the project?

8.3 Let us first look at the company's required rate of return. Suppose that it invested £1,000 for one year on 1 January, then on 31 December it would require a minimum return of £200. With the initial investment of £1,000, the total value of the investment by 31 December must therefore increase to £1,200. During the course of the year the purchasing value of the pound would fall due to inflation. We can restate the amount received on 31 December in terms of the purchasing power of the pound at 1 January as follows.

Amount received on 31 December in terms of the value of the pound at 1 January

$$= \frac{£1,200}{(1.10)^1} = £1,091$$

8.4 In terms of the value of the pound at 1 January, the company would make a profit of £91 which represents a rate of return of 9.1% in 'today's money' terms. This is known as the real rate of return. The required rate of 20% is a money rate of return (sometimes called a nominal rate of return). The money rate measures the return in terms of the pound which is, of course, falling in value. The real rate measures the return in constant price level terms.

The two rates of return and the inflation rate are linked by the equation:

$$\boxed{(1 + \text{money rate})} = \boxed{(1 + \text{real rate})} \times \boxed{(1 + \text{inflation rate})}$$

where all the rates are expressed as proportions.

In our example: $(1 + 0.20) = (1 + 0.091) \times (1 + 0.10) = 1.20$

Which rate is used in discounting?

8.5 We must decide which rate to use for discounting, the real rate or the money rate. The rule is as follows.

(a) If the cash flows are expressed in terms of the actual number of pounds that will be received or paid on the various future dates, we use the **money rate** for discounting.

(b) If the cash flows are expressed in terms of the value of the pound at time 0 (that is, in constant price level terms), we use the **real rate**.

8.6 The cash flows given in Paragraph 8.2 are expressed in terms of the actual number of pounds that will be received or paid at the relevant dates. We should, therefore, discount them using the money rate of return.

Time	Cash flow £	Discount factor 20%	PV £
0	(15,000)	1.000	(15,000)
1	9,000	0.833	7,497
2	8,000	0.694	5,552
3	7,000	0.579	4,053
			2,102

The project has a positive net present value of £2,102.

8.7 The future cash flows can be re-expressed in terms of the value of the pound at time 0 as follows, given inflation at 10% a year.

Time	Actual cash flow £	Cash flow at time 0 price level		£
0	(15,000)			(15,000)
1	9,000	$9,000 \times \dfrac{1}{1.10}$	=	8,182
2	8,000	$8,000 \times \dfrac{1}{(1.10)^2}$	=	6,612
3	7,000	$7,000 \times \dfrac{1}{(1.10)^3}$	=	5,259

8.8 The cash flows expressed in terms of the value of the pound at time 0 can now be discounted using the real rate of 9.1%.

Time	Cash flow £	Discount factor 9.1%	PV £
0	(15,000)	1.00	(15,000)
1	8,182	$\dfrac{1}{1.091}$	7,500
2	6,612	$\dfrac{1}{(1.091)^2}$	5,555
3	5,259	$\dfrac{1}{(1.091)^3}$	4,050
		NPV	2,105

8.9 The NPV is the same as before (and the present value of the cash flow in each year is the same as before) apart from rounding errors with a net total of £3.

The real rate of interest and the money rate of interest

8.10 In practice the **nominal or money rate** of interest or return is the **market rate** of interest or market rate of return. This is evident from the way in which rates of interest tend to rise whenever inflation rises. The real rate of return is not consciously used by investors, whose investment decisions are based on money rates of interest and the future money values of dividends and capital growth.

8.11 We must use the money rate of interest in our calculations when the money rate is below the rate of inflation, as it has been occasionally in the UK in the past, when the rate of inflation has been very high. When this occurs, the effective real rate of interest is negative and by investing his money, an investor's wealth will decline

BPP PUBLISHING

in purchasing power. Even so, an investor might prefer to invest some of his wealth now, even at a negative rate of interest, for the following reasons.

(a) There is a limit to the amount of money he wishes to spend now. It is better to invest any surplus funds now to earn some interest than to hold cash which earns nothing.

(b) There may be no better investments elsewhere offering a higher return at a satisfactory level of risk.

Costs and benefits which inflate at different rates

8.12 Not all costs and benefits will rise in line with the general level of inflation. In such cases, we can apply the money rate to inflated values to determine a project's NPV.

8.13 EXAMPLE: INFLATION (2)

Rice Ltd is considering a project which would cost £5,000 now. The annual benefits, for four years, would be a fixed income of £2,500 a year, plus other savings of £500 a year in year 1, rising by 5% each year because of inflation. Running costs will be £1,000 in the first year, but would increase at 10% each year because of inflating labour costs. The general rate of inflation is expected to be 7½% and the company's required money rate of return is 16%. Evaluate whether the project is worthwhile, ignoring taxation.

8.14 SOLUTION

The cash flows at inflated values are as follows.

Year	Fixed income £	Other savings £	Running costs £	Net cash flow £
1	2,500	500	1,000	2,000
2	2,500	525	1,100	1,925
3	2,500	551	1,210	1,841
4	2,500	579	1,331	1,748

The NPV of the project is as follows.

Year	Cash flow £	Discount factor 16%	PV £
0	(5,000)	1.000	(5,000)
1	2,000	0.862	1,724
2	1,925	0.743	1,430
3	1,841	0.641	1,180
4	1,748	0.552	965
			+ 299

The NPV is positive and the project would seem to be worthwhile.

Activity 11.6

The following information relates to two possible capital projects of which you have to select one to invest in. Both projects have an initial capital cost of £200,000 and only one can be undertaken. Profit is calculated after deducting straight line depreciation.

Project	X	Y
Expected profits	£	£
Year 1	80,000	30,000
2	80,000	50,000
3	40,000	90,000
4	20,000	120,000
Estimated resale value at end of Year 4	40,000	40,000

The cost of capital is 16%, relevant discount factors being as follows.

End of year	1	0.862
	2	0.743
	3	0.641
	4	0.552
	5	0.476

Tasks

(a) Calculate:

    (i)   The payback period to one decimal place
    (ii) The accounting rate of return using average investment
    (iii) The net present value

(b) Advise the board which project in your opinion should be undertaken, giving reasons for your decision.

Activity 11.7

Explain what is meant by the term 'cost of capital' and why is it important in coming to an investment decision.

---

9 TAXATION AND PROJECT APPRAISAL

9.1 The effect of **taxation** on capital budgeting is quite simple in theory. Organisations must pay tax, and the effect of undertaking a project will be to increase or decrease tax payments each year. These incremental tax cash flows should be included in the cash flows of the project for discounting to arrive at the project's NPV.

9.2 When taxation is ignored in the DCF calculations, the discount rate will reflect the pre-tax rate of return required on capital investments. When taxation is included in the cash flows, a post-tax required rate of return should be used.

ASSESSMENT ALERT

In any assessment involving taxation, check the rate of corporation tax which is assumed. For the tax year 2000/01, the main rate of corporation tax is 30%, with some companies qualifying for a lower rate.

Capital allowances

9.3 Capital allowances are used to reduce taxable profits, and the consequent reduction in a tax payment should be treated as a cash saving arising from the acceptance of a project.

BPP PUBLISHING

9.4 In the UK, writing down allowances are generally allowed on the cost of **plant and machinery** at the rate of 25% on a **reducing balance basis**. Thus if a company purchases plant costing £80,000, the subsequent writing down allowances would be as follows.

Year		Capital allowance £	Reducing balance £
1	(25% of cost)	20,000	60,000
2	(25% of RB)	15,000	45,000
3	(25% of RB)	11,250	33,750
4	(25% of RB)	8,438	25,312

When the plant is eventually sold, the difference between the sale price and the reducing balance amount at the time of sale will be treated as:

(a) A taxable profit if the sale price exceeds the reducing balance, and

(b) A tax allowable loss if the reducing balance exceeds the sale price

ASSESSMENT ALERT

Assessment questions often assume that this loss will be available immediately, though in practice the balance less the sale price continues to be written off at 25% a year as part of a pool balance unless the asset has been de-pooled.

The cash saving on the capital allowances (or the cash payment for the charge) is calculated by multiplying the allowance (or charge) by the corporation tax rate.

9.5 There are two possible assumptions about the time when capital allowances start to be claimed.

(a) It can be assumed that the first claim for capital allowances occurs at the start of the project (at year 0) and so the first tax saving occurs one year later (at year 1).

(b) Alternatively it can be assumed that the first claim for capital allowances occurs later in the first year, so the first tax saving occurs one year later, that is, year 2.

9.6 EXAMPLE: TAXATION AND PROJECT APPRAISAL

A company is considering the purchase of an item of equipment, which would earn profits before tax of £25,000 a year. Depreciation charges would be £20,000 a year for six years. Capital allowances would be £30,000 a year for the first four years. Corporation tax is at 30%.

Task

What would be the annual net cash inflows of the project:

(a) For the first four years

(b) For the fifth and sixth years

assuming that tax payments occur in the same year as the profits giving rise to them, and there is no balancing charge or allowance when the machine is scrapped at the end of the sixth year?

9.7 SOLUTION

(a)

	Years 1-4 £	Years 5-6 £
Profit before tax	25,000	25,000
Add back depreciation	20,000	20,000
Net cash inflow before tax	45,000	45,000
Less capital allowance	30,000	0
	15,000	45,000
Tax at 30%	4,500	13,500

Years 1 - 4 Net cash inflow after tax £45,000 – £4,500 = £40,500

(b) Years 5 - 6 Net cash inflow after tax = £45,000 – £13,500 = £31,500

Activity 11.8

A company is considering the purchase of a machine for £150,000. It would be sold after four years for an estimated realisable value of £50,000. By this time capital allowances of £120,000 would have been claimed. The rate of corporation tax is 30%.

Task
What are the tax implications of the sale of the machine at the end of four years?

---

10 PUBLIC SECTOR CAPITAL BUDGETING DECISIONS

10.1 There are differences between capital budgeting in the **public sector** and capital budgeting in the **private sector**.

10.2 Relatively few public sector capital investments are made with the intention of earning a financial return. Nationalised industries may be expected to earn profits on their investment, but spending on roads, hospitals, schools, the defence forces and the police service, nuclear waste dumps and so on are not made with an eye to profit and return.

10.3 When there are two or more ways of achieving the same objective the investment decision might to prefer the option with the lowest present value of cost. And if a cost-saving capital item is being considered for purchase, the decision might be to buy the item provided that the present value of savings exceeds the present value of costs. In these ways, capital budgeting decisions in the public sector might be based on financial considerations alone.

10.4 Rather than considering financial costs and benefits alone, capital budgeting decisions will often have regard to the **social costs** and the **social benefits** of investments. Social costs and benefits include non-financial aspects such as pollution (a cost) and better health (a benefit). An attempt can be made to quantify the social costs and social benefits in monetary terms, and to treat them as cash flows.

10.5 The **cost of capital** that is applied to project cash flows will not be a commercial rate of return, but one that is determined by the Treasury on behalf of the government.

Key learning points

- **Capital expenditure** results in the acquisition of fixed assets or an improvement in their earning capacity.

- **Revenue expenditure** is expenditure which is incurred for the purpose of the trade of the business or to maintain the existing earning capacity of fixed assets.

- A **long-term view** of benefits and costs must be taken when reviewing a capital expenditure project.

- The **accounting rate of return** method, sometimes called the **return on investment** method, calculates the estimated average profits as a percentage of the estimated average investment.

- The **payback period** is the time taken for the initial investment to be recovered in the cash inflows from the project. The payback method is particularly relevant if there are liquidity problems, or if distant forecasts are very uncertain.

- **Discounted cash flow** techniques take account of the **time value of money** - the fact that £1 received now is worth more because it could be invested to become a greater sum at the end of a year, and even more after the end of two years, and so on. As with payback, discounted cash flow techniques use **cash figures before depreciation** in the calculations.

- The **discounted payback method** applies discounting to arrive at a payback period after which the NPV becomes positive.

- **Annuities** are an annual cash payment or receipt which is the same amount every year for a number of years.

- The **net present value** method calculates the present value of all cash flows, and sums them to give the net present value. If this is positive, then the project is acceptable.

- The **internal rate of return** technique uses a trial and error method to discover the discount rate which produces the NPV of zero. This discount rate will be the return forecast for the project.

- **Inflation** is a feature of all economies, and it needs to be accommodated in financial planning. **Taxation** implications must also sometimes be considered.

- Capital budgeting decisions in the **public sector** are not often made with the intention of earning profits. Social costs and social benefits can be very important in public sector investment appraisals.

Quick quiz

1   What is a fixed asset?
2   What is revenue expenditure?
3   What is the formula usually used for calculating the accounting rate of return?
4   What is the payback period?
5   What is the yardstick for acceptance of projects when using the net present value method?
6   What is the discounted payback period?
7   What is the cost of capital?
8   What are the two steps involved in calculating the internal rate of return?
9   What is the relationship between the money rate of return, the real rate of return and the rate of inflation?

Answers to quick quiz

1   An asset normally used over more than one accounting period, acquired to earn profits for the enterprise.

2   Expenditure earned for the purpose of the trade or to maintain the earning capacity of fixed assets.

3    $\text{ARR} = \dfrac{\text{Estimated average profits}}{\text{Estimated average investment}} \times 100\%$

4   The length of time required before the total of the cash inflows received from the project is equal to the original cash outlay.

5   Accept the project if the net present value is positive.

6   The time after which the net present value of an investment becomes positive.

7   The weighted average cost of all sources of capital for an enterprise, used as the discount rate in investment appraisal.

8   Firstly, calculate the rate of return expected; secondly, compare the rate of return with the cost of capital.

9   (1 + money rate) = (1 + real rate) × (1 + inflation rate).

Answers to activities

Answer 11.1

(a)   If capital expenditure is treated as revenue expenditure, profits will be understated in the profit and loss account and fixed assets will be understated in the balance sheet.

(b)   If revenue expenditure is treated as capital expenditure, then the profits for the period will be overstated in the profit and loss account and fixed assets will be overstated in the balance sheet.

Answer 11.2

(a)   Depreciation is a way of allocating capital expenditure over future periods for accounting purposes. It does not reflect additional cash spent, and so is not a relevant cost.

(b)   The accounting rate of return method is based on accounting profits and therefore takes account of depreciation.

Answer 11.3

The contribution obtainable from putting the scarce resource to its alternative use is its opportunity cost (sometimes referred to as its 'internal' opportunity cost).

Quite simply, since the equipment can earn £7 per hour in an alternative use, the contract under consideration should also be expected to earn at least the same amount.

This can be accounted for by charging the £7 per hour as an opportunity cost to the contract and the total relevant cost of 5 hours of equipment time would be:

	£
Running costs (5 × £2)	10
Internal opportunity cost (5 × £7)	35
Relevant cost	45

The variable running costs of the equipment are included in the total relevant cost.

BPP PUBLISHING

Answer 11.4

Years	Cash flow £	Present value factor	Present value £	£
0	(24,000)	1.000		(24,000)
1	5,000	0.893	4,465	
2	5,000	0.797	3,985	
3	5,000	0.712	3,560	
4	5,000	0.636	3,180	
5	5,000	0.567	2,835	
6	5,000	0.507	2,535	
			20,560	
		NPV		(3,440)

The NPV is negative and so the project is not worthwhile.

Answer 11.5

(a)

Present value of £1 per annum, years 1-6	4.355
Less present value of £1 per annum, years 1-3	2.487
Gives present value of £1 per annum, years 4-6	1.868

Year	Cash flow £	Discount factor 10%	Present value £
0	(39,500)	1.000	(39,500)
1 - 3	10,000 pa	2.487	24,870
4 - 6	8,000 pa	1.868	14,944
		NPV	314

The NPV is positive, but only just (£314). The project therefore promises a return a little above 10%.

If we are confident that the estimates of cost and benefits for the next six years are accurate, the project is worth undertaking. However, if there is some suspicion that earnings may be a little less than the figures shown, it might be prudent to reject it.

(b) The project will just be worthwhile if the NPV is 0. For the NPV to be 0 the present value of benefits must equal the present value of costs, £75,820.

PV of benefits = annual savings × present value of £1 per year for 5 years (at 10%)

£75,820 = annual savings × 3.791

Annual savings = $\frac{£75,820}{3.791}$ = £20,000

This example shows that annuity tables can be used to calculate an annual cash flow from a given investment.

Answer 11.6

(a) Depreciation must be added back to the profits for each year to determine the cash flow for appraisal purposes.

Annual depreciation = $\frac{£200,000 - £40,000}{4}$

= £40,000 per annum

(i) *Payback period*

	Year	Project X £'000	Project Y £'000
Cash flows	1	120	70
	2	120	90
	3	80	130
4 Project	4	60	160
Resale value		40	40
Payback period		1 + (80/120) years = 1.7 years	2 + (40/130) years = 2.3 years

(ii) *Accounting rate of return*

The accounting profits are given in the question and we need to calculate the average over the four years. The average investment will be the same for both projects.

$$\text{Average investment} = \frac{£200,000 + £40,000}{2} = £120,000$$

	Year	Project X £'000	Project Y £'000
Accounting profits	1	80	30
	2	80	50
	3	40	90
	4	20	120
		220	290
Average (÷ 4)		55	72.5
Average investment		120	120
∴ Average accounting rate of return		$\left(\frac{55}{120}\right)$ 45.8%	$\left(\frac{72.5}{120}\right)$ 60.4%

(iii) *Using the cash flows from (i)*

Year	Discount factor 16%	Project X Cash flow £'000	Project X Present value £'000	Project Y Cash flow £'000	Project Y Present value £'000
1	0.862	120	103.44	70	60.34
2	0.743	120	89.16	90	66.87
3	0.641	80	51.28	130	83.33
4	0.552	100	55.20	200	110.40
			299.08		320.94
Initial capital cost			200.00		200.00
Net present value			99.08		120.94

(b) Project Y should be undertaken because it gives the highest net present value. This is a more important measure than the accounting rate of return because it takes account of the timing of cash flows and the time value of money. However the directors should bear in mind that project Y has a longer payback period which can lead to increased risk and reduced liquidity.

Answer 11.7

The cost of capital is the cost to the company of raising finance for capital expenditure projects, that is the cost of shareholders capital and the cost of any loans raised.

It is important in an investment decision because it is the minimum return that a project should earn. If a project does not earn a return which is at least equal to the cost of funds invested in it then it is not worthwhile.

Answer 11.8

There will be a balancing charge on the sale of the machine of £(50,000 – (150,000 – 120,000)) = £20,000. This will give rise to a tax payment of 30% × £20,000 = £6,000.

12 Analysing risk

Chapter topic list

1   Risk and why it arises

2   Sensitivity analysis

3   Probability analysis

4   Decision trees

Learning objectives

On completion of this chapter you will be able to:

	Performance criteria	Range statement
• Apply risk analysis techniques		16.2.3
• Calculate expected monetary values		16.2.3
• Analyse critical factors which may affect costs and revenues, using appropriate accounting techniques	16.2.2	

BPP PUBLISHING

1 RISK AND WHY IT ARISES

KEY TERMS

The term **risk** can be applied to a situation where there are several possible outcomes and, on the basis of past relevant experience, probabilities can be assigned to the various outcomes that could prevail.

The term **uncertainty** can be applied to a situation where there are several possible outcomes but there is little past relevant experience to enable the probability of the possible outcomes to be predicted.

1.1 A **risky** situation is one where we can say that there is a 70% probability that returns from a project will be in excess of £100,000 but a 30% probability that returns will be less than £100,000. If no information can be provided on the returns from the project, we are faced with an **uncertain** situation.

1.2 In general, risky projects are those whose future cash flows, and hence the projects returns, are likely to be variable - the greater the variability, the greater the risk. The problem of risk is more acute with capital investment decisions than other decisions for the following reasons.

(a) Estimates of capital expenditure might be for up to several years ahead, such as for major construction projects, and all too often with long-term projects, actual costs escalate well above budget as the work progresses.

(b) Estimates of benefits will be for up to several years ahead, sometimes 10, 15 or 20 years ahead or even longer, and such long-term estimates can at best be approximations.

Why are projects risky?

1.3 A decision about whether or not to go ahead with a project is based on expectations about the future. Forecasts of cash flows are made, however, on the basis of what is expected to happen given the present state of knowledge and the future is, by definition, uncertain. Actual cash flows are almost certain to differ from prior expectations. It is this uncertainty about a project's future income and costs that give rise to risk in business generally and investment activity in particular.

2 SENSITIVITY ANALYSIS

KEY TERM

Sensitivity analysis is one method of analysing the risk surrounding a capital expenditure project and enables an assessment to be made of how responsive the project's net present value (NPV) is to changes in the variables that are used to calculate that NPV.

2.1 The NPV could depend on a number of uncertain independent variables.

(a) Estimated selling price

(b)   Estimated sales volume
(c)   Estimated cost of capital
(d)   Estimated initial cost
(e)   Estimated operating costs
(f)   Estimated benefits

2.2   The basic approach of **sensitivity analysis** is to calculate the project's NPV under alternative assumptions to determine how sensitive it is to changing conditions. An indication is thus provided of those variables to which the NPV is most sensitive (critical variables) and the extent to which those variables may change before the investment results in a negative NPV.

2.3   Sensitivity analysis therefore provides an indication of why a project might fail. Once these critical variables have been identified, management should review them to assess whether or not there is a strong possibility of events occurring which will lead to a negative NPV. Management should also pay particular attention to controlling those variables to which the NPV is particularly sensitive, once the decision has been taken to accept the investment.

2.4   EXAMPLE: SENSITIVITY ANALYSIS

Nevers Ure Ltd is considering a project with the following cash flows.

Year	Purchase of plant £	Running costs £	Savings £
0	(7,000)		
1		2,000	6,000
2		2,500	7,000

Measure the sensitivity (in percentages) of the project to changes in the levels of expected costs and savings, assuming that the cost of capital is 8%.

2.5   SOLUTION

The PVs of the cash flows are as follows.

Year	Discount factor 8%	PV of plant cost £	PV of running costs £	PV of savings £	PV of net cash flow £
0	1.000	(7,000)			(7,000)
1	0.926		(1,852)	5,556	3,704
2	0.857		(2,143)	5,999	3,856
		(7,000)	(3,995)	11,555	560

The project has a positive NPV and would appear to be worthwhile. The changes in cash flows which would need to occur for the project to break even (NPV = 0) are as follows.

(a)   Plant costs would need to increase by a PV of £560, that is by $\dfrac{560}{7,000} = 8\%$

(b)   Running costs would need to increase by a PV of £560, that is by $\dfrac{560}{3,995} = 14\%$

(c)   Savings would need to fall by a PV of £560, that is by $\dfrac{560}{11,555} = 4.8\%$

Weaknesses of this approach to sensitivity analysis

2.6 (a) The method requires that changes in each key variable are isolated but management is more interested in the **combination of the effects of changes** in two or more key variables. Looking at factors in isolation is unrealistic since they are often interdependent.

(b) Sensitivity analysis does not examine the **probability** that any particular variation in costs or revenues might occur.

Activity 12.1

A company produces only one type of product. The budget for the year reveals the following.

Selling price per unit	£25
Variable cost per unit	£8
Total fixed cost	£210,000
Budgeted profit	£300,000

The level of profit is not regarded as acceptable and alternative proposals are put forward for evaluation.

Proposal	*Impact*
Reduce selling price by 10%	Increase sales volume by 6%
Increase selling price by 8%	Reduce sales volume by 4%

Tasks

(a) Calculate the breakeven point in sales volume and margin of safety in sales revenue for the budgeted figures.

(b) For the budgeted data, calculate by what percentage (to one decimal place) the selling price would have to change in order for a profit of £420,000 to be earned.

(c) Calculate for each proposal the profit for the year. (*Note.* You are required to present *two* sets of data. Each proposal is independent.)

3 PROBABILITY ANALYSIS

3.1 A **probability distribution** of expected cash flows can often be estimated, and this may be used to do the following.

(a) Calculate an **expected monetary value** of the NPV.

(b) Measure risk, for example in the following ways.

   (i) By calculating the worst possible outcome and its probability

   (ii) By calculating the probability that the project will fail to achieve a positive NPV

Let us look at an example.

3.2 EXAMPLE: PROBABILITY ESTIMATES OF CASH FLOWS

A company is considering a project involving the outlay of £300,000 which it estimates will generate cash flows over its two year life at the probabilities shown in the following table.

Cash flows for project

Year 1

Cash flow £	Probability
100,000	0.25
200,000	0.50
300,000	0.25
	1.00

Year 2

If cash flow in Year 1 is: £	there is a probability of:	that the cash flow in Year 2 will be: £
100,000	0.25	Nil
	0.50	100,000
	0.25	200,000
	1.00	
200,000	0.25	100,000
	0.50	200,000
	0.25	300,000
	1.00	
300,000	0.25	200,000
	0.50	300,000
	0.25	350,000
	1.00	

The company's investment criterion for this type of project is 10% DCF. Calculate the expected value (EV) of the project's NPV and the probability that the NPV will be negative.

3.3 SOLUTION

First we need to draw up a probability distribution of the expected cash flows. We begin by calculating the present values of the cash flows.

Year	Cash flow £'000	Discount factor 10%	Present value £'000
1	100	0.909	90.9
1	200	0.909	181.8
1	300	0.909	272.7
2	100	0.826	82.6
2	200	0.826	165.2
2	300	0.826	247.8
2	350	0.826	289.1

3.4   Next we set out the possible cash flows and their probabilities.

Year 1 PV of cash flow £'000	Proba- bility	Year 2 PV of cash flow £'000	Proba- bility	Joint probability	Total PV of cash inflows £'000	EV of PV of cash inflows £'000
(a)	(b)	(c)	(d)	(b) × (d)	(a) + (c)	
90.9	0.25	0	0.25	0.0625	90.9	5.6813
90.9	0.25	82.6	0.50	0.1250	173.5	21.6875
90.9	0.25	165.2	0.25	0.0625	256.1	16.0063
181.8	0.50	82.6	0.25	0.1250	264.4	33.0500
181.8	0.50	165.2	0.50	0.2500	347.0	86.7500
181.8	0.50	247.8	0.25	0.1250	429.6	53.7000
272.7	0.25	165.2	0.25	0.0625	437.9	27.3688
272.7	0.25	247.8	0.50	0.1250	520.5	65.0625
272.7	0.25	289.1	0.25	0.0625	561.8	35.1125
						344.4189

	£
EV of PV of cash inflows	344,419
Less project cost	300,000
EV of NPV	44,419

3.5 Since the EV of the NPV is positive, the project should go ahead unless the risk is unacceptably high. (The probability that the project will have a negative NPV is the probability that the total PV of cash inflows is less than £300,000. From the column headed 'Total PV of cash inflows', we can establish that this probability is 0.0625 + 0.125 + 0.0625 + 0.125 = 0.375 or 37.5%. This might be considered an unacceptably high risk.)

3.6 The **disadvantage** of using the EV of NPV approach to assess the risk of the project is that the construction of the probability distribution can become very complicated. If we were considering a project over 4 years, each year having five different forecasted cash flows, there would be 625 (5^4) NPVs to calculate. To avoid all of these calculations, an indication of the risk may be obtained by calculating the standard deviation of the NPV.

Activity 12.2

Killary Ltd, a manufacturer of airbeds, believes that the probabilities of different levels of sales being achieved in the forthcoming year 20X6 are as follows.

Sales Units	Probability
40,000	0.2
50,000	0.5
60,000	0.3

Each unit sells for £15.

The expected cost of materials is as follows.

Cost per unit £	Probability
8	0.1
9	0.2
10	0.5
11	0.2

Materials are the only variable cost. All other costs are fixed and are expected to total £140,000.

Calculate for 20X6:

(a) The expected total value of sales (in units)

(b) The total expected cost of materials

(c) The expected value of

    (i) Contribution, and
    (ii) Profit.

4 DECISION TREES

4.1 When appraising a project using the NPV method, it is possible that, of the many variables which affect the NPV, more than one will be uncertain. The value of some variables may be dependent on the values of other variables. Many outcomes may therefore be possible and some outcomes may be dependent on previous outcomes. **Decision trees** are useful tools for clarifying the range of alternative courses of action and their possible outcomes.

4.2 There are two stages in preparing a decision tree.

Step 1 Drawing the tree itself, to show all the choices and outcomes

Step 2 Putting in the numbers: the probabilities, outcome values and EVs

Drawing a decision tree: the basic rules

4.3 Every decision tree starts from a decision point with the decision options that are currently being considered.

(a) There should be a line, or branch, for each option or alternative.

(b) It helps to identify the decision point, and any subsequent decision points in the tree, with a symbol. Here, we shall use a square shape.

4.4 It is conventional to draw decision trees from left to right, and so a decision tree will start as follows.

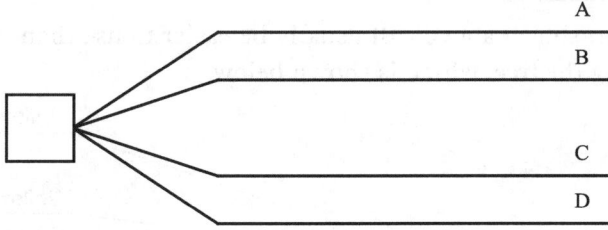

The square is the decision point, and A, B, C and D represent four alternatives from which a choice must be made.

4.5 If the outcome from any choice is **certain,** the branch of the decision tree for that alternative is complete. If, on the other hand, the outcome of a particular choice is **uncertain,** the various possible outcomes must be shown. We show this on a decision tree by inserting an outcome point on the branch of the tree. Each possible outcome is then shown as a subsidiary branch, coming out from the outcome point. The probability of each outcome occurring should be written on to the branch of the tree which represents that outcome.

4.6 To distinguish decision points from outcome points, a circle will be used as the symbol for an outcome point.

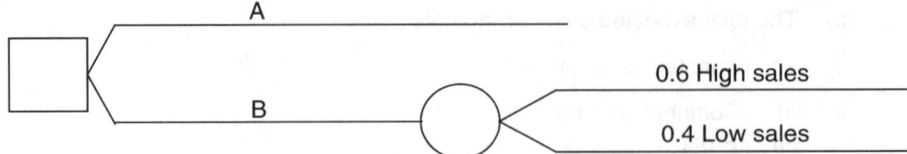

In the example above, there are two choices, A and B. The outcome if A is chosen is known with certainty, but if B is chosen, there are two possible outcomes, high returns (0.6 probability) or low returns (0.4 probability). When **several outcomes** are possible, it is usually simpler to show two or more stages of outcome points on the decision tree.

4.7 EXAMPLE: SEVERAL POSSIBLE OUTCOMES

A company can choose to invest in project XYZ or not. If the investment goes ahead, expected cash inflows and expected costs might be as follows.

Cash inflows £	Probability	Costs £	Probability
10,000	0.8	6,000	0.7
15,000	0.2	8,000	0.3

(a) The decision tree could be drawn as follows.

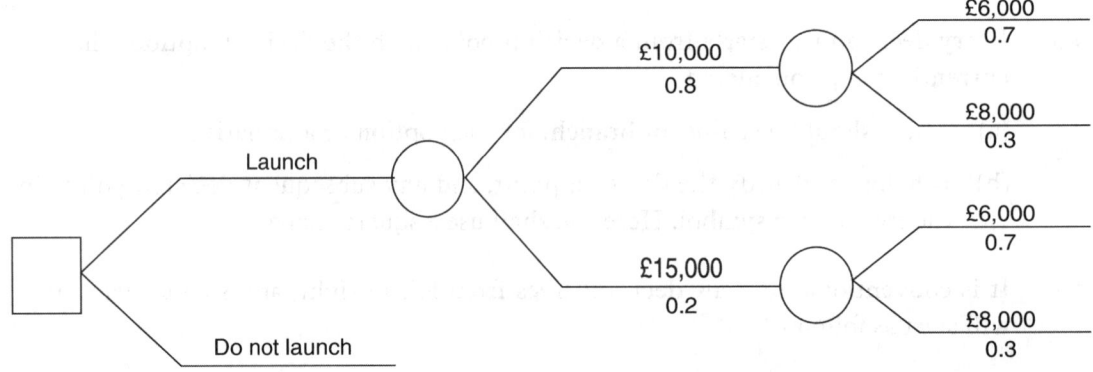

(b) The layout shown above will usually be easier to use than the alternative way of drawing the tree, which is shown below.

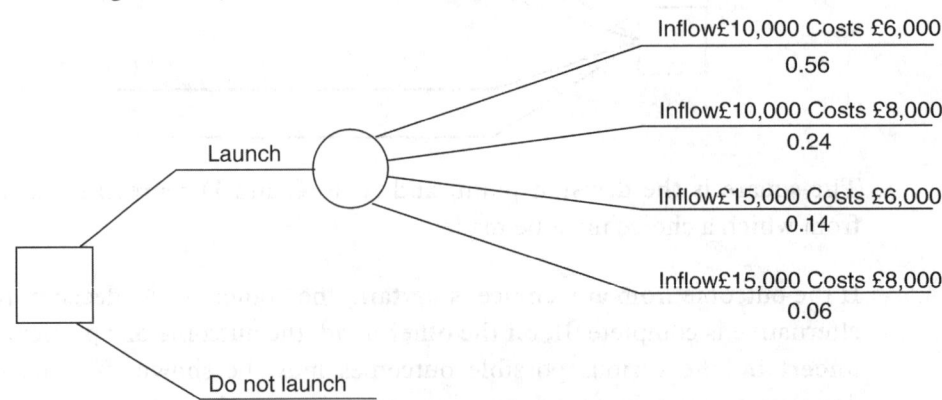

4.8 Sometimes, a decision taken now will lead to other decisions to be taken in the future. When this situation arises, the decision tree can be drawn as a two-stage tree, as follows.

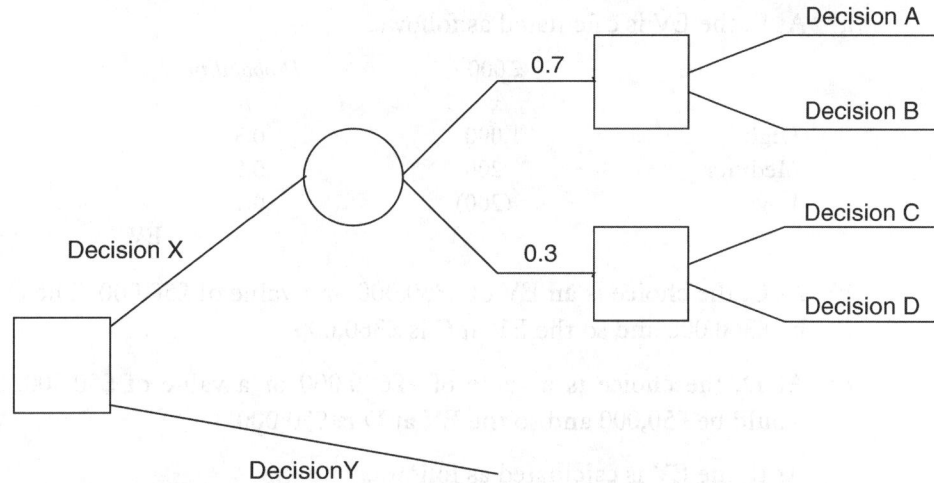

In this tree, either a choice between A and B or else a choice between C and D will be made, depending on the outcome which occurs after choosing X.

Activity 12.3

See if you can show the project cash flows for the example in Paragraph 3.2 on a decision tree.

Evaluating the decision with a decision tree

4.9 The EV of each decision option can be evaluated, using the decision tree to help with keeping the logic properly sorted out. The decision tree should be in chronological order from left to right. When there are two-stage decision trees, the first decision in time should be drawn on the left.

The basic rules are as follows.

(a) We start on the right hand side of the tree and work back towards the left hand side and the current decision under consideration.

(b) Working from right to left, we calculate the EV of revenue, cost, contribution or profit at each outcome point on the tree.

4.10 Consider the decision tree below.

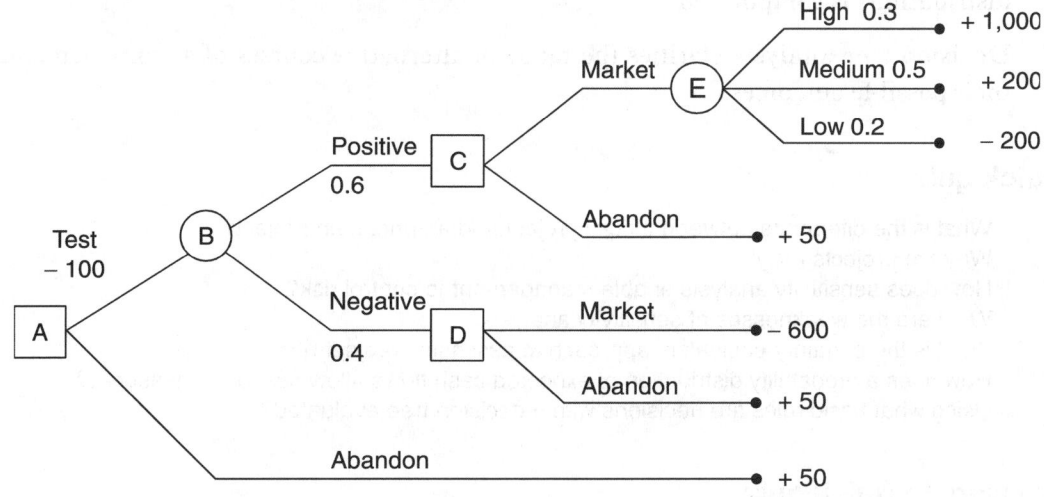

BPP
PUBLISHING

(a) At E, the EV is calculated as follows.

	£'000	*Probability*	
	x	*p*	*px*
High	1,000	0.3	300
Medium	200	0.5	100
Low	(200)	0.2	(40)
		EV	360

(b) At C, the choice is an EV of £360,000 or a value of £50,000. The choice would be £360,000 and so the EV at C is £360,000.

(c) At D, the choice is a value of –£600,000 or a value of £50,000. The choice would be £50,000 and so the EV at D is £50,000.

(d) At B, the EV is calculated as follows.

$$EV = (0.6 \times £360,000)\,(C) + (0.4 \times £50,000)\,(D) = £236,000$$

(e) At A, the choice is between an EV of £236,000 minus costs of £100,000 or a value of £50,000. The choice would be £136,000 and so the EV at A is £136,000.

Key learning points

- **Risk** can be applied to a situation where there are several possible outcomes and, on the basis of past relevant experience, probabilities can be assigned to the various outcomes that could prevail.

- **Uncertainty** can be applied to a situation where there are several possible outcomes but there is little past relevant experience to enable the probability of the possible outcomes to be predicted.

- There are a wide **range of techniques** for incorporating risk into project appraisal.

- **Sensitivity analysis** helps management decision making by assessing how responsive the project's NPV is to changes in the variables used to calculate that NPV.

- A **probability analysis** of expected cash flows can often be estimated and used both to calculate an expected NPV and to measure risk. The standard deviation of the NPV can be calculated to assess risk when the construction of probability distributions is complicated.

- **Decision tree analysis** clarifies the range of alternative courses of action open and their possible outcomes.

Quick quiz

1 What is the difference between a risky project and an uncertain project?
2 Why are projects risky?
3 How does sensitivity analysis enable management to control risk?
4 What are the weaknesses of sensitivity analysis?
5 What is the certainty-equivalent approach to assessing projects?
6 How does a probability distribution of expected cash flows allow risk to be measured?
7 Using what basic rules are decisions with a decision tree evaluated?

Answers to quick quiz

1 The term *risk* applies to a situation where there are several possible outcomes and, on the basis of past relevant experience, probabilities can be assigned to the various outcomes that

could prevail. The term *uncertainty* applies to a situation where there are several possible outcomes but there is little past relevant experience to enable the probability of the possible outcomes to be predicted.

2   Uncertainty about a project's future income and costs gives rise to risk in business generally and investment activity in particular.

3   The sensitivity analysis approach involves calculating the project's NPV under alternative assumptions to determine how sensitive it is to changing conditions. This indicates those variables to which the NPV is most sensitive (*critical variables*) and the extent to which those variables may change before the investment results in a negative NPV. Once critical variables have been identified, management should review them to assess whether or not there is a strong possibility of events occurring which will lead to a negative NPV. Management should also pay particular attention to controlling those variables to which the NPV is particularly sensitive, once the decision has been taken to accept the investment.

4   The sensitivity analysis method requires that changes in each key variable are isolated, while management is likely to be more interested in the combination of the effects of changes in two or more key variables. Looking at factors in isolation is unrealistic since they are often interdependent.

Furthermore, sensitivity analysis does not examine the probability that any particular variation in costs or revenues might occur.

5   This is a different approach to sensitivity analysis in which the expected cash flows of the project are converted to 'riskless equivalent' amounts. The greater the risk of an expected cash flow, the smaller the 'certainty-equivalent' value (for receipts) or the larger the certainty equivalent value (for payments).

6   By calculating the worst possible outcome and its probability or by calculating the probability that the project will fail to achieve a positive NPV, for example.

7   Start on the right hand side of the tree and work back towards the left hand side and the current decision under consideration.

Working from right to left, calculate the EV of revenue, cost, contribution or profit at each outcome point on the tree.

Answers to activities

Answer 12.1

(a)   Contribution per unit, from the budgeted figures £25 – £8   = £17

$$\text{Breakeven point} = \frac{\text{fixed costs}}{\text{contribution per unit}} \qquad = \frac{£210,000}{£17}$$

= 12,353 units

Budgeted profit	£300,000
Plus fixed costs	£210,000
Budgeted contribution	£510,000

$$\text{Budgeted sales volume} = \frac{\text{budgeted contribution}}{\text{contribution per unit}} = \frac{£510,000}{£17} = 30,000 \text{ units}$$

∴ Margin of safety = 30,000 units – 12,353 units   = 17,647 units

Margin of safety in sales revenue £25 × 17,647 units   = £441,175

(b)

	£
Budgeted profit for 30,000 units	300,000
Required profit	420,000
Required increase in sales value	120,000

Assuming that sales volume is to remain at 30,000 units, required increase in price per unit $= \dfrac{£120,000}{30,000}$

$= £4$

Percentage increase required £4 × 100% = 16%

(c)   *Proposal: reduce selling price by 10%*

	£
Selling price = £25 × 90%	22.50
Variable cost per unit	8.00
Contribution per unit	14.50

Sales volume = 30,000 × 106% = 31,800 units

	£
Total contribution	461,100
Less fixed costs	210,000
Revised profit	251,100

This proposal should not be adopted because it produces a lower profit than budgeted.

Proposal: increase selling price by 8%

	£
Selling price = £25 × 108%	27
Variable cost per unit	8
Contribution per unit	19

Sales volume = 30,000 × 96% = 28,800 units

	£
Total contribution (28,000 × £19)	547,200
Fixed costs	210,000
Revised profit	337,200

This is the most desirable of the two proposals because it produces a higher profit than budgeted.

Answer 12.2

(a)

Sales Units	Probability	Expected value Units
40,000	0.2	8,000
50,000	0.5	25,000
60,000	0.3	18,000
Total expected sales		51,000

(b)

Cost per unit £	Probability	Expected cost £
8	0.1	0.80
9	0.2	1.80
10	0.5	5.00
11	0.2	2.20
Expected cost of materials (per unit)		9.80

Total expected cost of materials = 51,000 × 9.80 = £499,800

(c)

	£	
Sales (51,000 × £15)	765,000	
Variable costs	499,800	
Expected contribution	265,200	(i)
Fixed costs	140,000	
Expected profit	125,200	(ii)

Answer 12.3 _____

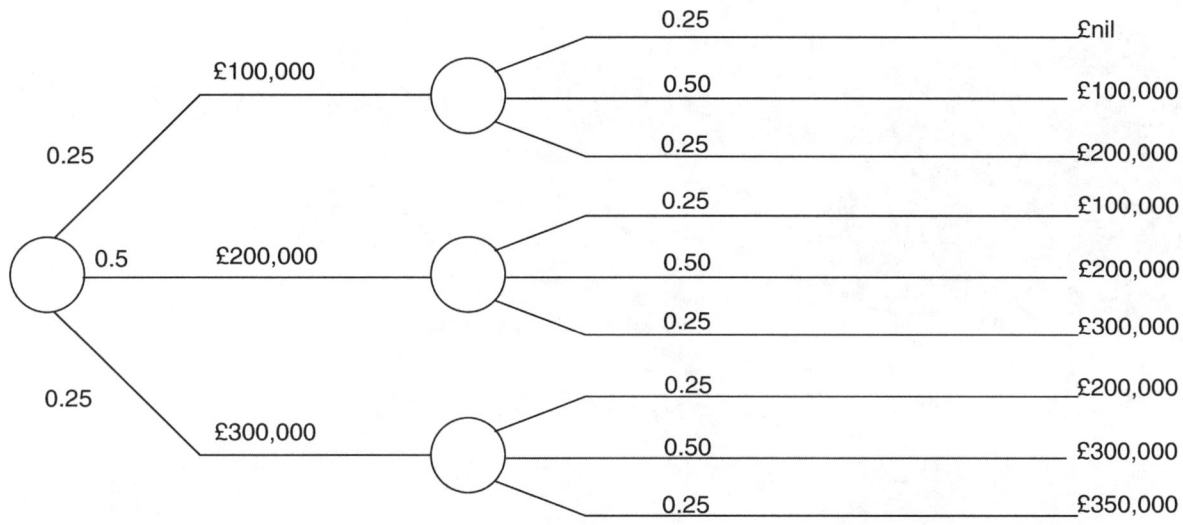

Year 1

Year 2

0.25	£100,000
0.5	£200,000
0.25	£300,000

Year 2 branches:

£100,000 node:
- 0.25 → £nil
- 0.50 → £100,000
- 0.25 → £200,000

£200,000 node:
- 0.25 → £100,000
- 0.50 → £200,000
- 0.25 → £300,000

£300,000 node:
- 0.25 → £200,000
- 0.50 → £300,000
- 0.25 → £350,000

Appendix
Present value tables

PRESENT VALUE TABLE

Present value of $1 = (1+r)^{-n}$ where r = discount rate, n = number of periods until payment

This table shows the present value of £1 per annum, receivable or payable at the end of *n* years.

Periods					Discount rates (r)					
(n)	1%	2%	3%	4%	5%	6%	7%	8%	9%	10%
1	0.990	0.980	0.971	0.962	0.952	0.943	0.935	0.926	0.917	0.909
2	0.980	0.961	0.943	0.925	0.907	0.890	0.873	0.857	0.842	0.826
3	0.971	0.942	0.915	0.889	0.864	0.840	0.816	0.794	0.772	0.751
4	0.961	0.924	0.888	0.855	0.823	0.792	0.763	0.735	0.708	0.683
5	0.951	0.906	0.863	0.822	0.784	0.747	0.713	0.681	0.650	0.621
6	0.942	0.888	0.837	0.790	0.746	0.705	0.666	0.630	0.596	0.564
7	0.933	0.871	0.813	0.760	0.711	0.665	0.623	0.583	0.547	0.513
8	0.923	0.853	0.789	0.731	0.677	0.627	0.582	0.540	0.502	0.467
9	0.914	0.837	0.766	0.703	0.645	0.592	0.544	0.500	0.460	0.424
10	0.905	0.820	0.744	0.676	0.614	0.558	0.508	0.463	0.422	0.386
11	0.896	0.804	0.722	0.650	0.585	0.527	0.475	0.429	0.388	0.350
12	0.887	0.788	0.701	0.625	0.557	0.497	0.444	0.397	0.356	0.319
13	0.879	0.773	0.681	0.601	0.530	0.469	0.415	0.368	0.326	0.290
14	0.870	0.758	0.661	0.577	0.505	0.442	0.388	0.340	0.299	0.263
15	0.861	0.743	0.642	0.555	0.481	0.417	0.362	0.315	0.275	0.239

	11%	12%	13%	14%	15%	16%	17%	18%	19%	20%
1	0.901	0.893	0.885	0.877	0.870	0.862	0.855	0.847	0.840	0.833
2	0.812	0.797	0.783	0.769	0.756	0.743	0.731	0.718	0.706	0.694
3	0.731	0.712	0.693	0.675	0.658	0.641	0.624	0.609	0.593	0.579
4	0.659	0.636	0.613	0.592	0.572	0.552	0.534	0.516	0.499	0.482
5	0.593	0.567	0.543	0.519	0.497	0.476	0.456	0.437	0.419	0.402
6	0.535	0.507	0.480	0.456	0.432	0.410	0.390	0.370	0.352	0.335
7	0.482	0.452	0.425	0.400	0.376	0.354	0.333	0.314	0.296	0.279
8	0.434	0.404	0.376	0.351	0.327	0.305	0.285	0.266	0.249	0.233
9	0.391	0.361	0.333	0.308	0.284	0.263	0.243	0.225	0.209	0.194
10	0.352	0.322	0.295	0.270	0.247	0.227	0.208	0.191	0.176	0.162
11	0.317	0.287	0.261	0.237	0.215	0.195	0.178	0.162	0.148	0.135
12	0.286	0.257	0.231	0.208	0.187	0.168	0.152	0.137	0.124	0.112
13	0.258	0.229	0.204	0.182	0.163	0.145	0.130	0.116	0.104	0.093
14	0.232	0.205	0.181	0.160	0.141	0.125	0.111	0.099	0.088	0.078
15	0.209	0.183	0.160	0.140	0.123	0.108	0.095	0.084	0.074	0.065

ANNUITY TABLE

Present value of an annuity of 1 ie $\dfrac{1-(1+r)^{-n}}{r}$

where   r = discount rate

n = number of periods

Periods					Discount rates (r)					
(n)	1%	2%	3%	4%	5%	6%	7%	8%	9%	10%
1	0.990	0.980	0.971	0.962	0.952	0.943	0.935	0.926	0.917	0.909
2	1.970	1.942	1.913	1.886	1.859	1.833	1.808	1.783	1.759	1.736
3	2.941	2.884	2.829	2.775	2.723	2.673	2.624	2.577	2.531	2.487
4	3.902	3.808	3.717	3.630	3.546	3.465	3.387	3.312	3.240	3.170
5	4.853	4.713	4.580	4.452	4.329	4.212	4.100	3.993	3.890	3.791
6	5.795	5.601	5.417	5.242	5.076	4.917	4.767	4.623	4.486	4.355
7	6.728	6.472	6.230	6.002	5.786	5.582	5.389	5.206	5.033	4.868
8	7.652	7.325	7.020	6.733	6.463	6.210	5.971	5.747	5.535	5.335
9	8.566	8.162	7.786	7.435	7.108	6.802	6.515	6.247	5.995	5.759
10	9.471	8.983	8.530	8.111	7.722	7.360	7.024	6.710	6.418	6.145
11	10.37	9.787	9.253	8.760	8.306	7.887	7.499	7.139	6.805	6.495
12	11.26	10.58	9.954	9.385	8.863	8.384	7.943	7.536	7.161	6.814
13	12.13	11.35	10.63	9.986	9.394	8.853	8.358	7.904	7.487	7.103
14	13.00	12.11	11.30	10.56	9.899	9.295	8.745	8.244	7.786	7.367
15	13.87	12.85	11.94	11.12	10.38	9.712	9.108	8.559	8.061	7.606

	11%	12%	13%	14%	15%	16%	17%	18%	19%	20%
1	0.901	0.893	0.885	0.877	0.870	0.862	0.855	0.847	0.840	0.833
2	1.713	1.690	1.668	1.647	1.626	1.605	1.585	1.566	1.547	1.528
3	2.444	2.402	2.361	2.322	2.283	2.246	2.210	2.174	2.140	2.106
4	3.102	3.037	2.974	2.914	2.855	2.798	2.743	2.690	2.639	2.589
5	3.696	3.605	3.517	3.433	3.352	3.274	3.199	3.127	3.058	2.991
6	4.231	4.111	3.998	3.889	3.784	3.685	3.589	3.498	3.410	3.326
7	4.712	4.564	4.423	4.288	4.160	4.039	3.922	3.812	3.706	3.605
8	5.146	4.968	4.799	4.639	4.487	4.344	4.207	4.078	3.954	3.837
9	5.537	5.328	5.132	4.946	4.772	4.607	4.451	4.303	4.163	4.031
10	5.889	5.650	5.426	5.216	5.019	4.833	4.659	4.494	4.339	4.192
11	6.207	5.938	5.687	5.453	5.234	5.029	4.836	4.656	4.486	4.327
12	6.492	6.194	5.918	5.660	5.421	5.197	4.988	4.793	4.611	4.439
13	6.750	6.424	6.122	5.842	5.583	5.342	5.118	4.910	4.715	4.533
14	6.982	6.628	6.302	6.002	5.724	5.468	5.229	5.008	4.802	4.611
15	7.191	6.811	6.462	6.142	5.847	5.575	5.324	5.092	4.876	4.675

List of key
terms and
index

These are terms which we have identified throughout the text as being KEY TERMS. You should make sure that you can define what these terms mean; go back to the pages highlighted here if you need to check.

BPP PUBLISHING

BPP PUBLISHING

ORDER FORM

Any books from our AAT range can be ordered by telephoning 020 8740 2211. Alternatively, send this page to our address below, fax it to us on 020 8740 1184, or email us at **publishing@bpp.com.** Or look us up on our website: www.bpp.com

We aim to deliver to all UK addresses inside 5 working days; a signature will be required. Orders to all EU addresses should be delivered within 6 working days. All other orders to overseas addresses should be delivered within 8 working days.

To: BPP Publishing Ltd, Aldine House, Aldine Place, London W12 8AW

Tel: 020-8740 2211   **Fax: 020-8740 1184**   **Email: publishing@bpp.com**

Mr / Ms (full name): _____

Daytime delivery address: _____

_____

Postcode: _____   Daytime Tel: _____

Please send me the following quantities of books.

	5/01 Interactive Text	8/01 DA Kit	8/01 Combined Kit	8/01 CA Kit
FOUNDATION				
Unit 1 Recording Income and Receipts (6/01 Kit)	☐	☐		
Unit 2 Making and Recording Payments (6/01 Kit)	☐	☐		
Unit 3 Ledger Balances and Initial Trial Balance (6/01 Kit)	☐		☐	
Unit 4 Supplying Information for Management Control (6/01 Kit)	☐	☐		
Unit 20 Working with Information Technology (8/01 Text)	☐			
Unit 22/23 Healthy Workplace and Personal Effectiveness	☐			
INTERMEDIATE				
Unit 5 Financial Records and Accounts	☐		☐	
Unit 6 Cost Information	☐			
Unit 7 Reports and Returns	☐	☐		
Unit 21 Using Information Technology	☐			
TECHNICIAN				
Unit 8/9 Core Managing Costs and Allocating Resources	☐			☐
Unit 10 Core Managing Accounting Systems	☐	☐		
Unit 11 Option Financial Statements (Accounting Practice)	☐			☐
Unit 12 Option Financial Statements (Central Government)	☐	☐		
Unit 15 Option Cash Management and Credit Control	☐	☐		
Unit 16 Option Evaluating Activities	☐	☐		
Unit 17 Option Implementing Auditing Procedures	☐			
Unit 18 Option Business Tax FA01(8/01 Text)	☐			
Unit 19 Option Personal Tax FA01(8/01 Text)	☐			
TECHNICIAN 2000				
Unit 18 Option Business Tax FA00 (8/00 Text & Kit)	☐			
Unit 19 Option Personal Tax FA00 (8/00 Text & Kit)	☐			

TOTAL BOOKS   ☐ + ☐ + ☐ + ☐ = ☐

Special offer   @ £9.95 each = £ ☐

Foundation units £80 complete set   £ ☐

Intermediate units £65 complete set   £ ☐

Technician units £100 complete set   £ ☐

Postage and packaging

UK: £2.00 for each book to maximum of £10

Europe (inc ROI and Channel Islands): £4.00 for first book, £2.00 for each extra   P & P   £ ☐

Rest of the World: £20.00 for first book, £10 for each extra

GRAND TOTAL   £ ☐

I enclose a cheque for £ _____ (cheques to BPP Publishing Ltd) or charge to Mastercard/Visa/Switch

Card number   ☐☐☐☐ ☐☐☐☐ ☐☐☐☐ ☐☐☐☐ ☐☐☐☐

Start date _____   Expiry date _____   Issue no. (Switch only)_____

Signature _____

REVIEW FORM & FREE PRIZE DRAW

All original review forms from the entire BPP range, completed with genuine comments, will be entered into one of two draws on 31 January 2002 and 31 July 2002. The names on the first four forms picked out on each occasion will be sent a cheque for £50.

Name: _____   Address: _____

_____

_____

How have you used this Interactive Text?
(Tick one box only)

☐ Home study (book only)

☐ On a course: college _____

☐ With 'correspondence' package

☐ Other _____

Why did you decide to purchase this Interactive Text? *(Tick one box only)*

☐ Have used BPP Texts in the past

☐ Recommendation by friend/colleague

☐ Recommendation by a lecturer at college

☐ Saw advertising

☐ Other _____

During the past six months do you recall seeing/receiving any of the following?
(Tick as many boxes as are relevant)

☐ Our advertisement in *Accounting Technician* magazine

☐ Our advertisement in *Pass*

☐ Our brochure with a letter through the post

Which (if any) aspects of our advertising do you find useful?
(Tick as many boxes as are relevant)

☐ Prices and publication dates of new editions

☐ Information on Interactive Text content

☐ Facility to order books off-the-page

☐ None of the above

Have you used the companion Assessment Kit for this subject?   ☐ Yes   ☐ No

Your ratings, comments and suggestions would be appreciated on the following areas

	Very useful	Useful	Not useful
Introductory section (How to use this Interactive Text etc)	☐	☐	☐
Chapter topic lists	☐	☐	☐
Chapter learning objectives	☐	☐	☐
Key terms	☐	☐	☐
Assessment alerts	☐	☐	☐
Examples	☐	☐	☐
Activities and answers	☐	☐	☐
Key learning points	☐	☐	☐
Quick quizzes and answers	☐	☐	☐
List of key terms and index	☐	☐	☐
Icons	☐	☐	☐

	Excellent	Good	Adequate	Poor
Overall opinion of this Text	☐	☐	☐	☐

Do you intend to continue using BPP Interactive Texts/Assessment Kits? ☐ Yes ☐ No

Please note any further comments and suggestions/errors on the reverse of this page.

Please return to: Nick Weller, BPP Publishing Ltd, FREEPOST, London, W12 8BR

REVIEW FORM & FREE PRIZE DRAW (continued)

Please note any further comments and suggestions/errors below

FREE PRIZE DRAW RULES

1   Closing date for 31 January 2002 draw is 31 December 2001. Closing date for 31 July 2002 draw is 30 June 2002.

2   Restricted to entries with UK and Eire addresses only. BPP employees, their families and business associates are excluded.

3   No purchase necessary. Entry forms are available upon request from BPP Publishing. No more than one entry per title, per person. Draw restricted to persons aged 16 and over.

4   Winners will be notified by post and receive their cheques not later than 6 weeks after the relevant draw date.

5   The decision of the promoter in all matters is final and binding. No correspondence will be entered into.